'Peter Murtagh's motorbike ride from [...] continent to the other is a gripping advent[...] political exploration and a rattling good ya[...] ears of a seasoned journalist, the brain of a [...] open-minded and sympathetic observer of [...], the sense of wonder evoked by such extraordinary landscapes and the saddle-sore humour of a not-so-easy rider.'

Fintan O'Toole

'Forget Boorman and McGregor - Peter Murtagh's longhaul motorbike ride through the Americas is a traveller's tale par excellence. From the land of fire to the continent's Alaskan extremity, here's a story full of curiosity and wonder, filled with stunning and diverse landscapes, buckets of humanity, and with some tight-spot tension on occasion. It's about places, yes, but, in the best travel-writing tradition, it's also about the lives of the ordinary people who inhabit them. Settle back in your armchair and enjoy the ride.'

Ros Dee

'Peter Murtagh fearlessly took on the rich and the powerful as a journalist. In this epic journey he faces different challenges and dangers. His journalistic skills brilliantly capture an epic journey as the world reopens post the pandemic. This book is for anyone who hears the call of the road and adventure.'

Tom Lyons

'Warning: erudite and entertaining.
Will result in severe attack of wanderlust. And possibly divorce.'

Geoff Hill

FROM TIP TO TOP

FROM
TIP to TOP

THE JOURNEY OF A LIFETIME
FROM CHILE TO ALASKA

PETER MURTAGH

GILL BOOKS

Peter Murtagh is an award-winning journalist and author. He spent almost forty years in newspapers holding several positions including chief editor, foreign editor, news editor, opinion editor and managing editor. As a reporter, he specialised in long form investigative pieces. His travel book with his daughter Natasha, *Buen Camino!*, was a bestseller.

SOUTH AMERICA

Chile and Argentina
- Puerto Williams
- Punta Arenas
- Torres del Paine
- El Calafate
- Puerto Guadal
- Bahía Murta
- Puerto Octay
- Lautaro
- Santiago
- Valparaíso
- San Pedro de Atacama

Bolivia
- Uyuni
- Oruro
- La Paz

Peru
- Puno
- Juliaca
- Cusco & Machu Picchu
- Lima
- Santa
- Paita
- Cabo Blanco

Ecuador
- Guayaquil
- Playas
- The Galápagos Islands
- Quito

Colombia
- Rosas
- Ibagué
- Bogotá
- Cúcuta
- Necoclí
- Capurganá
- Puente Linda

CENTRAL AMERICA

Panama
- Panama City
- Las Lajas
- Camp Los Planes

Costa Rica and Nicaragua
- Cahuita
- Puntarenas
- Managua

Honduras and El Salvador
- Coyolito
- San Salvador

Guatemala
- Antigua

Alaska

Yukon

Alberta

British Columbia

Washington

Oregon

California

Arizona

New Mexico

Texas

Mexico

Guatemala

El Salvador

Hondu

NORTH AMERICA

Mexico
- Santiago Matatlán
- Oaxaca
- Monterrey

Texas and Arizona
- Bandera
- Fredericksburg
- Austin
- Llano
- Study Butte
- Tucson

California
- Laguna Beach
- L.A./Hollywood
- San Francisco
- Gualala
- Avenue of the Giants/
  Redwood forest

Oregon and Washington
- Crescent Lake
- Longview
- Ilwaco/Cape Disappointment

British Columbia
and Alberta
- Vancouver
- Nelson
- Radium Hot Springs
- Mosquito Creek Campground
- Jasper
- Smithers

Yukon
- Whitehorse
- Carmacks
- Dawson City

Alaska
- Chicken
- Tok
- Fairbanks
- Deadhorse

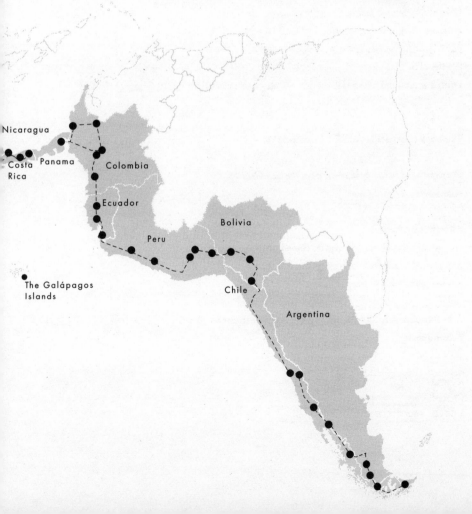

Nicaragua

Costa
Rica

Panama

Colombia

Ecuador

Peru

Bolivia

Chile

Argentina

The Galápagos
Islands

Gill Books
Hume Avenue
Park West
Dublin 12

www.gillbooks.ie

Gill Books is an imprint of M.H. Gill and Co.

ISBN: 9780717190027

Designed by Bartek Janczak
Print origination and illustration by Dexal Design
Edited by Ruairí Ó Brógáin
Proofread by Liza Costello
Printed and bound in the UK using 100% renewable electricity at CPI Group (UK) Ltd

This book is typeset in Adobe Garamond Pro.

*The paper used in this book comes from the wood pulp of
sustainably managed forests.*

A CIP catalogue record for this book is available from the
British Library.

5 4 3 2 1

For Ian Broad

1944–2021

And also in memory
of Patricio Corcoran

1954–2023

CONTENTS

INTRODUCTION

IN 2019, after nearly forty years working full time as a journalist, I retired from formal employment and faced all the anxieties that confront many retirees. Do I have a reason to get out of bed on Monday morning? What do I do with the rest of my life?

I had been a reporter and an editor, spending most of my career at the *Irish Times* and the *Sunday Tribune* (also in Ireland) and about a decade in the United Kingdom, working in London, briefly for the *Sunday Times* but mostly, for eight years, for the *Guardian*. I'm also a husband and a father and have lots of interests outside journalism. But still, for most of my life up to that point, the question 'What do you do?' – and the answer to it – was what defined me, to myself as well as to others. So now, entering retirement, what would the answer be? 'Well, nothing, actually. I'm retired'? The prospect induced a mild degree of terror in me. I wasn't ready to give up journalism. I didn't want to stop doing what had been my passion for all my adult life: reporting, getting out and about, meeting people, finding things out and telling others all about them.

The end of my formal career came on 11 April 2019, shortly after 5 p.m. in the *Irish Times* newsroom in Dublin, two days after I had turned sixty-six. I chose to work the extra year after sixty-five and also right up to my last day, eschewing the option of winding down by working one day a week less each month over several months, to the point where I would hardly be doing even one day a week. The idea of the wind down was that the cut-off moment, when it came, would seem less abrupt. Or so the reasoning went. No, I thought, I'll just carry on as normal right up to the end, and when it comes, well, that's it; it's over. I'll walk out the door and simply won't be working the next day.

Before I retired I attended a short course that included a lot of genuinely useful practical advice about pensions and other entitlements. There was also a pep talk about exercising. 'Practise picking yourself up off the floor,' said a Pilates lady. 'You'll find it easy enough now, but the day will come when you'll fall over and find it very hard to get back up without help. So practise now ...'

I remember wondering gloomily, 'Is this the future? Am I but an enfeebled stagger away from sitting in a winged armchair in the corner of a crowded old people's home, being spoon-fed puréed food by a care assistant?' I was, and remain, determined to be as active as I can, for as long as I can.

Within a few days of my final shift, I headed to south-west France to walk 350km of the Camino de Santiago, crossing the Pyrenees into Spain and going as far as the small town of Frómista, west of Burgos. I try to walk the Camino, or a good chunk of it, every year because of the great pleasure it gives me, a lapsed Protestant-cum-atheist, and because it's also a terrific way to keep fit. My wife and I then flew to America for the wedding of the son of some good friends. We tacked on a holiday during which I did some hillwalking in New Hampshire, and we roamed around Maine, enjoying the coastal beauty of that state. In July, with some friends, I went climbing in Switzerland, scaling three mountains in a week, each about 4,000m high, in support of a cancer research fund, the Caroline Foundation. But even with all this frenetic activity, at the back of my mind was another trip I wanted to undertake. It was one that had captured my imagination for a couple of years: riding my motorbike from the bottom of South America right up through the Americas to the very top of Alaska, to Prudhoe Bay and a place named Deadhorse, where the road ends and you can go no further. Far from being the first to undertake this journey, I would nonetheless be joining a select band of adventure bikers to have done it.

I was not a seasoned adventure biker, skilled in off-road riding (though I had done two brief off-road courses in Wales and Scotland), neither was I sufficiently mechanically minded to be able to fix the bike should it break down. I had gone to two demonstrations in emergency puncture repairing and bought the necessary equipment, but that was about it. However, I had been biking for over ten years and had ridden long distances around Ireland and the UK as well as several parts of Europe, including the Balkans, and also Chile and Brazil. The special feeling of freedom that comes with biking, of moving through the landscape but not being separated from it by travelling inside a metal box, is very seductive. And adventurous travel – the idea of just going, of coping with whatever happens along the way – appeals to me enormously and is a long-suppressed part of my make-up, going back to my twenties.

In 1979, while living in Denmark in my late twenties and working as a painter and decorator and as a gardener, I was asked by a woman whose garden I was doing whether I wanted to crew on a small wooden yacht owned by a man across the road who was sailing to Africa in three days' time. I jumped at the chance even though I had not sailed before, a detail that didn't seem to worry the boat owner or indeed me.

There were five of us: Lars, the captain; his friend Peter; Peter's wife; their son, aged about ten; and me. Soon after we left Copenhagen harbour, we were hit by a horrendous storm, forcing us to shelter in one of Denmark's many islands. After that we went through the Kiel Canal to Helgoland, where Lars caulked the yacht's timbers to seal several leaks. Later we rested in Dunkirk and in Guernsey's St Peter Port before crossing the Bay of Biscay in one go. We crewed by rota – a couple of hours on, then the same off for sleep – and my pulse still quickens remembering sailing alone at night, setting our course with the compass and then staying it by keeping the mast aligned with the stars. In our wake the sea was lit up by phosphorescence, glistening magically in the deep night blackness.

When we arrived in Vigo, north-west Spain, I left to go my own way, hitchhiking to North Africa and mostly sleeping rough. In Morocco I hated the hassle and constant pestering and, after Tetouan, got a bus east to Oujda, by the border with Algeria. The contrast between the two countries was immediate: whereas Morocco was desert burnt and poor, Algeria was irrigated and green, and the people were genuinely interested in who I was. They wanted to know what Ireland was like and took pride in telling me about themselves and their country.

I hitched to Oran (about which I remember absolutely nothing) and then south, in a great loop across the northern Sahara, taking in Laghouat and Ghardaïa, where I chickened out of going deeper into the desert, wheeling round instead to Touggourt and El Oued and on into Tunisia. There I got a lift in a Norwegian camper van heading for Genoa, where the Norwegian Seaman's Church served waffles daily to the homeless … and to young travellers chancing their arm. That adventure ended with the best hitch I've ever achieved: a single lift from outside Genoa to the central train station in Copenhagen, not far from where I lived. The driver was a Yugoslav shipyard worker on his way back to Sweden.

So adventure – and coping with the things that just happen, the people one meets, the other lives and the scenery – has a magnetic attraction for me. Retirement would not be an end but a beginning, a renewal while there was still time, a determination to keep grabbing life with both hands and living it to the full. That's why I did this journey.

This book is a compilation of my weekly reporting for the *Irish Times*, blogs written for my website, Tip2Top.ie, and extracts from my road trip notebooks. I hope you enjoy it and that it encourages others – especially anyone faltering at the thought of doing something similar – to steel themselves and just go for it!

Greystones, Co. Wicklow, and Louisburgh, Co. Mayo, October 2023

SOUTH AMERICA

ON 10 NOVEMBER 2022, American Airlines flight 723 took off from Dublin Airport, bound for Philadelphia and with me on board. I was anxious and excited in equal measure – anxious about the adventure I was resuming but excited also finally to be doing it. It had been aborted in late March 2020 because of the COVID-19 pandemic then sweeping the globe. Now that was all but over, conquered by vaccines. In Philadelphia I would catch another flight to Miami and, finally, a third to Santiago, capital city of Chile, arriving just before nine the next morning, Friday 11 November. A few days later I would fly further south, to Punta Arenas.

As the plane took off from Dublin, I thought to myself, 'At last, at long bloody last.' I had just one piece of luggage – my rucksack – packed with not very much: a sleeping bag and a change of clothes. Not a lot, considering I planned to be away for at least seven months. Everything else I reckoned I would need was with my motorbike, my Irish-registered BMW R1200 GS Adventure, which I hadn't seen since April 2020. A few weeks before that date, the bike had been airfreighted to Buenos Aires via Mexico City, and that February I had followed it to the Argentine capital. From there I rode 3,000km south, across the Patagonian Desert and over the border into Chile, to Punta Arenas, the capital of Chile's southernmost province, Magallanes y la Antártica Chilena.

In those early months of 2020, as I crossed the Pampas and was buffeted by the austral winds of Patagonia, I could sense the virus also creeping up behind me. In Buenos Aires everything seemed fairly normal: no one was wearing masks and there was little sign of hand gel, soon to be ubiquitous. But by the time I got to Río Gallegos, about 70km from the southern border with Chile, even the teenagers who hung round petrol stations, hoping to earn a few pesos helping motorists, were wearing masks and surgical gloves. At one station there were several bikers, and the word among them was that the frontier was closing at midnight. It would stay closed for at least two weeks, it was said, but that would be okay, I thought: there was enough for me to see and do for a fortnight in Chile's far south. So while the other bikers turned back, I sped on to the border and got to Punta Arenas just as the sun set on 16 March 2020.

Taoiseach Leo Varadkar's St Patrick's Day address the next day on the scale of the Covid crisis hit home and prompted anxious text messages to me from my wife. Within days it was clear that South America's borders wouldn't be reopening any time soon. After closing its border, Chile banned foreigners from using the country's ferries, meaning I could neither go further south within Chile, to Puerto Williams, nor turn north, using the Pacific Ocean to bypass the Southern Patagonian Ice Field and get into the rest of the enormously long country.

I was trapped in the far south, and even though life still seemed normal – people walked the streets or went to the supermarket, even if shops spot-checked shoppers' temperature – TV news reports told a different, and increasingly alarming, story. The dying had started and had reached Punta Arenas, including the house next door to my hostel. One day Eliana Valencia, the woman who ran it, was hosing down the entire exterior of the building, in the belief that she would wash away any virus that might be there. Inside, we were becoming inmates – Eliana and me, a young midwife named Anni, and Marcos, a chef from Ecuador.

The final nail in the coffin of my great adventure came soon after, on 22 March, when the Chilean government announced a nationwide curfew from 22:00 to 5:00, amid suggestions that it might be extended until June and become a twenty-four-hour curfew. During the curfew, no one would be allowed out of their accommodation save for medical emergencies or to get food. People were starting to lose their jobs as businesses, especially in hospitality, began shedding staff. It was obvious that I needed to get out of the country – if I could.

It took a few days to arrange, but I got standby on a LATAM flight from Punta Arenas to Santiago for 1 April and a seat on the last British Airways flight to London on 3 April. Eliana and Marcos drove me to the small airport in Punta Arenas, which was chaotic, as residents of other places in Chile, tourists and contract workers all tried to get home before the curfew came into force. Eventually, I got one of the last seats to Santiago, where I stayed two nights in a hostel near the airport, before getting the last BA flight to London. Both flights were crammed and I felt certain that I would catch the virus.

I got home to a virtually empty Dublin Airport, where my wife, Moira, and our children, Patrick and Natasha, threw me the keys to a second car so I could escape to our holiday home in Co. Mayo to isolate. On the way there, a garda stopped me near Croagh Patrick and asked where I was going.

'To Louisburgh,' I said.

'And where are you coming from?'

'Chile.'

He looked at me blankly, paused, and then, apparently deciding not to probe further, said, 'Grand, so. Carry on.'

Miraculously, I didn't catch the virus during my escape, but during the pandemic, 5.3 million Chileans would, with more than 62,000 of them dying.

Back home and safe, I was relaxed: my bike was secure, locked in a Punta Arenas warehouse owned by my new friend there, the Chilean Irish rancher, supermarket owner and local Kerrygold agent Patricio Corcoran.

I thought I'd be back in Chile after a few months at most, when all the fuss had died down, resuming my adventure. The naivety of it! It would be over two and a half years before I could return.

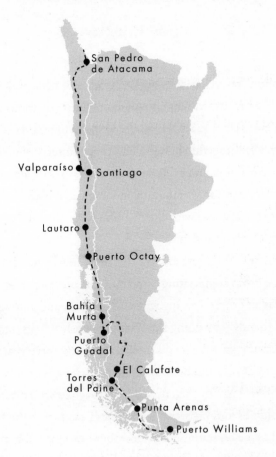

CHILE AND ARGENTINA

12–17 NOVEMBER 2022, PUNTA ARENAS, CHILE

The flight from Santiago began its slow but steady descent, wheeling left across the Strait of Magellan, the windows on the right side tilting upwards to give me a glimpse of the snow-capped Andes.

The Andes! Again, and at last, so close I could almost touch them – the same feeling I had two and a half years previously when mask-wearing soldiers stopped me just outside Puerto Natales to say, politely, no, I could not go further. 'Covid,' they said, as if I needed telling.

Now, with the curse lifted for almost everyone everywhere, I was back, a bundle of excitement and anxiety. Excitement because this was the resumption (resuscitation?) of the 'great retirement project', riding a motorbike from Tierra del Fuego to Alaska, alone and without the pressure of any deadline to get to place X by such and such a time or date. This would be no race, no 'lads together having a blast' expedition. I wanted this to be a journey of encounter and exploration, a journey partly along the famed Pan-American Highway – or the Panamericana, as it is known in much of Latin America – but one with the freedom to go this way or that as the mood or the moment took me.

But there was also more anxiety this time. Maybe it was post-Covid angst; maybe it was appreciating better than the previous time the anxiety I was causing in others – in my wife and children and among my wider family and friends – by doing this. But my selfish self was still doing it. Maybe it was the gnawing realisation that, nearly three years on, I was in my seventieth year and no longer had the strength or fitness I had as recently as 2020. I had by then developed a touch of arthritis in the joints where my thumbs join my wrist. Sometimes I can't twist the lid off a jar. My doctor has me on statins (a low dose, but heart pills nonetheless) and also something for blood pressure, and when I told him about the trip, he commented, 'Ballsy,' half admiring (I suspect), half thinking (I also suspect) that there's no fool like an old fool.

So what made me think I would be able to upright a toppled BMW R1200 GS Adventure, a vast machine by any measure – weighing over 250kg, luggage excluded – when, inevitably, somewhere along the way to Deadhorse, Alaska, it would indeed topple over? I didn't know, but I'd find out!

The Magellan Strait waters looked unusually calm from a few thousand feet up, but the bent-over trees around the airport reminded me that this is a place of extreme winds, the great south wind that blows, and blows and blows, seemingly without end. It was late spring in the Southern Hemisphere, but the ground below was visibly burnt and bone dry, showing little evidence of winter growth for grazing sheep.

When I came through the airport, there was no sign of Eliana, who said she might be there to meet me and bring me into town. Eliana runs the El Patagónico Hostel, on the way into Punta Arenas. I stayed there last time for no reason other than that hers was the first bed-for-the-night sign I saw. I thought then that I'd be there for two weeks, the initial period for which the border was due to be closed. In the almost three years since then, Eliana and I had kept in touch via Facebook Messenger. She's a hoot is Eliana – friendly and kind, funny and playful. Her hostel is an Aladdin's cave of stuff – stuff everywhere that hasn't been opened or used for yonks, broken-down stuff and other things that will probably never be used. It's like living in the centre aisle of Lidl.

I jumped into an airport taxi, and on my arrival the hostel door burst open. Eliana threw out her arms to give me a great big hug, laughing a laugh that said, 'Well, isn't this just gas?'

'Peeeeeeter! *¿Cómo estás, amigo?*'

'Grand, just grand. Great to be back!'

Inside, everything was much the same as before, except that the massive TV – it must be at least sixty inches across – that in March 2020 was blaring out the end of the world from its wall mounting now lay flat across the breakfast table, smothering it almost entirely. *'Muerta?'* I asked. *'Sí, muerta,'* she said. Never mind, I thought, feeling sure that it would be kept nonetheless ... finding a home with the two dead cars out back and the other bits of debris, a bicycle, some class of Husqvarna compressor and lengths of timber and plastic. Later, out there, Eliana showed me a small corner that had been cleared and wooden pallets that had been laid down to give an even, solid surface while leaving enough space for two plant beds along a rear and side wall.

'*Tomates?*' I asked.

'*Sí*, maybe,' she said.

On the way to my bedroom, at the turn in the creaking stairway, there was a three-foot pound-shop Santa Claus, smiling and wishing me a feliz Navidad ... and I got the eerie feeling that he had been there too when I stayed here first in March 2020.

After I unpacked my rucksack and caught my breath, I went back downstairs. Eliana had news for me: beaming, she told me that she had a new man. Two and a half years before, she was still in mourning for her then recently deceased husband – 'my best friend' she would say, eyes welling up. She said she thought of him every day but would try to lose herself in her hobbies: painting, photography and birdwatching.

'Alex!' she announced to me, simultaneously summoning the new man for presentation. He was a little stocky (Eliana herself is small in stature) but broad-shouldered and muscular. He had a big smile and shook my hand warmly. He told me that Eliana had spoken a lot about me. I asked whether they were married, pointing to my wedding ring to supplement my appalling Spanish. But, no, they were just together, they said. 'Living in sin,' I pronounce, and they both laughed uproariously.

'*Es un hombre muy excelente*,' Eliana said proudly of Alex, adding that he was her '*compañero de viaje*', her travelling companion, and that this was how they had got to know each other.

I went for a stroll to a nearby supermarket to acquire vital supplies, such as wine. It was strange to see spring flowers in suburban gardens – dandelions, millions of them everywhere, but also peonies, laburnum and yellow broom, sometimes fashioned into bright hedging. When I returned with the wine, Eliana invited me to join her and Alex's late-afternoon Sunday lunch of empanadas and pickles. The wine went down well, and I went to bed wondering what tomorrow would bring.

*

When in late March 2020 the Chilean government announced a curfew, it was clear that my plans were scuppered. I had just interviewed a local Chilean Irishman, Patricio Corcoran, who ran a food distribution company and three mid-sized supermarkets. I suspected that he had warehouses, or at least access to one, and might be able to store my bike for a couple of months, as I then expected I would need.

Patricio was quietly proud of his Irish heritage. In his office he kept two old British passports belonging to his grandfather and father, both of which show Irish birthplaces. His grandfather, Charles Peter Corcoran, was born in Co. Cavan but lived in Dublin. Patricio's father, Arthur Bartholomew Corcoran, was born in the city in August 1919 – a difficult time in Ireland, politically and economically. So when the Chilean sheep-farming company La Sociedad Explotadora de Tierra del Fuego recruited among the Irish and Scots for pioneers who would emigrate to Patagonia, Charles Corcoran signed up, taking with him his one-year-old son, Arthur.

When I met him, Arthur's son Patricio was the embodiment of the successful immigrant. He and Sylvia, his wife of forty-three years (she's a Blackwood, with lineage going back to Scotland), had three children and ten grandchildren. Apart from the food business, Patricio also owned a farm near Punta Arenas, which had some 2,500 sheep (the local average was closer to 5,000) and 500 Angus beef cows. The calves were matured on another farm near Puerto Montt, north of the Patagonian Ice Field, from where they were sold for slaughter.

Patricio was something of a local contact for the Irish embassy in Santiago, which put me in touch with him. My plea for his help in March 2020 was answered with an immediate and generous yes, and so I left my wonderful, almost-new bike on 31 March in a Corcoran Express warehouse, under a cover and with various bits and pieces stuffed into two bags and hoisted on a pallet up onto the top shelf of the huge building.

Now, two and a half years later, I really didn't know what to expect. The bike's battery would surely be dead, but could it be revived? And the tyres, had they deflated, and had the rubber cracked and perished? The petrol and oil would have to be drained. I'd have to get the whole bike serviced, surely.

I emailed him. 'Patricio! Am finally in Punta Arenas. Would it suit if I called around at 11 tomorrow morning?'

'Peter', came the reply, 'your bike is ready. We have to pick it up in a garage I sent them. 11.00 am would be great ...'

Down one of the roads near my hostel, Alejandro Lago runs a workshop where he services machines used by an adventure-biking company specialising in motorcycle tours of Patagonia. Patricio drove me there, and it was obvious from the workshop – from the equipment, the bikes being worked on, the big Dakar sign over his workbench and all the stickers left by visiting long-haul adventure bikers – that Alejandro knows his stuff and is a mechanic well trusted by bikers.

Mine was there – gleaming clean, fully serviced at Patricio's request. When I pressed the starter button it snapped into life with that deep-throated, satisfying GS purr. The years of enforced inactivity were blown away in an instant, and with them all my worries. A spin north, out across the Patagonian Desert by the airport and on towards the Argentine frontier, proved that everything was running perfectly. Everything I left behind in Patricio's care was retrieved: all the biking gear, the camping gear (an MSR Hubba Hubba NX tent – the most expensive item I took with me, after the bike and my laptop and phone – and as yet unused) and all the related equipment.

That night Patricio invited me to dinner in Sotito's, one of the best restaurants in Punta Arenas. Over locally caught king crab, octopus, abalone, grilled fish, pisco and wine, we talked Chile, Ireland, England, politics, family and climate change. The absence of new-season grass I had noticed from the plane was due to a lack of rain, he said. The relative lack of water meant that he was now drilling to get some, with pumps using solar power. From the actions of the restaurant owner and staff, it was clear that Patricio was well known and well liked. As we exited, he paused at one or two other tables to chat briefly with friends who were also dining.

I walked on slowly so as not to intrude. The waiter sidled over to me and smiled, gesturing towards Patricio. 'Rock star,' he said.

I could not but agree.

22 NOVEMBER 2022, PUERTO WILLIAMS, ISLA NAVARINO, CHILE

The main ferry port out of Punta Arenas was just down the road from Eliana's hostel, and that's where I headed in my quest to get as far south as I could before turning round and heading north. Ferry rides are generally perfunctory affairs. You get on board and do what you have to do to get through the tedium of the journey – play cards, fill in crosswords, read a book, whatever – except when you're on the Austral Broom's ferry *Yaghan* from Punta Arenas to Puerto Williams, the place farthest south in Chile that it's practicable to go, south of Argentina's Ushuaia, the better known 'most southern town in the world', which it really isn't. On this overnight journey, you don't need distractions because there's just far too much to see: epic seascapes churned up by the southern winds, seabirds performing aerobatics over the waves, raw and edgy landscapes and place names straight out of childhood adventure stories and geography class.

We set sail down the Strait of Magellan at about six in the evening, passing Cape Froward and its lighthouse, the final tip of the continental landmass of South America. In 2020 I had ridden there, and I did so again a few days before sailing, revisiting the grave of the luckless Pringle Stokes, captain of the first Beagle voyage, whose depression caused him to take his own life in August 1828. His grave overlooks the strait near Port Famine (Puerto del Hambre), about 50km south of Punta Arenas and near where the most southerly road on continental America ends a little further on, at Cape San Isidro.

As the ferry sailed past, in the far distance and in the fading gunmetal light of the night sky, I could just about make out the snow-capped mountains of the islands that make up the network of land and sea channels that comprise the toe-shaped formation of Tierra del Fuego and Cape Horn. It's an exhilarating sight. Not for no reason did the travel writer Bruce Chatwin describe the strait as a case of nature imitating art.

The *Yaghan* is a workhorse, a giant version of the sort of landing craft used on D-Day, with a bow door that opens down, creating a slipway for vehicles to gallop ashore. It's primarily a cargo vessel that also caters for passengers, and its deck was crammed with containers, vans and four-wheel drives, oil drums, wooden pallets, a dozen ton-bags of cement, lengths of steel and mesh for fencing. And now also my bike.

During the night, the ship threaded its way south like a darning needle, passing between islands and through channels whose names tell the story of the discovery of this place from the sixteenth to the nineteenth centuries.

We avoided fully entering the Pacific, passing instead on the inside of Isla London and into the Ballenero Channel, north of the islands of Stewart, Gilbert and Londonderry. The channel is squeezed narrow as it passes between Londonderry to the south and O'Brien Island to the north, before passing Darwin Island and entering the Darwin Channel.

North of us is Tierra del Fuego and the dark, brooding mountain range of the Cordillera Darwin – a set of snow-capped peaks and glacier tongues flowing off them but not quite dipping into the sea. They once did, before global warming began to eat away at them, as is evident from photographs taken a mere decade ago.

The ferry moved slowly, providing passengers – some locals and also some tourists, from France, Italy, the Far East and the United States – with ample time to take in the sights. The island scenery is astounding. Gigantic in scale and inhospitable in nature, the weather-beaten land masses are a shade of deep grey just short of black, their peaks white and their flanks broken by blotches of snow above the treeline. Despite some vegetation and forestry, there's no visible evidence of habitation. Seabirds abound and the star performer by a long shot is the petrel. Often flying solo, the bird moves upwards in graceful arcs, falling again to the water to glide at great speed and with seeming effortlessness, its wingtips almost brushing the tops of the waves.

We entered the Beagle Channel, which separates Chile and Argentina, and docked briefly at Yendegaia on Chilean Tierra del Fuego. Tierra del Fuego is an island that is split between Chile and Argentina; the Argentine town of Ushuaia, southernmost destination of most adventure bikers in the region, is a little further east of our landing place. At Yendegaia there's a small slipway but nothing by way of a settlement, save for a small Chilean Army presence and a rough road north, connecting ultimately with Porvenir, a Chilean town on the opposite side of the Strait of Magellan to Punta Arenas.

I walked about a bit while some building materials were offloaded, but I wanted to go further south still and stay with the ferry as it resumed its journey. A little further on through the channel, we docked at Puerto

Williams about midnight. Foot passengers alighted, but all remaining cargo stayed put, my bike included. 'Mañana,' said a crew member, adding that I shouldn't worry: I could sleep on the ferry. In the meantime we returned into the channel and dropped anchor, and I went to sleep for the night in a reclining chair.

Next day and back at the slipway, I disembarked and parked the bike immediately outside the Refugio El Padrino, a brightly coloured wood-and-tin hostel beside the harbour. But I had to move it almost at once. I was, apparently, taking up Cecelia's place. She was another larger-than-life *hospitalera*, who greeted me like a diva, proffering both cheeks for a kiss and administering a warm hug at the same time. 'Come in, come in,' she insisted, telling me that I was to have eggs and cheese and bread and coffee before we discussed matters. 'Sit!' she commanded, and who was I to question her?

The hostel kitchen–living room was typical: an amiable clutter of posters, maps, photographs and flags. There was a beaver pelt nailed flat onto the wall. The place was named in honour of Eduardo Mancilla Vera, an otter and sealion hunter who came to Puerto Williams in the 1940s and stayed until his death, aged eighty-one, in 2003. He spent his life helping create the town and championing its cause, lobbying the authorities for facilities and investment. He was so respected by the inhabitants that many of them named him as godfather to their children – hence his nickname, El Padrino ('the Godfather'). Eduardo was Cecelia's dad.

Puerto Williams has a real pioneer town feel to it: gritty, dusty and unkempt. Some roads are concrete but most are just compacted earth and gravel. They kick up dust when a vehicle passes. The original houses, those closest to the harbour, have a run-down, paint-peeling, shanty-town appearance. They're jumbles of plywood and sheet metal, often with satellite dishes nailed onto their fronts. Gardens, as generally understood, are virtually non-existent. The areas in front and around the sides of the houses are car parks and places for piles of timber, chopping blocks and other stuff. There are dogs everywhere. Many other homes further back from the harbour are owned by the Chilean Navy and are better kept.

The best buildings in the town are invariably associated with government. Puerto Williams as a town didn't come into being formally until November 1953 (the year of my birth), and there was to be an anniversary marked in the town the next day.

For now, however, I attempted my trek across the island to Lake Windhond, which is about 25km directly south from Puerto Williams and where there's a shack, the Refugio Charles, the most southerly place I could sleep before turning north and heading for Alaska, some 40,000km away. This was the bottom-most tip in this Tip2Top adventure.

The hike started at a small settlement named Villa Ukika, where the Ukika River enters the sea about 2km east of Puerto Williams. Villa Ukika is populated almost entirely by the surviving members of the Yahgan people, the Indigenous people who were 'transferred' there by the Chilean military in the 1960s. It's where they continue to live today in about a dozen wooden houses. I was curious about the Yahgan and the Ona, or Selk'nam, people of Tierra del Fuego, who had all but ceased to exist in any meaningful way outside of images on tourist tat. Recent scholarship has found evidence that the Sociedad Explotadora de Tierra del Fuego funded the murder of Selk'nam in the late nineteenth and early twentieth centuries, paying £1 for every person shot dead, the evidence for payment being the presentation of a severed hand or ear.

I walked to Villa Ukika from Puerto Williams and set off down the Ukika River valley through dense woods, on a trail indicated initially by two parallel red lines on a white background painted onto tree trunks. There was no road, just this trail. My compass bearing showed exactly 190 degrees, pointing precisely south. But after perhaps four kilometres, the trail marker signs disappeared, and soon I became hopelessly lost. For the moment, I was able to confirm my direction not just by my map and compass but also by following the skyline of the mountain ridges on the side of the valley. But what should have been a simple enough trek with these aids became more and more difficult as the woods thickened and fallen trunks and debris slowed progress to a painful crawl – sometimes literally. An ant would make faster progress through a ball of wire wool. I become increasingly concerned that if anything untoward happened – a fall, a sprain or, worse, a break – no one would know where to find me. The trail itself had disappeared, so how could they?

Forward movement became more and more arduous and, having zigzagged up and down the side of the valley, trying to relocate the trail, I descended to the valley floor. If nature does dystopia, this is maybe close to it. While it looks beautiful, the area is strewn with timber wreckage created by beavers chomping away at everything in their path. The creatures were introduced into Tierra del Fuego from Canada in the 1940s in the hope of creating an Argentine beaver fur industry, but it didn't work out. Some of the animals escaped, swam the Beagle Channel and populated Isla Navarino. Now the entire Ukika Valley floor is a maze of dams, lakes and swamp, of gnawed-off stumps and timber debris. Any trees left standing are dead, and the whole landscape looks not unlike bomb-blasted no man's land at the end of the First World War.

By 4 p.m., after some five hours' hiking, I had covered only about 12km – half the distance to the lake. I decided to give up and pitch my tent where I was, on a dry mound sandwiched between the forest and the swamp. I will sleep with the beavers, I thought to myself. At night, however, all I heard was the sound of bats and of wild dogs barking, four or five of them further up the valley – where no one lives ...

I awoke to find a lone goose, a Magellanic bustard, a grey-headed fellow with a lovely rust-coloured chest, standing by the beaver lake, just feet away. We sized each other up for a few moments before it waddled off, unfazed by my presence. I decided not to risk further trekking alone and, knowing the river would reach the sea, started to follow it back downstream. Wild horses had done the same and conveniently flattened out a path – not to Lake Windhond, unfortunately, but back to Villa Ukika.

Next day, back in Puerto Williams, they were getting ready in Plaza Bernardo O'Higgins to mark the town's sixty-ninth birthday. The school band, the Banda de Guerra, led the parade, followed by a marching column of about sixty naval ratings and a dozen or so officers, who were formally inspected by the regional governor, George Flies, and the commander of the navy's Beagle Channel operation, Comandante Cristián Yáñez. Flags of the town, the region and the country were raised and the national anthem was sung. The governor and the mayor, Patricio Fernández, made the sort of speeches governors and mayors make on such occasions, praising the people and their town for all they have accomplished and for the bright future that awaits them. Medals were presented to naval servicemen and servicewomen and local worthies; kindergarten and school children paraded.

Wearing a Sandeman port–style, broad-brimmed black hat, poncho and black leather boots with spurs, the traditional Chilean dancer Pablo Suaso led his troupe through several foot-stomping, skirt-and-handkerchief swirling numbers by the bust of Bernardo O'Higgins, Chile's liberator from Spanish rule. 'My hero,' said Pablo when I chatted to him. Bernardo O'Higgins was the illegitimate son of Ambrose (later Ambrosio) O'Higgins, late of Co. Sligo and Co. Meath, forced off his lands by Oliver Cromwell. Ambrose would become a servant of the Spanish crown, a merchant prince made viceroy of Peru, governor of Chile and marquis of Osorno.

Before leaving Isla Navarino the following day, I decided that, since I couldn't hike south, I should ride the road west as far as the island lets me. The way out of Puerto Williams is a dusty, gritty trail that wends its way hugging the south coast of the Beagle Channel. Up, down and over hillocks, on and on it goes for over 50km. Biking on dirt roads involves real concentration: front and rear wheels take on a life of their own when hitting a patch of loose gravel. But take it handy, stay under forty and you're okay. Besides, on this road, there's far too much to see, far too much beauty, to be rushing.

On that early summer's day, the water in the Beagle Channel was still and glistening in the sunlight. The sea is a mirror to all the world above it. The mountains of Argentine Tierra del Fuego on the far side were jet black and snow-capped; the sky was filled with big frothy clouds but sufficiently broken for there to be large patches of blue too. In the water of the channel, the world was displayed twice over.

On my side, the vegetation was surprisingly lush coming from ground so apparently dry and poor. There were banks of Chilean firetrees, with their bright orange-red flower. A group of condors circled above – wheeling in huge arcs, their wings outstretched and unmoving but held aloft on the wind, gliding effortlessly, as though by magic. As I biked along, I passed numerous apparently abandoned farmhouses – timber-and-tin shacks, for the most part, and pretty; but they're hard places in which to live, I suspect, in the winter. There's no question of electricity out here: gas if you haul the cylinders from Puerto Williams, logs otherwise.

Around a corner I came to a sign, *Cementerio Indígena de Bahía Mejillones*. In the graveyard, large plots were enclosed by low picket fencing, but there were no individual markers or names, save for one plot in which a weathered board announces that the plot was for the Familia Torres, with occupants dating from 1931 to 1946 and one later interred but with the date indistinct.

At the back of the graveyard there was a single grave, a new arrival in a plot delineated by fresh timber edging and newly planted flowers, some plastic. Behind the grave was a tiny glass-fronted shrine with a small pitched roof. Inside were more flowers, a statue of the Virgin and a framed photograph: a picture of a woman glancing sideways and showing a wonderful face, weathered and lined but alert and with glistening eyes.

A cross states that she was Cristina Calderón Harban and gives her dates as 24 May 1928 to 16 February 2022. She lies in one of the most beautiful places I have seen. I didn't know it when I stumbled upon her grave, but Cristina Harban was the last full-blooded Yahgan, known to all as Abuela Cristina ('Grandmother Cristina'). She was a basket-weaver, ethnographer and cultural activist who lived in Villa Ukika and had ten children and nineteen grandchildren. One of her daughters, Lidia González, was elected to the Chilean Constitutional Convention and served as deputy vice-president.

The convention was designed to write a new constitution for Chile, replacing the 1980 one that was devised by the Pinochet regime and amended no fewer than fifty-two times since. The new body had 154 elected members, and it was heavily politicised, unlike Ireland's Citizens' Assembly, on which it was partly modelled and which comprises ninety-nine randomly selected citizens and the chairperson. In September 2022 the Chilean electorate, by a convincing margin of 62 per cent to 38, rejected the new convention-drafted constitution. One of the main reasons (among many) was a sense that, by saying Chile should be a 'plurinational' state, thereby recognising the rights of its 13 per cent Indigenous people, a nightmare of disputes over land and resources could be opened up.

At the celebrations in Puerto Williams marking the town's sixty-ninth birthday, I noticed that the regional governor, George Flies, gave a particularly warm embrace to an elderly woman, a member of the Indigenous community, leaning down to hug her warmly – a gesture she reciprocated with equal warmth.

On the overnight ferry back to Punta Arenas on the *Yaghan* ferry once again, the walls of the cafe area were lined with sepia photographs of Yahgan people: naked and semi-naked people living in the wild, their bodies painted, and carrying simple tools and weapons. A photo portrait had been added recently – that of Cristina Harban. A tribute to the last native speaker of the Yahgan people, says the inscription under a shot of her looking sideways over her spectacles, out on a world of which she is no longer part.

26 NOVEMBER 2022, EL CALAFATE, ARGENTINA

The ferry from Puerto Williams didn't stop again at Tierra del Fuego, which was a pity. Had it, I'd have been able to offload my bike at Yendegaia and ride it back to Punta Arenas, via Porvenir. Instead, I had to stay on board, all the way back to Punta Arenas, where we docked about midnight. But unlike at Puerto Williams, the crew would not allow passengers without accommodation in the city to sleep the night on the ferry. I settled down instead on the ferry terminal building floor … Surprisingly, alone, in full biker gear, minus the helmet, I got some sleep.

At 5:15 the sun, not yet quite over the horizon, was nonetheless brightening the sky, and it was time to start the trek north. The 250km road to Puerto Natales was empty – not even a guanaco in sight – and the wind only slight. The guanaco, first cousin to the llama, is ubiquitous in Patagonia, especially to the east of the Andes and right across the Patagonian Desert steppe to the Atlantic. An attractive animal, with its brushed-rust brown coat and pert tail, it is, however, easily spooked as well as rather shy. This does not discourage it, however, from gathering in large numbers beside busy roads. Whenever a vehicle approaches, your average guanaco will look up and start fretting. Despite there being millions of hectares of desert scrub on each side of the highway, the guanaco will observe the approaching vehicle and, taking decisive action to get away from it, run straight onto the road in front of it!

For this reason, dead guanacos are not uncommon sights, distressing as they are for all concerned, save for the grateful birds of prey and insects, whose work ensures that soon all that is left of the late guanaco is an empty hide flapping in the wind and bones rapidly bleached white in the sun. There was no sign either of the flock of flamingos I observed at a lake last time I passed this way in March 2020.

By the time I got to Puerto Natales, breakfast was calling and the wind had whipped up. I ate at Noi Indigo Patagonia, a hip restaurant and hotel with great views over the sea. The town, one of the main set-off ports for vessels touring the many islands off Chile's west coast and venturing as far as Antarctica, is flat, weather-beaten and rather dull-looking. It too has a frontier feel about it, but the most abiding feature was, without doubt, the wind, which was churning up the sea and battering everything in its path. The westerlies blow in from the Pacific, whipping round Cape Horn as well as over the Andes. As they reach the mountain range, moisture is released as rain and snow, so that, by the time the wind swoops down the eastern side of the range and onto the Patagonian steppe, it's bone dry but fierce in its intensity. Throughout the spring and into the summer, the wind speed increases at times to 120km/h.

It felt like that on the road out to Torres del Paine, the Chilean national park that has become a Mecca for hikers because of its striking granite peaks (the 'Towers') and glaciers that feed a series of lakes and rivers, one of them the River Paine. The park is 181,400 hectares and attracts a quarter of a million visitors a year, half of them foreigners who pay a premium surcharge compared with Chilean visitors. On my visit, they included a busload of tourists for whom I was seemingly far more interesting than the Cordillera Paine mountain range rising above Lago Nordenskjöld, at which we were all, at least initially, gazing.

The Cordillera is the star of this place. I baulk when I hear someone describe a half-decent cup of coffee as 'awesome', but the mountains here truly are awesome in that they inspire awe in those who gaze upon them. It's not just their Tolkienesque appearance – black, brooding and snow-capped – it's their massive bulk, their scale and their imposing presence, as opposed to their mere size (the tallest is only 2,884m above sea level; for reference, the Matterhorn is 4,478m). The impression they make is due to the scale and the sense that, when standing even hundreds of feet away, one is in the presence of something truly massive. It was all a little overwhelming.

The lakes – Nordenskjöld, Pehoé and, nearby, the glacier-fed Grey Lake – are a striking azure. Their beauty appears somehow unreal, but there they were, one after another, right in front of me. Rivers flowing off the snow-topped mountains, or straight out of glaciers, are blue-grey. Add to that the effect of a clear blue sky, and all the waters became a pure, painted blue.

I rode on and later crossed the frontier into Argentina, heading for El Calafate, a small resort town and playground for the country's well-heeled younger set and for backpackers. The main attraction for me was the Perito Moreno Glacier, the largest in the country and the second-largest in South America. It's unusual in that it's melting and accumulating ice at roughly the same pace, and so it's classified as stable in terms of the effects of global warming. It flows out of the Southern Patagonian Ice Field, which contains an astonishing one-third of the Earth's reserves of fresh water. The glacier is 30km long and 3km wide at its mouth, where it's also some 70m tall.

Directly opposite the mouth, on a slope of land facing it, a series of gantry walkways and platforms allows visitors to get to within what seems like touching distance of it. The front nudges into Lago Argentino, and slowly but inexorably the ice dies. Every now and then the silence is broken by a great cracking noise, sometimes a thunder-like snapping, that sends a sharp splitting sound through the air. Sometimes it's more a dull thud, as if a shotgun is being discharged in the distance. And with the noise, another giant shard of ice falls into the water, sometimes moving as though in slow motion, the way giant things sometimes seem to – slow and powerful, even in death. I cannot stand before such a sight except in silence, scanning the details of it, the size of the mass in front of me, and just taking in what I'm seeing.

I jumped on the first available bus back to the car park from the edge of the glacier. There you can wander down to the shore of Lago Argentino and scan the blue water all the way back across the lake to the glacier. Standing there for a while, I knew before long that this was the right place to do something that I had resolved would be part of this trip.

I had brought with me some of the ashes of the man to whom this book is dedicated. Ian Broad was my geography and geology teacher in my secondary school, the High School, Dublin. Ian had a profound influence on me, and on the things I grew to love, second perhaps only to that of my mother. He fired in me an interest in buildings and building materials and, through his imaginative, field-trip-led teaching of geomorphology and glaciation, in the natural forces that have shaped Ireland and the world. He taught me how to read landscape, which I do all the time, however inadequately, and this has been a source of pleasure my whole life. Geography and geology have enriched my time, something of which I'm conscious almost every single day and was especially so on this trip.

But Ian was so much more than a teacher, so much more than a figure in a classroom who would drill us sufficiently to get us through the Leaving Certificate and on into whatever it was we chose in life. He was an inspiring educator, an irrepressible and sometimes chaotic force of nature himself. He had us climbing up the sides of the valley in Glendalough in Co. Wicklow looking for galena and garnets or rummaging for amethyst among the rocks above Keem Bay on Achill Island. He took us potholing in Co. Fermanagh and Co. Clare, where we would break open rocks looking for fossils, and to Connemara beaches to examine coral. He brought the streets of Dublin alive by showing us the visual effect of different natural materials used in walls – coloured bricks, limestone, chert and granite – and the quietly pleasing effect when marble, granite and oolitic limestone or Portland stone are combined with Victorian red brick. The multiple rock types inside the Museum Building at Trinity College were to me like an Aladdin's cave of treasures. To this day, I marvel at the skill and artistry of the O'Shea brothers, John and James, and their nephew Edward Whelan in their extraordinary rose carvings that encircle that whole building.

Ian taught us about town planning, about the evolution of architectural style from medieval to Georgian to Victorian and how to look at details in a wider picture. He revealed to us that a streetscape – the building facades and roofs, doors and windows, seating, lamp standards, railings, granite flagstones and kerbs and coalhole covers – comprises a unified whole and that if a part is damaged or removed the whole ensemble is diminished, if not ruined. Ian fought many battles to try to save Dublin's heritage, taking part in 1970 in the Hume Street Occupation, an unsuccessful struggle to prevent the demolition of Georgian houses on the corner of Hume Street and St Stephen's Green. For a time he ran the Dublin Arts Festival, on which I also worked, with others, including the publisher Michael O'Brien and the future presidential advisor Bride Rosney. All of these interests, these passions, helped form much of my own outlook – and that of others, I have no doubt. The rage I feel at the destruction of heritage in Dublin goes right back to Ian inculcating in me an appreciation of all that surrounded me as a boy. That several of Ian's pupils became geography teachers speaks to the impact he had on others as well.

Ian was gay and was never entirely at ease, if that is the appropriate term, with his sexuality. None of that was known to us when he was our teacher; but I learnt later that it tortured him and that he lived in terror of being forced to quit his job if anyone found out and took against him. That fear was the main reason he quit High School, in the early 1970s, and went to work as a teacher in China, then in Bhutan and finally in South Africa. He eventually came home to an Ireland that had changed but that still had some way to go in treating gay people without prejudice. But it was too late for him. He spoke of his sexuality sometimes with the obsessiveness of someone you knew had been damaged by the world, but at least he could now be open. He never found the love he so deserved, or at least I don't think he did, but he did find spiritual solace with the Quakers.

Covid killed Ian. He died a horrible death in February 2021, doctors and nurses doing everything they could to get oxygen into his lungs, including puncturing his neck and chest in a desperate but ultimately futile effort to inflate them. He was seventy-six.

His sister Pamela offered me some of his ashes, and I knew immediately that I had to take him with me on this journey. I like to think that he would approve of the place of their scattering. At the Perito Moreno Glacier the Argentine authorities have worked hard to present the spectacle as an educating experience, explaining the forces that created the glacier and how it works. If some of that rubs off on visitors and helps them appreciate the natural world around them, I think Ian would approve. So I knelt down at the edge of the lake, unscrewed the lid of a small jar and tilted Ian's ashes out and into the water. They floated gently and then sank to the bottom. They will be washed through the great lake and eventually, somewhere, will form a tiny part of the Earth. I was pleased to have done this – pleased for Ian and grateful for all that he had given me.

I rode back to El Calafate and camped for the night in a site just off the main drag. A man about my own age wandered over to my tent and introduced himself as Jaime. He looked at me, my tent and the bike as though he was about to cry. He used to ride bikes, he told me. There was mention of a Kawasaki. 'But this,' he said looking at mine while holding both hands to his chest, palms open, before gesturing to the machine itself. 'This ...' He wanted to know where I was from and where I was going. I told him and he immediately hugged me, a sort of comfort hug as though I had suffered a great loss. But I realised that the loss was his. He hugged me, and implored the blessings of God upon me, because of what I was doing. And because of what he was not.

Next day I rode north out of El Calafate. The wind was ferocious, battering and buffeting me constantly. You have to lean well into it as you ride just to stay upright and, even though you get used to it, regular gusts produce scary moments. I eventually rode onto an unpaved part of Route 40, a road idolised by bikers that runs north–south for almost the length of Argentina. The gravel stretch was about 70km long and the stones were rounded; they hadn't been steamroller-crushed into angular rocks, thereby binding them into a hardened surface. They were mostly loose and in places were many inches deep, almost like you'd find on a beach. Inevitably, I took a slow-motion tumble as the front wheel veered and the bike skewed over onto its side. Thankfully, there was no injury (to man or bike), and I discovered that I had the strength to upright the machine – which isn't bad considering my age and its weight.

29 NOVEMBER 2022, PUERTO GUADAL, CHILE

I spent the night in a smart but inexpensive hotel in the town of Gobernador Gregores and the following one at a dingy truck-stop joint named Bajo Caracoles in Argentina's Patagonian Desert. The mangy dogs that hung about it were better presented than the place itself. I slept on the bed fully clothed. Had I entered the shower, I reckon I would have emerged dirtier. The toilet was to be avoided entirely. I stayed there because, having thought about a particular unpaved road west – out of Argentina and back into the Chilean Andes – and having tentatively set out on it at about 4 p.m., the wind was so ferocious that I thought better of it and reversed.

I tried again next day, but after perhaps two kilometres into a stiff headwind, I admitted defeat again, turned round and resumed the (longer) tarmac route north to another border crossing. I eventually turned west off Route 40 and left Argentina at Los Antiguos.

The Chilean town on the other side, Chile Chico, is a pretty lakeside affair and noticeably more prosperous than many similar places on the Argentine side, with the exception of El Calafate. I couldn't help wondering what role stiffing the international banks, a policy driven by populist politics, had played in Argentina's current down-at-heel state. There was an air of decay to much of the country. Many cars still on the roads there were old, bashed and dusty. Homes looked dishevelled; people appeared poorer than they should be. Public spaces were shabby and unkempt. Chile, on the other hand, looked and felt different, more prosperous. The place had a spring in its step.

Chile Chico sits on the southern shore of a lake that itself straddles the Chile–Argentina border. On the Argentine side the lake is called Lago Buenos Aires; on the Chilean side it's Lago General Carrera, named in honour of one of the country's founding fathers. There was a small ferry port, and I wondered whether I might be able to circumvent some 200km of gravel road by crossing the lake on it. In the restaurant beside the slipway, the staff said the ferry had left that morning, and they didn't know when there would be another. A man eating lunch, an Australian geologist, piped up on overhearing our conversation. There would probably be another on Thursday morning, he said. It was now Tuesday and I didn't fancy kicking my heels for two days. 'If I were you,' said the geologist (he worked at a nearby silver mine), 'I'd take the gravel road around the lake. It's really something.'

I thought I'd give it a go and, my God, what a road! This secondary, unpaved road, the R265 from Chile Chico to El Maitén, presents the traveller with vistas of jaw-dropping magnificence. The sky was clear blue, the lake a corresponding azure. The Andean peaks on the far side were dark, angular and snow-capped. On my side of the lake, the land was poor scrubland but beautiful. Frequently wide enough for just one vehicle, the road at times hugs the side of the mountain, bare sandstone escarpments towering above me, matching in scale a sheer drop below. The road rises and falls, twists and turns. And despite its being gravel, the grit is compacted and easy to ride on.

WhatsApp advice from a pal and a bit of 'Swallow hard and get stuck in' self-belief helped. I was familiar with the basics of off-road biking from the two courses I had done. What I lacked was the confidence to put lessons learnt into practice. When riding over rough ground, with the bike slewing this way and that, the best thing to do is to stand fully upright on the footrests (the 'pegs', as they're known). As a means of exerting greater control, it seems counterintuitive, but standing upright and forcing your upper body weight forward, over the fuel tank and the handlebars, does increase your control over the bike. Somehow, instead of twitching your backside while sitting down, haplessly trying to control the machine as it slithers on the slippery gravel, standing upright and channelling control through your knees and ankles enhances stability and really puts you in charge.

Skirting round the edge of the lake, one fabulous vista appears, and then another. I stopped to stare, in the stillness of the moment, at the beauty that time and nature had conjured. And it's just there – free and not asking for anything, other than to be enjoyed and respected. The road seemed never to end – and very soon one is hoping it does not. The stretch I did was a bit over 100km and has to be one of the best, one of the most beautiful, drives anywhere.

Afterwards, I came to Puerto Guadal and decided to settle down for the night. It's a little town of some 700 inhabitants, some making a living from sheep farming, others from tourism. It's at the heart of Chile's Aysén region and is right by Route 7, the Carretera Austral ('Southern Way'), a road of growing and deserved renown. The 1,200km Route 7 runs between Puerto Montt at its northern end and Villa O'Higgins at its south, after which southern Chile is cut off from the rest of the country by the Southern Patagonian Ice Field.

I pulled up outside Hostal Janito, a wooden house with a red tin roof, typical of the town. A man inside indicated that the owner wasn't there but would be back in about an hour. I established that he was at the funeral I had just seen, proceeding at a walking pace to the local graveyard. Next door was a small supermarket, where I got pasta and wine. Coming out, I noticed that people were examining my bike – always a source of interest and a conversation starter. A minibus had also pulled up. 'You want room?' asked Lautaro, the driver and apparently a tour guide. I said yes, and a few minutes later he announced with great authority that he had arranged for me to take Room 2 in the hostel and that I must install my belongings there and settle in.

That night, much wine disappeared, along with pasta and tomatoes and onions and garlic – lots of garlic. I felt lucky to be alive, a master of the gravel roads, and I slept so well.

30 NOVEMBER, BAHÍA MURTA, CHILE

The prospect of about 200km of unpaved road to Coihaique didn't faze me. I set off in good cheer and rode the gravel like a pro before dropping into Bahía Murta. I mean, with a name so close to my own, how could I not? To be honest, after a cursory ride through, the place didn't have a huge amount to recommend it, so I rode on for maybe 8 or 10km until I noticed the tyre-pressure warning light. And then the rear-wheel sensor told me that my rear pressure was down to 16psi when it should, with the load I was carrying, be about 42psi. Within minutes, it was down to fourteen. Then ten, nine, eight and six, and I was in the middle of nowhere.

I had an emergency kit to plug a leak, but my instinct was to press on, until common sense dictated that I return to my namesake – but fairly forgettable – village and try to deal with the problem there, where at least there was food and shelter, if I was really stuck. I didn't fancy camping in the wild and having to deal with such a problem.

I limped back into the village with the rear tyre pressure down to 4 and then 2psi, that is, almost totally deflated and running on the rubber. At the edge of the village I asked a passer-by whether there was an hombre moto around. I made a hissing noise as I pointed to by deflated rear, as it were.

I was directed first left, then first right and ... well, somewhere up there. As I searched for the *vulcanisa* man, a car approached. The couple in it were also looking for the tyre man, though without obvious need. They were French tourists and urged me to stay put while they searched.

Within minutes we were all standing on a stony incline outside a ramshackle yard, with a shed and an awning, under which was one of those machines that takes tyres off wheel rims. So at least we were at the right place. Soon after a few phone calls with a helpful neighbour, a slightly worse-for-wear Nissan pickup truck with a barking dog in the back appeared, and out hopped a man. The dog stayed put but continued barking.

'*¿Qué pasa?*' the man asked.

I explained, attempting Spanish, 'Hmm, me no moto,'

But – and this was the worrying bit – he indicated, Irish-style, that he'd give it a go! His name was Andres, and he set about trying to work out how to take the wheel off the motorbike – his first. He was initially stumped, until his brother Enrique appeared. '*¿Enrique comprender el moto?*' I asked. No, they both answered. I rather feebly suggested the emergency plugging, achievable without removing the wheel, but they were having none of that half-measure stuff.

And lo and behold, after a while, they worked out how to do it (and it turned out to be simple) while Andres's eleven-year-old son Marrin was deploying his full arsenal of school English on me. Where are you from? How old are you? Where are you going? For how long? How old moto? You wife? You son?

In no time at all, once Andres and Enrique got the wheel off, they detached the tyre, found the tiny hole and sealed it with a mushroom-shaped patch. From inside the tyre, the stem of the 'mushroom' is pushed through the hole, while the mushroom cap, as it were, is glued to the inside of the tyre. With the tyre reinflated, the air pressure also forces the cap tighter onto the inside of the tyre. The lads were as delighted as I was with their success. There was much shaking of hands and embracing. I gave them $100 – a small fortune, yes, but I was very grateful, the more so too for their cheerful have-a-go attitude.

6 DECEMBER 2022, PUERTO OCTAY, CHILE

As I moved north along the Carretera Austral, through Patagonia and towards Chile's lake district, a Germanic influence became more and more apparent. Beside the campsite in Puyuhuapi, a small fishing settlement of fewer than 1,000 people on the edge of a fjord, Hostería Alemana, which is run by Otto, has two flagpoles in the front garden – one sporting the Chilean flag, the other a German one.

The Austral is now also mostly paved – thank God. But just before Puyuhuapi the road slips between mountains, the (appropriately named) Cerro Elefantes and the Queulat National Park range, which has a hanging glacier. On one short and very steep unpaved stretch, there are no fewer than fourteen hairpin bends – a nightmare to negotiate on gravel that in places is as deep, and therefore as unstable for motorbike wheels, as a dry riverbed. I failed on two of the bends, toppling over but without serious damage or injury, because I was moving slowly (which was perhaps part of the problem).

Later, at a petrol station in La Junta, I met four Argentine bikers heading south and into this stretch. Three were riding suitable bikes: a Royal Enfield Himalayan, a Ducati and a Benelli. But one was on a Harley V-Rod (think Batman movie) – a long, low-slung streak of jet-black US highway testosterone. A machine less suitable for what they were facing into I cannot imagine.

After one more puncture (repaired for €10 after a ferry ride and a night's sleep in Hornopirén) I was in the small lakeside town of Puerto Octay, simply because it was on the map and I didn't fancy stopping in the city of Puerto Montt. It's not easy exploring a city of 300,000 people, navigating busy streets while riding a fully laden motorbike. I couldn't just park it and leave it to ramble on foot, a rucksack and two large bags strapped onto my panniers easy prey for thieves. So I scooted on through to the more manageable Puerto Octay. Like several small towns in this region, it has a pronounced German feel to it, rooted in the design, shape and style of the buildings and in occasional other things, such as signs for German beer that use Gothic lettering. I came to the town via Lago Llanquihue, a substantial lake. The first town on the lakeshore is Llanquihue itself, and it looks as though it wants to be in Bavaria. The architecture and setting, and hence the whole feel of the place, is Germanic, with many buildings, especially the more modern ones, presenting a Teutonic solidity.

Riding down a steep hill leading to the main square, you are invited to drop in to the Club Alemán, which announced on its Facebook page that it would soon host a Weihnachtsmarkt (a Christmas market also known in Germany as a Christkindlmarkt). The club's logo includes the German coat of arms, that splayed black eagle, head turned sideways. A large sandwich board outside the club entrance advertises bratwurst. None of this is so very different, of course, from the legion of global 'Irish pubs' flogging nostalgia for the old sod – whether to the Irish abroad, to local people or to foreign tourists who, in Chile or wherever, fancy a night of 'Irish'.

The story of German migration to this part of the world goes back to the middle of the nineteenth century, when poverty and hunger were prevalent throughout much of what today are prosperous parts of Europe and countries like Chile and Argentina were looking for settlers. Part of the attraction must surely have been the landscape. The topography of the Chilean Andean slopes is not dissimilar to what one sees in Bavaria but also in Switzerland, Austria and Slovenia. And the style of homes and farming reflects that: lots of shallow-pitched roofs with gable overhangs and long balconies, fir forests and cattle grazing meadows that slope down from the lower treelines or along valley floors and field fencing that is visually Alpine. What attracted a later generation of German migrants was different. The cultural familiarity of where they were going was surely a huge part of it, even if the compelling reason for leaving Europe was a hoped-for obscurity and avoidance of accountability for leaders and collaborators from Nazi Germany.

The current generation of German Chileans seems to me to be very much part of where they are, rather than trying to keep alive what they, or their ancestors, used to be. They're all Chilean now but, like the Irish in America, they keep alive a sense of who they were. In Llanquihue I managed to acquire a pliers (I now know that the Spanish for pliers is alicates, something I probably won't need to know again) to adjust one of my wing mirrors. Perhaps more memorably, I stopped at a German-looking cafe and had a huge slice of carrot cake. Further along the lakeshore, I came to Puerto Octay and spotted the El Molino campsite sign.

For €10 a night I had a lakeside perch where I could sit and listen to the southern lapwings that scamper in fits and starts about the muddy bits at the water's edge, squawking to each other. What really made its presence felt was the bandurria, the buff-necked ibis. This chicken-sized creature has pink legs and grey wings and a black torso or lower body. Its neck is russet brown or gold, and it has a brown cap and a long curlew-like bill. But what distinguishes it more than anything else is its endless chattering. Either alone or, more often, in pairs, they like to perch high in trees or on rooftops and, especially in the early morning from about five and in the late afternoon and early evening, indulge in non-stop yak, yak, yakking.

The sound accompanied me on the morning I wandered around Puerto Octay looking for eggs for breakfast. Going up through the town, one is immediately struck again by the German or colonial old-style buildings. One of them, the former (or so it seemed) Hotel Haase, is just aching to be restored to its former grandeur. It is listed on Booking.com, so it may still be functioning, but it is not, apparently, at present. In fact, when I passed later in the day, it was open but just as a restaurant, and then only till 7 p.m. The inside is beautiful, full of Old World charm but still noticeably the family home and business it once was. Photos of the man and woman who made it what it was are in the hall, and the woman at reception allowed me to wander and take photos. It really could be something special ... in the right hands.

Later, I had a coffee in the coolest cafe in town. It's owned and run by Pauline, who told me that it used to be a workshop (I think for vehicles) and then a shoe shop. She opened the cafe in February 2020 but had to close for a time because of Covid. She noted that I was a biker and said I must contact her friend, Francisco Maturana, who had several motorbikes and lived just up the road, opposite a restaurant named Anita's.

'I'm sure he'll show you,' she said. 'He'd love to meet you.'

The 'several motorbikes' turned out to be at least 130 – an amazing collection, including several seriously rare machines, all of them lovingly restored. On entering a large wooden barn (like something from the film Witness), the visitor is met by three bikes displayed vertically against a wall. There's an 1890s pedal bicycle with wooden wheels sheathed inside rubber, and below it is a 1909 250cc Alcyon, an early French-built machine. Finally, there's one of Ducati's revolutionary Bimotas, a strange-looking bike with front forks replaced with a joint, front and rear suspension, slung under the engine. 'It is very unique,' Francisco explained. 'There were only twenty-nine of the first edition made.'

The aim of the display is to show the evolution of two-wheeled transport. The entire collection will form the core of a motorbike museum and family-fun activity centre park on the edge of Puerto Octay. For Francisco, who is supported by his wife, Loreta, the whole thing has become a passion and is now his life's work (facilitated by the proceeds from the 2014 sale of his online real estate business). In 2024, a permanent home for the collection, emerging on the grounds and project-managed by Francisco, who trained as a civil engineer, will open ... all going well.

But, for now, everything is in the modern wooden barn, itself a beautiful building. The ground floor opens into a restoration workshop, with offices and a range of machines on display, culminating in my own BMW R1200 GS Adventure – 'the only bike for Alaska', says Francisco. And he knows: he did the trip a few years back, north to south, the opposite direction from me.

Upstairs, large picture windows look out to the surrounding lush countryside. And here the extent of the collection becomes clear. It includes a Belgian FN 1913, a 1926 Henderson (like the one used in 1912–13 by Carl Stearns Clancy, the first person to ride a bike around the world, starting in Dublin) and an extremely rare 1928 500cc, pressed-steel Opel (known as the Rocket). There's a 1929 James, a 1958 Adlerwerke 100, a 1958 Horex Imperator, a TWN (short for Triumph-Werke Nürnberg, a plant run by the

German engineer who founded Britain's Triumph), a 1935 Royal Enfield, a 1950 Benelli and several Harleys, Nortons, Triumphs and BMWs.

Then there's a 1938 Excelsior, a couple of BSAs, an AJS, a Matchless, a Suzuki, a Kawasaki, a Honda, a 1960 Panther and a 1959 Motobi, along with several smaller bikes and scooters. There's a collection of sidecar bikes, including a 1930 Harley, a 1956 Zündapp and a 1943 BMW Afrika Korps. And the collection also includes the bike of one of the outrider policemen who accompanied Bill Clinton when he visited Chile in 1998.

To put it mildly, this is not what one expects to find in a little town like Puerto Octay, and, boy, is it worth the stop! Anyone interested in motorbikes or motor engineering, design and development – from the ungainly and clunky to the sexily sleek and dangerous – will love this place. For me, biking is less about the machines and very much more about the freedom they deliver – the freedom to just go to places, anywhere and any time you want, and meet people – people like Francisco and Loreta – and the generosity they display when someone arrives on their doorstep, unannounced and unexpected.

But if the machines are what do it for you, this is a place to visit!

8 DECEMBER 2022, LAUTARO, CHILE

My next stop was Lautaro, a small town in south-central Chile further up Route 5 and to which I went for a very particular reason. Over the previous number of years, when I had mentioned my desire to ride a motorbike from Tierra del Fuego to Alaska, countless people responded along the lines of 'Aha! The old "Motorcycle Diaries" trail, eh?' – a reference to Che Guevara's famed journey and book of the same title. Guevara's 1951–52 motorbike escapade has become very much part of the wider Che story and, let's be honest, is also something of your average adventure biker's fantasy. My problem is that it's mostly myth, or rather it has evolved into a narrative that essentially isn't true. In many ways, Che is an attractive character. Unusually handsome, he had a terrific smile and a charming personality, even if he was also a ruthless militarist. In the 1960s and '70s, many left-leaning young men wanted, in effect, to be Che. But the essential proposition about his biking adventure doesn't bear scrutiny.

The myth is that in late 1951, twenty-three-year-old Che, an Argentine medical student of sometime Irish extraction, and a pal, Alberto, hatched a plan to ride a Norton 500cc bike, which they nicknamed La Poderosa (the 'Mighty One'), from Buenos Aires through Latin America and up into North America. Although the journey, such as it unfolded, helped radicalise Che because of the poverty and grinding inequality he saw, little of the adventure actually happened by motorbike. The pair did indeed head west from Buenos Aires, riding across Argentine Patagonia to the Andes and into the town of Bariloche, from where they crossed a lake into Chile and rode down onto that country's central valley. It was then a case, as with me, of heading north. Today that journey can be done on a modern motorway, but seventy years ago it was mostly unpaved gravel roads and, in the diary that became the book, Che described repeated punctures. I know the feeling ...

Just short of the town of Lautaro, La Poderosa crashed. The bike 'took a sharp twist sideways sending us flying to the ground,' Che wrote. 'Alberto and I, unharmed, examined the bike – finding one of the steering columns broken and, most seriously, the gearbox smashed.'

They hitched a ride to the town. Having come here myself because of that, I wondered what they'd make of it now. It's a medium-sized place of maybe 25,000 people and is dusty and unkempt, like a lot of others in the region. That said, the main drag, Avenida Bernardo O'Higgins, was getting a makeover, and despite the roadworks, on that Friday evening it was busy enough. The shops are a typical hotch-potch selection, selling everything under the sun. Bra, knicker, fabric and drapery stores vie for attention with hardware outlets and vegetable and dried-bean shops; small corridors at right angles to the pavements grandly call themselves 'malls' but contain only a handful of shops. Gaudy neon signs flash Open or Closed, as the case might be. There are several of those oversized, Chinese-owned stores, places so crammed with goods they make TK Maxx and pound shops appear empty by comparison.

There's a fashion outlet called Vintage Paris, a builder's suppliers, a petrol station and several motor- and tyre-repair shops, numerous fast food places and several banks and dentists. There are at least three one-armed bandit gaming joints, pathetic, gloomy places filled with flashing neon lights, garish pictures of pneumatic young women, techno 'music' and, in each outlet I peered into, a single elderly player working a machine on their own.

One block back from it all, a railway line slices through the town, with precious little separating it from everything else. Children play ball in dusty corners, and dogs roam freely or just loll about, waiting for something interesting to catch their attention – a passing wheel or a scrap of food. There are plenty of vehicles that look new and would have cost a lot of money. Equally, while not everyone is poor, those who have a lot less are equally visible, as are those who have fallen through the cracks. Che would have noticed that.

Many of the buildings are from after the early 1950s, but several others are clearly older and would have been there when Che and Alberto limped into town. They're mostly timber-clad and painted fading shades of white, pink, yellow or red. They look strangely Russian and, in snow, they could be in scenes from Dr Zhivago. Just off Vicuña Mackenna Street (named after the Chilean writer of Irish and Basque lineage, a grandson of Monaghan-born Juan Mackenna), round the corner from my hostel, there's a defunct garage, and I wonder whether Che and Alberto might have brought the bike there. It's possible, I suppose, but I had no way of finding out, at least not in the few hours I was there.

Che wrote that the pair divided their time in Lautaro between working to fix the bike, scrounging food and drink from strangers and trying to seduce the wife of one of the mechanics. When they left Lautaro – Che driving, Alberto riding pillion – they careered into a herd of cows, 'at good speed', according to Che. A screw came off the back break, and Che threw the handbrake – a handbrake on a motorbike, imagine! – which, soldered ineptly, broke too.

For some moments I saw nothing more than the blurred shape of cattle flying past us on each side, while poor Poderosa gathered speed down the steep hill ... in the distance a river was screaming towards us with terrifying efficacy. I veered to the side of the road and in the flash of an eye, the bike mounted the two-meter bank, embedding us between two rocks, but we were unhurt.

They had gone only a few miles north from Lautaro, but that was that – little more than six weeks of an adventure that continued for a further six months ... and none of it on motorcycle. Thereafter, they hitched rides on lorries and ferries, north into the Atacama Desert, Peru, Colombia and Venezuela. But the motorcycle diary myth endures, inspiring young people (and the not so young) to embark on daft adventures.

*

As I moved ever further north up the country, some of the reasons for Chile's wealth became more evident. Riding along Route 5, the 3,364km spinal transport road linking northern, central and southern Chile, it's apparent that logging is a huge part of life, from the lake district into the neighbouring Los Ríos region. Huge pine and eucalyptus forests line the road all along the way and, at regular points, there were enormous lumber yards, where tree trunks, in various stages of transformation into usable timber, were stored and stacked. Some stacks of dark black trunks were being sprayed with a liquid that I assumed was part of a preservative process. In other places the piles at sawmills were being processed into fence posts or planks; sometimes, off-cuttings and bark were pulverised into what looked like dunes of sawdust, I assumed for processing into chipboard and the like.

At various points there were outlets advertising casas – whole houses, small readymade wooden homes that could be transported and plonked wherever one wished. And with all the forestry there was evidence too of the wildfires that can lay waste to large tracts of brush and forest. In 2022 over 7,000 hectares were destroyed by fires. When I passed through, firefighters were battling eighteen fires, many of them close to Santiago, which was itself under a public health alert because of the density of smoke in the air.

The road sliced through the landscape, passing over riverbeds in parallel with the main railway line, whose mostly yellow-painted old bridges of bow-shaped steel girders bend in graceful lines leaping the valleys. They can appear like a family of dolphins, flipping in and out of water. As fields gradually took over the landscape, the soil was dark and appeared to be rich in nutritious humus. Already in the south, many fields had been harvested for silage, and gradually, as I progressed north, fruit trees took over – apples, peaches, apricots and cherries – as well as hazel and walnut trees.

And then came the roadside fruit sellers and the processing operations – factories where the produce is cleaned and packed, where the crates that are filled in fields are stacked and stored. One of the giants in Chile is the Irish-owned Dole Plc, part of the Total Produce group, whose lineage included Fyffes and whose global corporate HQ is 29 North Anne Street, Dublin 7. Route 5, now branded on hoardings as the Panamericana, is filled with mid-sized pickup trucks, flatbed trucks and some massive transporters – Macks and Freightliners, those bottle-nosed American giants best given a wide berth.

Around Talca, I began to see the first evidence of Chile's wine industry, and before long, grape production, and all that goes with it, started to dominate – together with roadside corporate advertising by the major brands and wine tours for the curious and the thirsty. The importance of the industry to Chile can be illustrated by one fact alone: 83 per cent of production is exported, which is the second highest ratio of any wine-producing country, after New Zealand. There are over 800 wineries, employing 100,000 people, about half of them in production, the rest in logistics, sales and marketing. The industry constitutes 0.5 per cent of the country's GDP and 2 per cent of all exports – and Ireland is one of the leading takers.

14 DECEMBER 2022, SANTIAGO, CHILE

Jaime de la Barra is the viticulture manager at Santa Rita, whose vineyards, for their various Santa Rita labels and also their Carmen wines, are produced in Buin, just south of the capital, Santiago, where they also run an upmarket hotel, restaurant, museum and visitor centre. The particular vines receiving his attention – and which pass the test – will shortly produce grapes for the vineyard's iconic class, special reserve red wine, Casa Real. Jaime strokes the leaves on a row of cabernet sauvignon vines with his open palm, in a loving and gentle way, as he might stroke his child's hair.

'If [the rustle] sounds like paper,' he says, 'too much water [has been applied]. It needs to sound like the wind blowing on leaves, like in the movies.' He also wants the leaves to appear a light green, not a deep dark green.

It's a bit odd to think that vines could receive too much water, because Chile has an extreme water shortage problem that shows every sign of getting worse – not because of profligate use or leaking pipes, though presumably both happen to some degree, but because of climate change. The country had just entered its fourteenth year of continuous drought, and the strain was showing. According to a February 2020 study of a river valley some 200km north of Santiago, the country was experiencing its worst drought for 700 years. In the last century, Chile averaged just over 900mm of rain a year; today that has fallen by 30 per cent. In the few days in December 2022 during which I was around Buin, Santiago and the Pacific coast city of Valparaíso, temperature records were broken. Valparaíso recorded Chile's highest known temperature to date – 41.6°C – while Santiago fried in 33°C, a temperature normally experienced six to eight weeks further into the Southern Hemisphere's summer. According to Sustainable Solutions Development, in fifty years' time, the amount of water available to Santiago will have reduced by 40 per cent, through a combination of climate change and population growth. The capital city has 6.8 million residents, but that is expected to grow to eight million by 2030. Earlier in 2022, water rationing was announced for the first time.

At Santa Rita – one of the country's top wine producers and the largest exporter of Chilean wine to Ireland – de la Barra explained what he and his colleagues were doing to address the water problem. We drove to a vineyard named Hill 93, looking down on the village of Alto Jahuel and beyond it to the Maipo Valley. The ground is bone dry and dusty. Extreme heat from mid-December to mid-January is not that unusual, he said, 'but it is definitely getting more extreme'. Not only has the volume of water from the Andes diminished significantly as demand has grown, but the quality of such water as now flows has also decreased. This is because concentrations of carbonates and chlorine in Andean lakes have built up as the volume of water passing through them has decreased. By the time the water reaches the valleys below, it has become mineral-heavy.

'So there is a lot more concentration of minerals into the water and into our three reservoirs on the estate,' he said. The effect for vine growers is that this mineral-heavy water reacts with lime in the soil and forms a surface crust, causing water from irrigation drips to flow away from the stem of the vine rather than sink into the soil where it falls. This in turn causes vine roots in effect to chase the water and, by growing up towards the surface rather than down to other minerals that are wanted to make the best wines, the vine eventually dies. One solution is to treat the water, with sulphur or by ionisation or with sun-wave technology (developed by Israel to desalinate seawater but very costly) to break its surface tension and encourage absorption. But de la Barra prefers a more holistic approach. Part of that is to sow mustard between the vines, cutting the plants and ploughing the crop into the ground.

Another solution is to identify, from among the 300 different bacteria and 170 types of fungus that are in the soil, which ones contribute to vine health and use them to create natural fertilizers. The bacteria and fungus also take carbon from the atmosphere. 'It can be three or four times more than is produced by the vineyard,' said de la Barra, adding that while viticulture generates fifteen tons of CO_2 per hectare, forty-five tons can be extracted from the atmosphere using this natural tool. 'The maths is that the most realistic thing is not related to biofuels or a different tractor engine.

It's about biodiversity and biology in the soil,' he argued. 'For us as a team this is our number one priority. We are not going to be bankrupted as a company [by using this method], and we are using technologies which are already having a positive side effect by using fewer insecticides, and fertiliser use is dramatically reduced.'

Santa Rita has almost 400 hectares devoted to wine production in Chile and in Argentina (for its Doña Paula wines), and by 2025 it aims to have 30 per cent of its vine-growing land using the carbon-reducing system described by de la Barra. Just 3 per cent of global CO_2 emissions is related to wine production, and so while the industry itself is not a major contributor to the problem, it's highly vulnerable to the effects of climate change.

Dealing with the water issue is one problem. Another is changing planting positioning. De la Barra said some vineyards had been replanted by sowing vines in parallel to the sun's daily movement. By doing so, and not allowing the sun's rays direct access to the grapes by shining on the side of the plant, the top of the vine becomes a protective cover for the fruit underneath. Similarly, in the vineyard's nursery, where new vines can take six years to reach production maturity, plants are now protected by a sunray-reducing mesh.

Grinding down the 3 per cent global CO_2 contribution is especially difficult as 64 per cent of that 3 per cent relates to activities not entirely within the industry's control: it involves barrel production, glass manufacture and shipping. Without major technological change in shipping (which means reducing use of diesel engines), what Santa Rita as a company, and indeed the entire Chilean wine industry, can do is limited. Santa Rita exports 91 per cent of what it produces – of which a surprising 36 per cent goes to Ireland.

One of the reasons I wanted to visit the Santa Rita vineyard was something their main man in Ireland, Terry Pennington, said to me a while back about climate change, the drought and how the company was trying to mitigate the effects of global warming on wine production. Another reason was to visit Casa Real, the former estate house and now upmarket hotel that specialises in low-key excellence. The winery was founded in 1880 by Domingo Fernández Concha, whose family owned it until it was bought by the Grupo Claro in 1980. What is now the hotel was the Concha family summer residence. As a hotel, it just oozes an Old World charm, with squeaky polished floorboards, family portraits and chintzy furniture. Notwithstanding its current function, the place still manages to feel like a family home.

It sits in a forty-hectare park, designed by the French landscape gardener Guillaume Renner. From the front terrace, guests look out on mature trees, a lake and formal beds framed by privet hedging and defined by elegant garden statues. The front of the hotel is festooned by an enormous pink bougainvillea, reputed to be the largest in all of South America. Beside the hotel is a medium-sized chapel, built in 1885 and combining Roman, Norman and Neo-Gothic styles. The whole ensemble is delightful.

One of the many charms of the place is that one day every mid-week, Doña María Luisa Vial, the widow of Richardo Claro, group founder and purchaser of the winery, and who is in her mid-eighties, comes from her home in Santiago to walk the gardens and reassure herself that everything is just as it should be. Unfortunately, I have never managed to bump into her.

The winery is also open to day visitors, and offers tours of the vineyard, including cycling tours, entry to a museum (which has artifacts from Chile's ancient history), a cafe and restaurant and, of course, a wine shop. In December 2022 the winery received Chile's best wine experience tourism award.

The aim, according to the hotel's tourism manager, Diego Valenzuela, is to preserve the heritage both of the wine that is produced and of the place itself – and also to make guests feel they're in a home. 'This is not a museum hotel,' he says, 'because you come inside here and you can touch everything. You can sit in the chairs.' The hotel has sixteen accommodations, a mixture of bedrooms and suites. But the defining feature, for me at any rate, is the dining room – a lovely elevated conservatory-style high-ceilinged room whose three sides overlook an inner courtyard, with dappled light, a fountain and a gazebo. There are also the walkthrough drawing rooms, all of them with that slightly lived-in feel of sofas you want to flop onto and those family portraits – all the complete opposite of the personality void of some other upmarket hotels.

Oh, and there's a full-sized billiard table too, not to mention the fine dining. And the wines are not to be beaten ...

16 DECEMBER 2022, VALPARAÍSO, CHILE

Oliver St John Gogarty's poem 'The Ship', famously translated into Irish as 'Valparaíso' by Pádraig de Brún, bestowed something magical on the Chilean port city. It became for me that sunlit kingdom ... a place of romantic attraction to which I longed to go. The poem is filled with memorable imagery – the lure of a country far away, to be taken there by a ship shining like gold. I heard and remembered the ship's siren call from the mists beneath the Andes in youth, inviting us to this jewel by the sea.

I rode into Valparaíso on a sweltering December day and went straight to the La Joya Hostel near the seafront, which promised safe parking for the bike – albeit in a garage with a roller door open permanently to the street! Throughout Latin America I found myself staying mostly in hostels, sourced mainly through Booking.com and Hostelworld, both reliable for inexpensive and generally well-run places to stay, costing usually €10 to €15 a night for a dorm bed. La Joya was one such, even if the entrance – a stairwell from a grotty street to the first floor – was unpromising. The first floor was in fact uber cool, full of black-and-white signs and lots of post-industrial chic tubular-steel furniture. There was a low-slung sofa and wooden pallets fashioned into coffee tables. On an adjoining top floor there was a pub and burger joint doing a roaring trade, and not just from backpackers at the hostel.

Outside was typical Valparaíso urban chaos. Crowded, noisy streets and footpaths. But awful graffiti almost everywhere gives the place a deeply run-down feeling; shops were apparently so fed up that they had given up trying to protect their facades and had their shutters down all the time. The city, in effect an amphitheatre looking out onto the Pacific, used to have twenty-six funiculars, but only sixteen remain functioning. One of the closed ones was by the hostel, and a sad sight it was, all broken timber and twisted rusty metal.

Across the main thoroughfare, by the hostel, was the city's fruit and vegetable market – though as much seemed to be going on outside the market hall as inside it. Farmers, middlemen, sellers and household buyers (some doubtless small traders intending to sell on) filled the footpaths as people and lorries lugged produce this way and that. Cars tried as best they could to make their way through. Liberal use of the horn was employed by all.

My favourite part of the city is the far southern end, the hill known as Concepción, which overlooks the rest of the chaos. In front is the sea; to the right is today's bustling city; and to the left and below is the Barrio Puerto, with its buildings that remind one of a different, possibly more prosperous era. Valparaíso's heyday was from the mid-nineteenth century to the mid-twentieth. What spelt the end, or at least a major change, was the opening in 1914 of the Panama Canal. Before that, all shipping from the east going west, or vice versa, had to round Cape Horn and generally stopped at Valparaíso for R&R and any fresh supplies needed for the onward journey, often up the west coast of the Americas.

The port was also the main route out of Chile for the country's vast mineral treasure trove. Since the opening of the Panama Canal, and with it the loss of a big chunk of business for Valparaíso, other ports have been developed on Chile's Pacific coast, notably in the north. Despite all that, Valparaíso remains a major port.

Why do I like Concepción? Because on that hill there's the most extraordinary collection – spread across a warren of streets and walkways – of timber buildings made to serve the needs of the community that built and operated the port: their homes, machine workshops, retail outlets, offices and churches. The roofs are almost invariably corrugated iron, and if the external walls are also, they're usually clad in another flatter but also ribbed metal.

As the port declined and other changes of modernity kicked in, Concepción went downhill as well. Today it's on the up, thanks to gentrification. But it remains a beguiling mix of the shabby and the chic. Some buildings are run-down and some are simply falling down, all peeling paint and windows askew; others have been restored and are super trendy, or they're merely occupied by artists and the like while owners ponder what to do with their asset.

Some terraces, such as Paeso Atkinson, are a mixture of done-up and still run-down. One suspects there may be more than a few squatters about. The whole area is a firm favourite of artists, students and intellectuals, as well as dropouts. There are lovely hostels and hotels such as the Bristol Hotel (but don't lean on the balustrade: it's so rotten that you'll probably plunge into the barrio below), and there are boutique stopovers, cafes and restaurants.

Concepción is the one place in the city where I think it's fair to refer to much of the graffiti that covers many of the buildings as art. Walking tours abound, and well-informed guides, often retirees or students earning beer money, have a good knowledge of many of the artists. Some of the huge, full-facade or gable-end paintings are commissioned by the property owners. Some of the artists have become known by name, such as Sebastián Varas Mackenzie, who specialises in black-and-white works, marking him out from the rest, and Mauro Goblin, who some liken to Banksy. Several have graduated from the street, take commissions and have their own galleries. One of the best known is Cuellimangui, whom I met while on a walking tour, flogging his work on Paeso Atkinson. This part of Valpo is worth visiting for the graffiti art alone: a riot of vibrant primary colours and figures, some mythical in style, others cartoonish, some surreal but all arresting, many brightening what otherwise are frequently dilapidated, grungy alleyways and derelict eyesores.

18 DECEMBER 2022, NORTHERN CHILE

A few days before Christmas I decided I needed to cover some serious ground and make haste for northern Chile. And so I hit the road, covering, on three successive days, 435km, 445km and 473km – 1,353km in all. On the fourth day I miscalculated and ended up doing another 443km, for a grand total of 1,796km. Truly, this is not to be recommended, but the GS Adventure is designed for such journeys, even as tiredness becomes the enemy. Physically, however, one dismounts at the end of a hard day's travelling none the worse for wear. And, as always, along the way there were sights to be seen and places to be experienced.

I had returned to Santiago for a seasonal function at the Irish embassy but was now ready to make tracks again. The city is a sprawling place of over six million people, but the way north was easy enough to find. My hostel, an arts and crafts gem called the Aji, was just off Avenida Providencia, which in due course becomes the grandly titled Avenida Libertador Bernardo O'Higgins. This in turn leads directly to Route 5 and the way north. At a filling station I got chatting to a biker couple who said I must stop at Guanaqueros. It is a small town beside the sea, which I said appealed to me, and they said it had a nice campsite.

When I got there the site looked a bit shambolic, but it was indeed right by the sea, and the woman who emerged from the house at the entrance that doubled as the site office said I could pitch my tent anywhere I wanted and use the loo and showers. The fee was 10,000 pesos (about €10).

There were some Chilean families there enjoying barbecues, but they all left as the sun set. I went to sleep with my tent door open, wondering what the rows of black dots were on the water about a kilometre out to sea. I slept to the sound of waves breaking on the shore in a melodic, arching roll, from one end of the beach to the other, and to the sound of gulls. There wasn't another soul about.

Next morning I got up, took down the tent, repacked and rode off into the town to see what the place was about. The black dots turned out to be the floats of a shellfish farm, working exactly like the mussel farms on the Killary in Connemara. But here the floats were holding up large tubular nets filled with scallops – small ones about half the size of what you will see in Spain and Ireland but scallops nonetheless. In the early morning, which was dull, cool and slightly misty, caused by the cool Pacific air, small boats were going to and from the farm, bringing in nets bulging with scallops. At a small two-storey processing plant beside the harbour they were emptied out, washed and packaged for sale. Essentially, they were plucked from the sea ready to be eaten.

Beside the plant, fishermen were gutting and cleaning fish, thereby attracting the interest of sea lions. Several of these vast animals were lolling about in the water just below where one man was working, his arm swishing guts off a wooden block onto the concrete just below his feet ... and into the grateful mouth of one elderly sea lion that had jumped out of the harbour water with surprising agility and slobbering enthusiasm. He was an ugly brute, and I'd say his breath could have stripped paint. In appearance, he was to a seal what a hippopotamus is to a piglet. There were also lots of pelicans observing everything from elevated positions in a statuesque manner but ready should lunch appear suddenly.

By the sea a desert landscape was beginning to emerge, along with extreme temperatures in the mid to late afternoon. There was something disconcerting about riding along a road and seeing, on the left-hand side, the vast Pacific Ocean, blue and beautiful, its white rollers crashing onto shoreline rocks or small beaches and, at the same time, on the right-hand side, a bone-dry desert landscape, endless stretches of lunar-like landscape and pink-tinged mountains that could double as a Martian film set.

Just north of La Serena I came across a disused narrow-gauge railway line and stopped to examine it. The wooden sleepers were gnarled and split; the rails had evidently carried nothing for decades but were not really rusted because, of course, there's no rain here. I assume the line was connected to a mine, but it clearly hadn't been used for years.

As I went further north into the Atacama, which starts here as a defined political and geographic region, I came across several such disused railway lines. But despite the desert conditions, nature can still thrive: there were two types of flowers and some cactus plants, like the ones you see in cartoons, and one that had a huge rock embedded in its trunk and lower branches. I guessed it must have grown that way, embracing the rock as it grew and eventually lifting it off the ground.

North of Vallenar, on a perfectly straight stretch of road, I saw the aftermath of a serious crash. Two vehicles, a small white van and a Hyundai four-wheel drive, apparently travelling in the same direction, had collided. Both were smashed to such a degree that they looked like write-offs. Traffic had ground to a crawl and several people stopped to help. I did as well, thinking that my first aid kit could be of use. As I crossed the road to a wreck lying on its side, a man emerged from the back of it with blood on his hands and face, but he seemed more distraught than wounded.

'Can you help me? Can you help me?' he said. I asked what I could do. He then tumbled out what was essentially a chunk of his life story. He had worked in a mine, but he hated that life and was going to Los Angeles to make a new life for himself. His vehicle was the other one, about 100m away, embedded in the roadside bank of sand and gravel. It had a *Se Vende* ('For sale') sign on the back windscreen. He was going to, or coming from, seeing his daughter, but the car sale was clearly what had been going to fund his escape to California. I told him that he was alive and that this was the most important thing. He would see his daughter again, and wasn't that great? We hugged before he wandered off, dazed.

I then went over to the van. The driver was trapped inside but conscious and being looked after by another passer-by – someone with a first aid kit and evident medical knowledge. An ambulance had been called.

I walked back to my bike and packed away my kit. The man on his way to California had walked back to his car. His emotions were clearly as wrecked as the vehicle: he seemed to look at it for confirmation that his dreams were just as smashed. He came back to me. 'Have you any words for me, sir? Have you any words for me?'

I didn't know what to say. He said I must be a very successful person in my country to be riding a motorbike in Chile. He pulled out his wallet to show me his ID. His name was Steve Verdugo, and he was thirty-four. He said he spoke English well because either he or his mother (I can't recall which) had been born in the Philippines. He wanted me to take a photograph of him. He didn't ask me for money. And I didn't offer any. He stood there on the side of the road clutching his wallet and a water bottle, fighting back tears as he gave a thumbs up for the picture. We hugged once more and said our goodbyes.

I couldn't stop thinking about Steve for some days after, and I reproached myself for not doing more for him. I couldn't have given him a lift, but I could have given him money. I didn't and I felt, and still feel, ashamed about that. I rode on and camped the night in a site at Bahía Inglesa.

The next day took me into the capital of northern Chile, Antofagasta, a big city with all the grime and glam of a place serving heavy industry and reaping the rewards. I stayed at a small hotel and next morning found Luis, a bike mechanic who could service the bike and supply me with a set of new tyres. He runs Big Trail Service, a workshop that does for the local police as well as for adventure bikers. I figured that if the cops trust Luis with their bikes, so could I. In any event, I didn't fancy tackling unpaved roads in Bolivia and Peru with a back tyre already weakened by two punctures, even though it was about halfway through its natural life in terms of the mileage notched up.

I then rode north from Antofagasta along the increasingly desert-like coast to a place named Mejillones. There was a string of what appeared to be huge but distinct industrial operations. I counted thirteen, and each one seemed to be the size of massive operations in Ireland, such as Aughinish Alumina in Co. Limerick. Each had chimneys and venting stacks and production buildings the size of aircraft hangers, and they were fed by a battalion of giant pylons marching across the desert landscape that, on inspection, turned out to be nothing more than sand and crushed shells. All were related in some way to Chile's huge mining industry in the Atacama Desert. The whole area had a Mad Max feel to it, accentuated by a mass of petrol tankers – I estimated 200 – just hanging about for no obvious reason at the junction of the main road and the turn down to the industrial zone. It looked like they were waiting for work. From there I rode east, deep into the Atacama.

23 DECEMBER 2022, PAMPA UNIÓN AND THE ATACAMA DESERT, CHILE

Having entered the Atacama Desert – the driest place on Earth other than the poles – by following the Pacific coastline, I turned inland and headed for Calama along Routes 5 and 25. About 30km south of Sierra Gorda there is what I first thought was a long-abandoned Indigenous settlement. For about 2km on one side of the road there are hundreds of ruined mud-brick buildings, a cluster that was obviously once a town. The buildings are behind one of those green mesh fencings that gardeners use to keep harsh winds off plants, but such is the harshness of the Atacama that the mesh was mostly blown away. Clearly visible behind it were streets, a grid pattern layout, what were at one time homes – many homes, in fact, and probably enterprises of one sort or another – and something of a town square. It all just stands there now, beaten down daily in the Atacama sun, lashed by the winds but never worn away by rain, because it never rains here.

A sign said keep out. So I went in.

So too did Gustavo and Stephanie and their children, a boy of perhaps seven and a girl of maybe five. They had been wandering about the old main square area (as I call it – perhaps it was something totally different), and Gustavo and his son were kicking a ball between them. I parked the bike and did my own wandering. When I came back to the bike, I approached Gustavo and asked him about the place. I later did a little research of my own.

The town was known as the Pampa Unión, and it appeared, to me at least, to have had a short and unpleasant existence, the origins of which are not entirely clear. In the first decade of the twentieth century, some people were living at the northern end of the town, apparently digging saltpetre for mine owners who had little to no interest in their welfare. The miners too appear to have lived in ignorance of their health, or they felt that they had no choice but to take risks in order to live. There were numerous accidents as well as problems resulting from overexposure to the mineral, which can cause chronic blood pressure and respiratory problems. Community health was poor.

Enter, in 1911, Lautaro Ponce Arellano, a thirty-four-year-old physician and Freemason from Valparaíso, who decided to set up a sanatorium there, seemingly for altruistic reasons. This appears to have fostered the consolidation of the settlement, then known as the Pampa Blanca, and fuelled its growth along the Antofagasta–Calama railway line. It quickly became known as the Pampa Unión. Numbers grew rapidly, from about 2,000 to anything between 10,000 and 15,000, many of them Chinese, Croatian, Palestinian, Syrian, Argentine, Peruvian, Bolivian and, of course, Chilean.

There were few laws, and those that existed were enunciated by the Nitrates Office, that is, by the people who bought the saltpetre and hence controlled the local economy. An 'administrator' appointed by the Nitrates Office ruled unaccountable and in a manner that history seems to agree promoted debauchery and social vices. No money circulated in what was a barter economy: you got what groceries you needed, and what beer or wine you wanted, by exchanging tokens earned at the nitrate mine.

The streets were mostly mud-surfaced, but the main thoroughfare, Sotomayor, onto which the train station fronted, ran six or seven blocks and was floored in timber. There was a theatre that could fit 200 people, a boxing stadium for 250, a printing house and a civil registry that may or may not have been related to the fact that brothels – several of which existed around the edges of the town – also thrived. They never got round to building a church, but those who wanted to worship did so in a room at the school.

Whatever about Dr Arellano's altruistic or Masonic motives, he wasn't beyond putting himself around. Married twice, he had five children with his first wife and another son resulting from an affair with a woman known as Pampina Mima, about whom my limited research suggests nothing; but the name itself suggests something. For all sorts of reasons not difficult to imagine, the place became notorious and was finally 'disestablished' by the regional authorities in 1954. Dr Arellano died aged ninety-one in 1967.

'There's a cemetery over there,' said Gustavo, pointing to an unkempt collection of many graves blasted by the desert wind, some half buried now by wind-blown sand. It could be a set from a spaghetti western. Some of the plots are simple graves – many containing the remains of children, apparently more susceptible than adults to nitrate poisoning – while other, grander memorials have been burst open by grave robbers, leaving and their mummified corpses visible and open to the elements. I chatted a bit more with Gustavo and gave his boy some stickers. Gustavo rushed to his car and returned with a lump of rock 'from my mine', he said, pointing out streaks of malachite and purple amethyst–stained quartz. He gave it to me and we shook hands and waved our goodbyes.

Further along the road towards Sierra Gorda, the presence of a huge Polish-controlled open-cast copper mine, south and west of the town, was evident from huge piles of mine tailings, the debris left over once the mineral-bearing lode has been extracted from the rock. Something caught my eye as I passed on a day when the wind was blowing dust clouds and tornado eddies across the landscape before they vanished as suddenly as they appeared. Peering between several huge tailing mounds perhaps a hundred feet tall, I noticed a strange, almost sinister, beacon. It was perhaps 5km back from the main road at any one point but must have been hundreds of feet high. It looked in one sense like a lighthouse, except that there was no flashing – no pulse or rhythm to suggest it was a signal – just a constant, slightly throbbing beam of pure white light atop what looked like a huge column. Like the eyes of a portrait, as the road bent past the tailings, over a stretch of maybe 5km, the beam seemed to follow my own gaze. It was creepy.

I asked in Sierra Gorda and in Calama about the beam but, strangely, no one knew anything about it. It may have had nothing to do with the mine; from a distance, its light appeared to be entirely unfocused in terms of what it might be projected to illuminate. But it reminded me of nothing less than the Eye of Sauron, casting an evil gaze over a wasteland filled with slag heaps and things abandoned.

25 DECEMBER 2022, SAN PEDRO DE ATACAMA, CHILE
San Pedro is the centre of tourism in the northern part of the Atacama Desert and a backpacker haven. Calama is another dusty city of about 200,000 people and exists really only for the mine at Chuquicamata, the

largest open-cast copper mine in the world, and for serving other mineral extraction operations in the region. Chuquicamata is, simply, a vast hole in the ground with resultant mine tailings the size of mountains. San Pedro is about 100km south-east, close to the border with Bolivia. The road crosses a desert plain before dropping into what is essentially an oasis. The way down is through Valle de la Luna ('Valley of the Moon'). Everyone stops there to gaze in wonderment at the aptly named, barren mountainous landscape sculpted by heat and wind, everything a sort of burnt red.

San Pedro was where I spent Christmas Day, in a hostel where we had a communal barbecue, about which I remember very little, not because of the quantity drunk but just because it was all so ordinary! I missed my family back home, and the highlight of the day for me was a parade of Indigenous people to the town's simple, single-storey whitewashed adobe church, where gaily coloured costumes, music and dancing clashed in a joyous celebration.

San Pedro has been lived in for about 8,000 years. The town and surrounding area has a population of about 11,000, about half of whom are Indigenous Lickan Antay people. The area in fact once comprised eighteen settlements, each with their own way of doing things and their individual sense of identity, but over time these grew into one organic socioeconomic unit called an 'ayllu'. That whole order was irrevocably changed, of course, with the arrival of the Spanish, and today San Pedro trades on its past and its location and is a magnet for tourists.

The little town has a few shady enclaves where trees have grown sufficiently to provide shade for outside eating; but mostly the narrow streets of hardened mud are lined with white single-storey adobe terrace houses. In the centre, around the main drag, named Caracoles, every outlet is a tour operator, a restaurant or a shop selling souvenirs. San Pedro might just have the highest density of backpacker hostels anywhere. An arcade beside the municipal offices near the church is reserved for Indigenous people selling souvenirs; on the footpaths of Caracoles, latter-day dropouts try their luck selling bead bracelets and other handmade trinkets, usually involving copper wire and bits of rock.

The tour operators flog bicycle trips to the nearby Salar de Atacama, the largest salt flat in Chile and one of the largest in the world; minibus rides to the geysers at El Tatio, high in the Andes close to the Bolivian border, and to Valle de la Luna and its sister nearby, Valle de la Muerte (Valley of Death); and star-gazing expeditions. The Atacama is famous for its clear nights and moisture-free atmosphere, with the latter adding enormously to the clarity of what can be seen above.

Fifteen minutes east of the town is the entrance to Alma – the Atacama Large Millimeter Array. Ireland is one of the twenty-two countries participating in and helping to fund the project, albeit to a modest degree. Alma is home to the world's largest collection of space-observing antennae, assembled at the highest altitude. Sixty-six mobile antennae, fifty-four of them with 12m diameter dishes and weighing up to 110 tons, trundle around the Array Operations Site (AOS), 5,050m up the Andes, looking at the universe just after the Big Bang.

I met Alma's director, the Canadian astrophysicist Sean Dougherty, at the Irish embassy in Santiago (his mother came from Co. Tyrone) and asked whether I could visit. He kindly said yes, and so, on St Stephen's Day, I went with Danilo Vidal, Alma's community and media relations officer, to the facility's Operation Support Facility (OSF). To describe it as a city would be an exaggeration, but spread over many acres is a series of low-lying rectangular modern buildings set into the flank of the bare mountain and sitting at 2,950m above sea level. It looks like a cross between an Antarctic scientific base in the sun and Blofeld's lair.

Anyone can go to the OSF, but to travel higher to the AOS you must undergo a health check and record a blood pressure reading of 140/90 or lower. To my great disappointment, I failed the check three times. I returned to San Pedro dejected – and doubled my dose of blood pressure tablets.

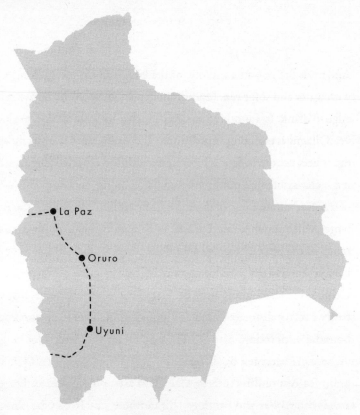

BOLIVIA

30 DECEMBER 2022, UYUNI

I headed north-east out of Chile, riding from San Pedro to Ollagüe on the border with Bolivia. For the first time on this adventure, I was about to enter pastures entirely new to me. Before this visit to Chile I had already been to Patagonia, the Central Valley and the Atacama. But I had never been to Bolivia or Peru and, even though neither is exactly what you'd call the dark side of the moon, I felt a bit nervous.

For a time on the way to Ollagüe, the road ran along the flank of a string of volcanoes straddling the frontier, the last one of which was active, a puff of smoke being released from just below the lip of its cone every couple of minutes. But the landscape was noticeably less desert-like than further south. This was no longer the deep Atacama: there were plants – desert plants but plant life nonetheless – and therefore other forms of life too.

And before the frontier, among the volcanic peaks, there was a large salt lake with water and some birds paddling about. Guanacos ambled to the water's edge to drink. It was odd to see life in such a harsh, seemingly barren place.

Ollagüe is essentially a train stop on the Chilean side of the frontier and exists because of Chile's victory in the War of the Pacific (1879–83), which it fought against Bolivia, with Peru dragged in on Bolivia's side because of a secret alliance between the two. It was also called the Saltpetre War, which tells you what it was actually about. At the time, Bolivia controlled much of the Atacama north and east of Antofagasta, which it regarded as part of its territory. Having lost the argument in battle, Bolivia accepted Chilean occupation of the entire region in 1884, and in 1904 it signed a treaty ceding all of Antofagasta Atacama to Chile, creating the national boundaries of today.

Bolivia became landlocked, but part of the deal was that Chile would grant Bolivia unhindered commercial access to the Pacific by a rail link across the Andes and the Atacama and down into Antofagasta. Ollagüe is the Chilean railhead of the line out of Bolivia and is today a desolate place. It has no earthly reason to exist: it's 3,660m above sea level, nothing grows there, and it appears to have no purpose other than to receive trains from Bolivia, from the city of Uyuni and, beyond it, the capital, La Paz. All that happens at Ollagüe is a cursory inspection of freight carriages and their manifest, after which the lumbering trains are allowed to proceed. There's a large railyard with maybe a dozen tracks all flowing east to west and, spread around the facility, piles of old timber sleepers, twisted rails and other bits of discarded metal and abandoned cargo carriages. There are lots of buildings too: wooden ones from the early twentieth century that must have served as offices or waiting rooms.

When I was there, bright orange closed-door cargo carriages, each labelled Ferroviaria Andina, lined one track. There was also a Bolivian passenger- and cargo-train company that operates a service on narrow-gauge lines criss-crossing Bolivia's altiplano, the high plateau between La Paz and Uyuni. I wandered about the railyard unimpeded and approached the only person I could see, a fellow named Bernardo, who was in a hard hat and denim jacket and peering under the carriages.

'¿*Aduanas* [customs]?' I asked.

'*No*,' Bernardo answered, '*mecánico*.'

We chatted briefly, and he told me that the border inspection takes place at the frontier, a kilometre or two further along the road, and that the carriages were carrying zinc bound for Antofagasta.

Incidentally, the only other thing of interest in Ollagüe is a giant metal condor standing on the ground, its wings half open and its neck outstretched. It's three or four metres tall and looks as much like an oversized chicken as a condor.

Down at the frontier there was something of a queue on either side because the staff members inside the customs and passport frontier terminal building were having lunch. I parked, went inside and sat down beside another biker. He introduced himself as Michael Brinch and turned out to be particularly good company, allowing the lunch hour to pass without too much frustration as the queue grew ever longer. Michael is from Roskilde in Denmark, a place I happen to know. He started adult life as a civil engineer and worked variously for Lego as a systems manager and then in their education department before becoming a software troubleshooter and systems manager at a video technology company. Michael is a really positive guy and is one of those people who can instinctively analyse personal situations, take a positive approach and come up with a solution. He lost his wife to cancer over a decade ago, when in his mid-forties. His wife told him to go on living life to the full and to do everything he wanted to do. 'And so that's what I'm doing,' he said. He was now fifty-seven and looked fit, bright and brimming. As we waited – he coming from the Bolivian side and heading south into Chile and me going the opposite way – he marked my cards.

'Just about fifty kilometres after the border,' he said, 'there's a section of the road – it might be five kilometres long – that's all sand, and it's really, really hard. It's awful. Just be careful.'

Once the passport and customs staff got back to work, the queue ran down quickly, and there was no pushing or shoving to get ahead. The train heading to the Pacific was one of the first to get the all-clear and trundled off. Michael rode down into Chile to meet his children, who were on their own South American adventure, while I went off in the opposite direction.

Instantly, it was obvious that I had left Chile. The road deteriorated so rapidly that it quickly gave up and became an earth-and-gravel trail, but it was okay because it was hard and well ridden. I kept an eye on the mileage, wating for the 50km mark and heeding Michael's warning. In fairness, a new road was being built and, for large stretches of the old road, the new one – a perfectly flat tarmac affair, nicely elevated from the surrounding desert landscape – followed essentially the same route; but, maddeningly, it was still sealed to traffic. The route, Highway 701 to Uyuni, drops down just after the frontier crossing before turning east and, in a big arc, swings further east and then north, eventually to Uyuni – a journey from the frontier of about 230km.

And then what Michael warned of was there in front of me: about 5km of narrow road, twisting and turning, up and down over hillocks and round acute bends, snaking its way through a boulder-strewn desert. And virtually no hard surface or defining edges: nothing but deep, powdery sand. 'My mistake was to approach it too fast,' Michael had said to me. 'I must have been doing fifteen kilometres per hour.' As a result, he came off twice – without, thankfully, hurting himself.

I went at it very, very slowly – first gear only and with both feet off the pegs, hanging down and skimming the powdery surface. Every now and then, the bike lurched sideways, putting me off balance, or the front wheel suddenly took on a life of its own, causing the bike to slew into a drift of sand and threaten to topple over. My feet would stop it, but the strain on my upper body from trying to maintain an upright position, with the enormous weight of the bike itself and all that it was carrying, was great. Huge clouds of dust, whether ahead or in the rear-view mirror, put the heart crossways on me, as each heralded an approaching lorry, usually a monster

Freightliner or, worse, some bashed-up old thing with a devil-may-care driver at the wheel, often moving at reckless speed. In fairness, some drivers were considerate and slowed, but the majority just put the foot down, blew their horn and ploughed on past.

I didn't fall once, and my sense of elation was heightened when, a kilometre or two further on, access to the new road was permitted. I opened the throttle and leant into the curves as they approached, almost caressing the road as the bike glided effortlessly through its paces. I sailed into Villa Alota – a half-horse collection of buildings and a hostel, Hospedaje des Andes, on one side of the road – exhausted but feeling like I'd just won my first under-tens football medal.

Uyuni is famous for two things: its train cemetery and its enormous salt flat. Transport and minerals – the story of Bolivia, in so many ways. The city's main drag is called Avenida Ferroviaria, and the raised median dividing the two directions of traffic is used to display bits of disused machinery related to the railways or to mining – train engines small enough to run through mine tunnels or ore-carrying buckets filled by the miners. There's also a bright-silver statue, in the style of socialist realism, of a railway worker striding into the future, all muscles and confidence and wielding a monkey wrench, a train wheel beside him. I looked at it and thought it could double as the Tomb of the Unknown Motorcycle Mechanic.

Along much of the street, and in an elongated plaza off it, there are many restaurants and other outlets run by descendants of Chinese people who came here, and to Peru, in the late nineteenth and early twentieth centuries, lured by the promise of work in the mines or building railways. A similar pattern of migration occurred in California. But the most common outlets by far are small tour operators, selling day trips to all there is to be seen. All the buildings are in the regional style – that is, half finished: a single-storey is followed by a three-storey, is followed by a single-storey, is followed by a six-storey ... and none of them is remotely near completion above the ground level.

Next morning, the street was packed with Toyota Land Cruisers, Nissan Patrols and similar four-wheel drives, all with large roof racks, lashed-down spare wheels and plastic drums containing extra fuel. You, too, can be an adventure tourist!

For my day trip, I was paired with a family from Oruro, a city halfway between Uyuni and La Paz. There's the father, Freddy, an engineer whom I suspect was partly retired; his wife, Amelia; their children Maurico (a student engineer), Laura (an engineer) and Gabriella (a student engineer); and Gabriella's son Leonardo (an engineer-in-waiting, I suspect, and a right little chatterbox!). Our driver and guide for the day was Roger Copa. First stop: the train cemetery ...

Once upon a time, there were great plans for Uyuni: it would be the hub of a trans-Bolivian rail network and a funnelling point through which all goods in and out of the country would flow via the Bolivian Atacama Desert. And then that war happened, and Bolivia lost the Atacama to Chile. Mining faltered, and expansion plans were shelved. Uyuni tried to keep going as a train maintenance hub, but it all ground to a halt ... leaving lots of trains, mostly European-manufactured ones, high and dry, as it were. And now they sit in the middle of the desert, right on the edge of Uyuni, very slowly being eaten by the salty wind blowing off the nearby flats. The trains suffer the indignity of a million and one youngsters (and the not so young) clamouring atop them and, against a clear blue sky, getting their picture taken while making a V for victory sign.

There are more than one hundred trains there, it is said. I didn't count them, but there were certainly dozens of engines and many carriages and bits and pieces of rolling stock lying about. The engines were wonderful, even if dead and a little forlorn. They were made of large sheets of metal, buckled into shape and held together by pop rivets of the sort you'd see Harland & Wolff shipyard workers smashing into place – red-hot metal beaten with lump hammers.

Anything there worth taking – nameplates, bits of other metal such as brass and copper – is long gone, but you still get a great sense of what fine works of mechanical engineering these beasts once were. They lie on rails, their huge clunking wheels sometimes derailed and sinking into the sand.

You can stand on the footplate and pretend to be a driver or a stoker. You can jump onto the roof and pretend to be Butch Cassidy or the Sundance Kid. (According to one account, the pair of bandits died in 1909 in San Vicente, about 100km south of Uyuni, their hostel surrounded by a Bolivian cavalry unit.)

Trains and bandits are only a small part of Uyuni's story, however. Far larger is the city's salt flat. The meeting points of Chile, Argentina and Bolivia contain about 75 per cent of the world's known deposits of lithium, which is contained within the region's many salt flats. These are lakes of salt sealed on top by a layer of rock-solid salt several feet thick. These are now being mined by means of cutting out blocks of salt and leaching out the lithium, rather like getting sea salt to crystalise in large evaporation pools.

Uyuni's vast salt flat, known by local people simply as the salar, is a terrifying place. The largest in the world, it's 130m deep and covers 10,000km2 – about one-eighth the size of Ireland. It's easy to get disoriented while out on it because, in whatever direction you look, the landscape is the same: blindingly white, flat and seemingly unending. Truth be told, you could easily be burnt to death by the relentless sun. At night the temperature can plunge to minus eight or nine degrees.

Approached from the train cemetery, the salar appears initially in the distance as a white neon strip along the horizon, sealing the joint between land and sky. As one gets closer, a mirage makes the mountains seem to detach themselves from the earth and shimmer and float in the air. Gradually, the strip expands, closing the gap between bleached white earth and sky. When you drive onto the salar, it takes over the landscape completely: whichever way you look, there's nothing but the intensely white salt flat.

Our tour guide, Roger, drove us across it. There's no road as such, of course, and yet he followed a well-worn track to a point where an enterprising local man has used salt blocks to make statues and a pyramid, charging tourists who want to wander about taking pictures. Next, we stopped in the middle of nowhere, set up a table and ate lunch in the vast, burning expanse of white silence. Afterwards, we took lots of photos, using perspective and the pure white backdrop for trick photography.

Then it was off to an island, Isla Incahuasi, the top of a former volcano that got trapped, as it were, in the geological turmoil and now sits in the middle of the salar. It's so strange: you drive out to it over miles and miles of salt, and, yes, it really is an island ... of lava and cactus plants. And tourists – lots of tourists. In the distance across the white salar, one sees little black objects beetling across the vast whiteness – people, just like us, careering about in four-wheel drives. When we go, there will be our wheel tracks and nothing more. There's nothing living there, save for some organisms deep beneath the crystalline salt in the gloopy stuff at the bottom of the lagoon. We passed a cross stuck into the salt – a memorial cross to a twenty-year-old man whose vehicle overturned a year before, killing him.

Our day on the salar ended at sunset – a spectacular sunset during which the sky turned Technicolor red and orange and the reflection of water atop the salar merged earth and sky into one vast saline nothingness.

1 JANUARY 2023, SICA SICA

I spent the night in a hostel in the middle of Uyuni, where the elderly mother and daughter who ran the place kindly let me park my bike in their unused dining room, at that moment being decorated. For dinner I ate at a nearby Chinese restaurant. The impact of China – both historically, from the railway-building era of the late nineteenth and early twentieth centuries, and more recently, through new waves of migration – is evident in shops and restaurants here and through much of South America.

Next day, passing graffiti portraits of Che Guevara (he was killed in 1967 near the mountain village of La Higuera, about 600km east of Uyuni, today part of a tourist trail, the Ruta del Che), I headed north to Oruro, a city of over a quarter of a million people set in the middle of the Altiplano that links Uyuni and the capital, La Paz. In Oruro I had my first exposure to the sort of inequalities and grinding poverty common throughout much of Latin America. I had booked a room in a hostel-type hotel that looked like it was built about ten years before. But what the photos didn't show was the surroundings: a mixture of something like a warzone and an open-top landfill, in high wind. The filth was simply incredible. It was everywhere, and there was no apparent effort to keep the place clean. The only ones doing that were the stray dogs that were everywhere feeding on mounds of rubbish.

Apart from the hotel, there was a warren of mud-and-gravel roads and walled-off sites, some of which had homes in them. Most were half finished, or certainly works in progress, and not a lot of progress at that. The ring road, off which the hotel was located, was the only hard-surface road around. Everything else was mud and piles of builder's waste, plastic – loads of plastic – and domestic garbage. And so when it rained, which it did for most of the night, the result next morning was medieval looking in terms of the squalor everywhere. And a few feet from the hotel there was what might have been a small river but was more of an open sewer. My bathroom stank of sewage.

I slept badly, woke at 5:00. and got up to do some writing, checking out soon after to continue north, where there was lots of tillage and quite a few dairy and beef cattle farms, all facilitated by the rain, such as that of the night before. Small towns and villages along Route 1 to the capital, La Paz, appeared to have little to offer. Most straddled the highway and, even though it was Sunday, you could tell from the shops what went on most of the time: mini-markets, puncture-repair outfits, metal workshops, clothes shops and outlets supplying machinery and other items to agriculture. I reckoned that, behind all this, there was nothing much of interest, and so I ploughed on. The road was good, there was little traffic and it was nice to ride at 100km/h.

Just south of La Paz, Sica Sica,one of the nondescript towns straddling the road, had a largish brown stone church that looked interesting. By then I needed a break, so I turned in and rode up yet another battered and bashed mud-and-gravel road, around a small square and down a narrow lane to the church. When I came to the gates, people had started pouring out, and it was immediately apparent that a special event was taking place.

There were perhaps seventy or eighty people in traditional Bolivian dress. The women wore brightly coloured woven shawls, multi-layered skirts and hats (sometimes the traditional Bolivian hat favoured by women, a cross between a bowler and a pork pie hat). The men were similarly colourfully attired. And when they filed out of the church, they lined up in front of it, I assumed for family photos. But others began moving along the line, shaking hands, embracing and throwing confetti-like pieces of white paper over their heads. At first I thought it must be a wedding. The churchyard was thronged with people, some wearing non-traditional clothing, and there was also a band. In fact, several bands soon converged on the churchyard and began belting out, on drums and woodwinds, traditional Bolivian music, somewhat in competition with each other.

It was a joyous and laughter-filled occasion. I parked the bike immediately and wandered in. Everyone was taking photos, so I did too. There was nothing stiff or formal going on. There was lots of embracing and shouts of 'Feliz Año Nuevo!' which made me think maybe the whole thing was a special Mass for New Year's Day. Eventually, I spotted a real photographer, a professional named Juan Carlos. With his bit of English and my bit of Spanish, he was able to tell me that what I was witnessing was a special New Year's Day church service for the incoming members of administrative bodies, serving the four areas around the district. Sica Sica, I now know, is the capital of Aroma Province in the department of La Paz, and the stone church is a significant building, with twin bell towers.

I think, but can't be certain, that the local bodies to which the people being sprinkled with good-luck confetti had been drafted, or elected, were special councils for Indigenous people and were to come into being, in effect, on 2 January. Of course, they might have been straightforward ordinary local municipal councils, but they were a cause for celebration nonetheless.

What they must have made of me I haven't a clue. There I was moving in and out of the crowd, taking pictures and videoing, carrying a motorcycle helmet and lumbering about in motorcycle gear. I must have seemed like something from NASA and, very obviously, was the only outsider there. But their reaction was nothing but curiosity, warmth and friendship. I was approached repeatedly and asked where I was from – everyone there confuses Holland and Ireland and so I had to whip out my passport to be sure – and what I was doing. They embraced me and shook hands and laughed great happy laughs. It was very moving, the warmth of their greeting for a total stranger. Me, the odd one out, could not have been made to feel more welcome. After the dirt and awful poverty in Oruro, here was colour and happiness and richness that was like a balm.

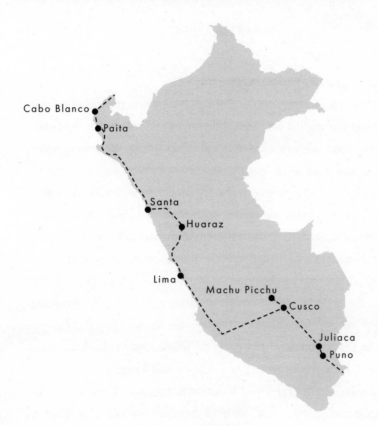

PERU

I SPENT A COUPLE OF NIGHTS AT A HOSTEL IN LA PAZ, catching up on my sleep and trying to assess the situation in Peru. The word from other travellers who had come south from there was of political upheaval, with multiple roadblocks and aggressive protesters turning everyone back, tourists included. Despite advice to avoid the protest areas, which were mainly in the south-east and the Indigenous-dominated mountain region, up to and including Machu Picchu, I had to go and see for myself. Besides, there was a lull in the protests – a Christmas–New Year truce, if you will – but they were due to resume on 4 January. I set off the day before, armed with a 'safe passage' request letter from Irish diplomats assigned to the country. It might have been of use in an emergency, and I wondered how far I'd get.

3 JANUARY 2023, PUNO AND JULIACA

I entered Peru on 3 January via the main crossing where the highway from La Paz starts skirting the southern shore of Lake Titicaca. Maybe 20km inside Peru, there was evidence of the protests – large mounds of earth had been dumped across the road, a wide and otherwise well-maintained highway, Highway 3S, leading to the regional capital, Puno. The earth mounds, at the entrances and exits of each town and village, were maybe two metres tall and straddled the full width of the road. However, they had been breached in the middle, and so traffic was able to move freely, if slowly. Besides, there were no protesters manning the barricades. I got to Puno and spent the night in a hostel before heading north again the following morning. Next city: Juliaca.

Exiting Puno, I quickly came upon my first manned roadblock about halfway to Juliaca. About twenty men had formed a large circle and were standing in the middle of the road, listening to a speaker. They held a large banner that said (in Spanish), 'Unified defense front against pollution of the Coata River basin and Lake Titicaca,' which seemed rather beside the point. After all, the crisis engulfing Peru went back to the June 2021 presidential election run-off. The contest had been won on the slimmest of margins – 50.13 per cent – by Pedro Castillo, a former primary school teacher and trade union organiser. He stood for the Free Peru party, which has a Marxist ideology, although Castillo himself is personally socially conservative. In Peru the president has executive powers to appoint and run the government, but Congress (the parliament) has a break on presidential overreach. Congress remained politically conservative after the election and was implacably opposed to Castillo. In six months he appointed no fewer than four separate governments, unprecedented in Peruvian history.

In December, and after several attempts, Congress impeached Castillo after he declared that he would sack all of the governments, write a new constitution and, in the meantime, rule by decree. By the time of the Christmas and New Year protests, he was in prison, and his former vice-president, Dina Boluarte, took over as president, an act of treachery in the eyes of Castillo's supporters. The protests were strongest in the south-east of the country, where government buildings were attacked and road toll booths wrecked.

As I approached the circle of protesters, they looked at me with suspicion and were determined to stand their ground. Luckily for me, there were no other vehicles trying to get through, so there was little tension in the air. I stopped the bike, turned off the engine, took off my helmet, dismounted and approached them, my hand outstretched. We got talking. I explained who I was and what I was doing, and they let me pass without demur.

By the time I got to Juliaca, the atmosphere had changed. About 270,000 people live in the city, and when I arrived, just before 10:00., a good number of them were out on the streets. The main drag through the city is simply the regional highway between Puno and Cusco. It enters the city as a four-lane highway, slicing through the heavily built-up downtown area, with a series of roundabouts, a flyover and, on both sides of the highway, parallel local service roads allowing access to the buildings flanking the highway and the rest of the city. The first roundabout was blocked by a large crowd, maybe 300 or 400 strong, many holding placards ... and sticks and rocks. As I approached, they became agitated and began shouting at me, '*¡No pasar! No pasar!*' Several picked up rocks.

I did as before – stopping the bike, removing my helmet and approaching with my arm outstretched. '*¡Hola!*' I said. '*Soy periodista a Irlanda.*' A poor attempt at 'Hello! I'm a journalist from Ireland,' but it was enough to be understood. I took out my passport and press card, holding them up, and a man with a megaphone approached me. We chatted a bit, the conversation limited only by my lack of good Spanish. There followed a somewhat surreal situation in which he handed me the megaphone and told me to address the crowd. In what can only have been Spanish that was far below primary school level, I told them who I was and that I was travelling to Alaska and writing as I went for my newspaper in Ireland.

As I ran out of things to say (and how to say them), I asked them to tell me why they were protesting, before handing the bull horn back to the man. I fear much went missing in translation but not their warmth and appreciation of my interest in them. They spoke Spanish and Quechua, the Indigenous language of the Peruvian Andes. The man with the megaphone spoke to them for a moment. He referred to President Boluarte as an assassin and then raised his arm. With clenched fist, he shouted, '*¡Viva Peru!*' and '*¡Viva la prensa!*' ('Long live the Press!') – then the ubiquitous favourite: 'The people united will never be defeated'. There were cheers and applause and then selfies. There may even have been a clenched fist or two raised in solidarity. I may even have indulged myself. At one stage, one of the women asked me to pose with her while holding her poster. I obliged willingly, so somewhere in Juliaca there are smartphones with the incriminating evidence. I had reported on many demonstrations and more than a few riots but never one quite like this.

'*Pasar, pasar,*' they said and, amid hugs and handshakes, they waved me on my way. And so the scene was repeated every fifty metres or so along the highway for perhaps a kilometre, as I threaded my way gingerly through glass and wire, around boulders and over mounds of clay and rubble. Occasional threats to ram nails into my tyres were subdued with conversation and my insistence of '*¡Soy periodista, soy periodista!*' I saw one young woman out of the corner of my eye pick up a rock. I looked straight at her and said '*¡No, soy tu amigo. Soy periodista!*' She looked down and dropped the stone.

Similar admonitions mixed with expressions of friendship worked with the nail women. The whole scene was edgy and potentially dangerous. I felt that at any moment my luck might run out. I'm not sure what to make of it, but the only people who threatened me – and, truth be told, not terribly seriously – were women. The men on the barricades seemed much more laid back. There were some police around, but they lurked in side streets, out of the way of the protesters.

I moved onto the no man's land earthen track that separated the main highway from the parallel service road running with it and continued to ride, very slowly and all the time looking at the protesters and greeting them. That I got past each block, or cluster, of protesters seemed to have an effect on the attitude of the next group approached, and so I was able to move forward gradually.

But when I came to the flyover, I could see that I would have to go under it to progress. I feared that those on the bridge might throw things down on me. At that point, a friendly man suggested that I go into the city along a road at right angles to the blocked highway and then turn left – a route that would take me right out of the city. And as I moved further north towards Cusco, the scenes were repeated in smaller towns and villages along the way, although with smaller groups of protesters. I never had to resort to the safe passage letter: my strategy of engagement worked fine.

Some days later, I headed west towards the coast. By that stage I had made a large PRENSA! sign in large red letters, which I taped to my windscreen. When I approached any further protesters at roadblocks, there could now be no doubt as to what I was claiming to be. At Puquio, on the road west towards the coast, the town of some 15,000 people had been cut off for several days. Substantial mounds of clay and dozens of large boulders, pieces of wood and metal, mounds of dirty black silt and tangles of wire – the remains of burnt tyres – made the road impassable. The backlog of lorries wanting to get out of the town stretched right back into the centre – with huge Freightliner, Mack and Volvo lorries dwarfing many of the buildings around them – clogging the streets. On the other side of the roadblock, which was on the western edge of the town, the queue of immobile lorries stretched for several kilometres, their drivers hanging about in groups by the roadside or sleeping in hammocks slung beneath their trailers.

At the makeshift roadblock, some of the protesters were standing on a hillock where the road wound through several sharp bends. It was a strategic position, just like those castles medieval warlords would build on river bends. From their elevated position, the protesters observed and shouted to the others below whenever anything seemed to be inching forward to break the blockade. There were no posters expressing what the protest was about, and neither were there national flags, which attended both of the roadblock protests I had seen before. But the mood was clear enough. 'The people are angry,' a young woman told me. She seemed to have a position of some standing with the others but was reluctant to accept a leadership role.

'*¿Esta una comandante?*' I asked her, hoping to find an organiser – someone in charge, as it were.

'*No,*' she said, '*no commandante.*'

The people, the angry people, were in charge and speaking with one voice. The woman was clearly motivated and was completely on the side of the protesters, whose resolve she sought to stiffen. But she was reluctant to direct them. And so I was able to move about, chatting to them and taking pictures.

Eventually, they let me through, pushing boulders aside sufficiently for me to thread my way through slowly. I think it helped that I never tried to push my way through, never challenged their actions or argued with them, as I heard some bikers did, and to little good effect, from their own point of view.

Later, passing through a town named Chao that straddled the Panamericana north of the capital city, Lima, the same lack of protest leadership resulted in the centre of the town being turned into a dystopian wasteland, where desultory gangs of young people roamed the highway or hung round burning tyres that belched deep black smoke into the air. The road was covered in debris – broken bricks, smashed bottles and wheelie bins – and the whole scene looked aimless and destructive. I parked my bike in the middle of it all and wandered among them, chatting and taking photos, almost invariably without objection.

In Lima, by contrast, protesters who had gathered on a Saturday evening at Plaza San Martín, a square on the edge of the historic centre, were marshalled by stewards along a protest route and shouted slogans as they went along. They seemed to be people well versed in the art of protest: professional agitators, political activists and students. The city's historic centre, with its cathedral, presidential palace and preserved old streets, was beautiful, as was the plaza.

Lima has several statement structures from the nineteenth and early twentieth centuries that would not look out of place in any central European capital city. There is the Teatro Colón, a beautiful corner building dating from 1914 ... but it has been dark since 2000 and is awaiting new life as a 'cultural centre'. There is the Edificio Sudamérica, another sturdy but elegant building, well looked after and in use. One side of the square is taken over by a single block, with a colonnade at street level filled with shops and restaurants and something inside it that billed itself as a military hotel, whatever that was.

On the other side of the square, near the theatre, is the Gran Hotel Bolívar, which dates from 1924 and is still a hotel. They were happy enough for me to wander about the interior, which is approached by passing a twin set of tall brass lamps leading to a hallway and then a rotunda with a magnificent Tiffany-style domed glass ceiling. The elegance and slightly faded charm of the interior contrasted starkly with what was going on outside.

On that particular Saturday night, more than 5,000 protesters marched twice round the plaza and then off into the modern city, with a police escort front and rear – a flowing mass of banners, flags and noisy hand-pumped horns and whistles. They marched, without explanation as to destination, to Miraflores, about 10km away.

Miraflores turned out to be probably the most fashionable inner-city suburban place I saw in Peru. It was dripping in nouveau riche wealth, modern high-rise office buildings, brand-name fashion outlets and the sort of chichi restaurants and resto-bars that go with them. This, then, was the 'other Peru' and it seemed to me that the protesters were making sure the people there knew something was not right in what should be their shared society. They didn't just stay on the main route that led straight to the park: they wound their way round the residential streets behind the main drag – streets lined by either medium-height apartment blocks or individual homes, many of them with that 'architect-designed' look about them. My impression was that the protesters were saying, 'We're here, and we're very, very unhappy. This is our country too, and we're not going away..

The weekend after I had been in Juliaca, seventeen people there were shot dead by police. According to the prime minister, Alberto Otárola, some protesters had attacked a police car, beat and handcuffed a policeman and set fire to the vehicle, burning another policeman alive. 'We call for peace. We cannot murder one another,' said Otárola, according to the local news agency Andina. TV footage showed injured protesters being taken to hospital. Reports said that some had gunshot wounds and that the police car was set alight after shots were fired. The only people known to have been armed in the situation were the police. Later, a civilian was shot dead in Cusco, and a few nights after the protest that I observed in Lima there was rioting during which a large empty building beside the plaza was set on fire, apparently by protesters.

Established politicians, such as the prime minister and others, denounced the protesters as violent agitators, terrorists intent on overthrowing the government. Certainly in the towns and villages outside Lima, I saw obviously poor people who wanted something more than the little they had and who felt that their man – the first Indigenous person, the first of them, to sit in the presidential palace – had been done down by the elite in the capital. They were not so much the dispossessed as the never possessed it in the first place, and they knew it. They were contemptuous of Congress, which they called corrupt – a mantra heard everywhere.

4–8 JANUARY 2023, CUSCO AND MACHU PICCHU

After the eventful ride from Puno, I needed a few days calm in Cusco. The Andean mountains of central Peru nestle the country's ancient capital of the Incas in their palm. The shoulders and valleys of several mountains converge, and where they meet there's something of a natural bowl in the landscape. That's where Cusco is, 3,416m above sea level – high but not that high, considering, and that's where the Incas long ago decided to build their most important city. It was their capital until the Spanish came along and made it their city, the capital for a time of what is now Peru. (Lima came a long time after.)

It's no surprise to learn that Cusco's pink-stone cathedral basilica that dominates the old town, overlooking the beautiful Plaza des Armas, was built between 1560 and 1668 on the spot where the Incas had their most important temple. That's what the Christians did: everywhere they sought to establish themselves, they simply grafted their faith onto what was already there, either suffocating the old faith or tweaking and rebranding it as their own – and a remarkably successful strategy it has been too.

All the churches of Cusco were doing flying business on my second day in the city. I got there late on 4 January after a tough but interesting day negotiating with protesters, and so the following day was spent resting and indulging in food and drink. Two days later, 6 January, was, of course, Little Christmas, or Nollaig na mBan, as it's increasingly known in Ireland. Well, something similar applies in Peru: on the 6th the Christmas season officially comes to an end ... and Cusco goes bananas! The whole historical centre of the city was thronged with families out enjoying themselves. Women carried small baskets containing crib-like assortments of extravagantly dressed dolls. At Masses they brought the baskets forward for blessing by the priest. In one church, the Iglesia de la Compañía de Jesús, which was opposite the cathedral basilica (a complex of three separate churches), I attended a packed Mass at about noon. There was just one priest, and when I put my head round the door again early in the evening, he was still there saying Mass. It was one Mass after the other, with no breaks, as far as I could tell.

In front of the cathedral, a ceremony was taking place involving a small version of one of those religious statues that, in Spanish towns and villages, are placed on platforms and carried through the streets on people's shoulders on a given saint's day. Inside, the cathedral was typical of its type: over-the-top side chapels dripping in silver and gold, sixty-four carved wooden choir stalls dating from 1636 and the almost inevitable statue of the legendary Santiago Matamoros, St James the Moor-Slayer. There was a crib with gaudy flashing lights and, by far the most noteworthy item, an arch of flags over the whole crib, the top one being the LGBTQ+ rainbow flag.

As the morning wore on, the police took centre stage in the plaza, with the canine patrol putting on a display that delighted children and parents alike. The dogs leapt through hoops and danced on their hind legs for their uniformed handlers. A particular favourite was Tiana, a black lab wearing an Inca-style colourful skirt. When the dogs were finished, Santa arrived, accompanied by three young women in short skirts and 'Where's Wally' style striped leggings. They danced about in front of the cathedral, a police officer with a microphone encouraging mums and dads and children to join in, which many did.

Suddenly, Santa and the dancing Wallies were gone ... disappeared into the crowd, as far as I could tell. There were lots of policemen around – uniformed police mingling with the crowds and riot police with helmets and shields lined up at strategic locations, especially anywhere to do with the administration of justice. And there were soldiers too.

In relation to tourism, Cusco lives off its Inca heritage far more than its Spanish colonial one, even though the latter is physically far more obvious – at least in the city. To see the other Cusco, you have to travel to Machu Picchu, about five hours away by road. Fleets of minibuses, each carrying eighteen people, set off from Cusco close to midnight in order to reach a hydroelectric station near the foot of Machu Picchu by dawn. I was by far the oldest in our minibus: the average age was probably thirty-five. We were disgorged in the half-light in front of a shabby food and soft drink outlet and directed to start walking. Soon we were on a railway track that appeared to be linked to the hydroelectric operation but that also, it transpired, was the main access to a small town at the foot of Machu Picchu called, perhaps inevitably, Inca City. It's also known as *Aguas Calientes* (Hot Springs in English, because it has them).

The walk along the railway track was really pleasant, as it turned out. No train was running, for reasons never entirely clear though that seemed to be linked to the anti-government protests. But the scenery was magnificent. We were passing through what was essentially a narrow gorge whose sheer cliff-face sides were enormously high. In places, I would estimate the rock face to have been a vertical 500m top to bottom. The vegetation was sub-tropical.

We were, in reality, walking along a train track through jungle (think *Bridge on the River Kwai*) with all the sights and sounds you'd expect. The river flowing down the gorge was muddy brown and flowing in places with a sort of wild rage, bashing off granite boulders the size of houses. Every now and then we'd pass a homestead – somewhere to sleep and not much else, it seemed. Living was largely in the open, especially the cooking and eating elements of daily life. Chickens scurried through vegetable patches, pecking here and there, as they do. Some of the homesteads were also hostels; others, especially one or two on the far side of the river that could be reached only by precarious basket chairs slung beneath cables above the torrent, appeared to be efforts to escape conventional life.

At the foot of Machu Picchu there was no transport. The fleet of buses that normally ferry tourists up the mountain were all parked in a line and going nowhere, their immobility linked absolutely to the anti-government protests. We would have to climb the stairs. It was 450m and not a gentle gradient either. By chance, while trying to find out what was happening, I came upon the English-speaking guide assigned to our group – which in reality appeared to mean assigned to me (as everyone else was Spanish-speaking and happy to do their own thing) and a young Swiss woman named Nicole.

The guide, Ruth Maribiel, lived in Inca City and is married to Robert, also a guide. The first and most startling thing she told me was that before Covid, in the high season, Machu Picchu was visited by 6,000 to 8,000 people every day. Once you see the place and its narrow walkways, and imagine the noise and clamour of such a huge number of tourists, visiting in such conditions sounds like hell on earth. Luckily for me, there couldn't have been more than a few hundred on that day.

On reaching the top of the stairs, you pass through the ticket turnstiles to emerge slightly above Machu Picchu itself. You know that feeling of elation when, climbing a mountain, you reach the final ridge and, surmounting it, realise you are at the top and there's nothing above you now? Well, that moment on Machu Picchu comes as you round a bend behind the ticketing and cafe complex ... and realise you are actually a little above the Inca city. There below you is Machu Picchu (2,350m), spread out across the top of the mountain; beyond, other mountains encircling it, each topped by whisps of candyfloss cloud. The name means 'Old Mountain', and opposite it, so close that it seems you could almost touch it, is Huchuy Picchu (2,479m), which means 'Young Mountain'. The young mountain looks down on the old one, almost with a protective posture.

Machu Picchu is a stone city – a small city but a city nonetheless. The stone is granite, mostly boulders, though some stones were cut to shape and fitted in place without mortar, like the huge rectangular lintels above doorways or the squared-off corner pieces of buildings. According to Ruth, the Incas 'came here because they studied astronomy' and because 'the light was clear here, and because of the magnetic concentration in the valleys from the rotation of the earth.'

To be honest, I was slightly underwhelmed with the place after a while. I thought its scale would be greater, more epic, as it were, and would set me back on my heels. I had expected something much larger, more visually impressive. But there is something ethereal, something otherworldly about the place. And it is one of the great wonders of the world, one of the great achievements of ancient society. The top of Machu Picchu slopes to one side, and the city therefore faces predominately in one direction, looking out on the ring of other mountains in the area. All the mountains are granite and, unlike in Ireland, where glaciation has fashioned granite into gentle slopes like the backs of whales, the mountains here are like pointed towers whose sides are almost right angles, with only the tops rounded.

From the vantage point of where one enters the city, you can see how it was laid out. It was built around 1450 by about 20,000 people, none of whom slaves. Inca society functioned according to several principles: there were rules to be obeyed, people had to work, there was a quest and respect for knowledge and there was love. Boys learnt maths, astronomy, science and physics until they were ten or so. After that they left Machu

Picchu for Cusco to teach others until they were sixteen, and then they led whatever life they wanted. 'For the Incas it was very important to spread the knowledge and to love it,' Ruth explained. 'In the Inca's time, the rich people have not a lot of money but a lot of knowledge.' Sounds good to me.

According to Ruth, 600 to 800 people lived in Machu Picchu at any one time, and the great focus – apart from the daily routine of growing maize, potatoes and tomatoes on numerous terraced fields for survival and the maintenance of an irrigation system – was astronomy. The city was also something of a summer residence for Inca royalty. There was no army to defend the city: the only protection from attack was a perimeter wall. The place was abandoned in about 1530 because of the Spanish invasion – it's amazing to think that it was lived in for little over one hundred years – and it was lost for centuries until European and American explorers began visiting it in the nineteenth century.

It was German surveyors who may have associated the name Machu Picchu with the city. But the substantial rediscovery, and the basis of our understanding of the place now, came in the early twentieth century. An American explorer, the academic and later politician Hiram Bingham, excavated the site, sponsored by Yale University and National Geographic in 1911. Bingham took thousands of objects – ceramics, human remains and jewellery – back to the university, where most remained until a few years ago, when they were finally returned to Peru.

The ancient city has essentially two distinct clusters of buildings, separated by a central green area. The left side, Ruth explained, was dominated by religious buildings, whereas the right side was for living, for the most part, even though on that side there's the wonderful Temple of the Condor. Two huge boulders with dark streaks are splayed in a V shape, and they look something like a giant bird. There's also the Temple of the Sun, with a window placed strategically to catch the dawn sunlight of the December solstice – shades of Newgrange. Inside the Temple of the Sun, water was decanted into shallows in rocks, creating pools so that the reflection of the stars could be studied at night. Ruth explained that, far below Machu Picchu, at the bottom of the valley, the river was named Willkamayu ('Sacred River') because 'the shape of the river looked like the Milky Way.'

Ruth added that the Incas 'didn't take water from the river but used spring water from the mountain. The Incas said the river gave them fish. Today, there's no fish because the river is always polluted.' Foul water from Machu Picchu itself was mixed with ash and used as fertiliser on the vegetable terraces.

You can pause and look down on the city, and you can walk through it, seeing up close the small houses, narrow streets, temple building and open green space between the two clusters. It's kept very well, and there's a sense of respect for the place and the people for whom this was somewhere important, sacred even. But I didn't get a sense of those people, the Incas, of who they were and what they were about. Maybe that's my shortcoming: there is, certainly, something magical about the setting – a city perched atop a pinnacle of granite, surrounded by mountains of like shape, all covered in jungle-like vegetation.

The Temple of the Condor had a specific purpose: it was used for a ceremony to mummify the dead, who were then placed in urns that were taken higher up, above Machu Picchu itself, closer to their gods. 'They were embalmed in the fetal position in death,' said Ruth, 'because that is the way we came out, and that was the way to go back to Mother Nature.'

13 JANUARY 2023, LIMA

A few days later, while I was in Lima, I received the most awful news. My friend and guardian angel in Punta Arenas, Patricio Corcoran, had died on 12 January. He was only sixty-eight and looked healthy when we met in November, when he was in great form, brimming with life, full of enthusiasm and optimistic about the future. I was shocked and saddened by the news – for him and for his family. He had told me, more than once, how much they all meant to him.

A mere seven weeks before his death, we had dined together, embraced afterwards and said our goodbyes. At the meal, we chatted about Chile and about some of the things that made the country different from the English-speaking world. Patricio explained to me the meaning of the Spanish honorific 'Don'. Thanking him by text next day, I signed off *'Gracias, Don Patricio'*. I think that would have made him smile, and he certainly deserved that degree of respect. I felt certain that we would meet again, and I hoped that it would be in Ireland, so I could have the opportunity to be as kind to him as he had been to me.

Patricio was a lovely man – handsome, smart, warm and successful and big into his family, his ranching, his businesses and Punta Arenas, and he was quietly proud of his Irish roots. He ran a food distribution company and medium-sized supermarket in Punta Arenas and was also a sheep and cattle rancher. I had been introduced to him in early 2020 by Ireland's then ambassador to Chile, Paul Gleeson, and I wrote a piece about him. Patricio was a mechanical engineer by training but, like his father, Arturo, had gone into business and became a major player in the economy of Magallanes y la Antártica.

When I was returning to Punta Arenas, I struggled to think what I could bring Patricio as a present from Ireland to thank him for looking after my bike during Covid. I didn't really know him that well, or his likes and dislikes, but I did know that his Irish heritage meant a lot to him. So I got him a hand-painted heraldic family scroll of the Corcoran clan. And I got his wife a thick Irish woollen throw, together with one of my wife's oil paintings, a scene from the west of Ireland. He seemed chuffed and told me later how pleased his wife, Sylvia Blackwood, was too. Together they had three children and ten grandchildren. I really hoped they would come to Ireland for a holiday when he retired, which he was thinking about. It would have given me such pleasure to share our place in Co. Mayo with them and show them the sights in Dublin and the beauty of the West.

I don't know exactly what happened, but some sort of medical emergency in December caused Patricio to be put into an induced coma in hospital, and he just never came out of it. His funeral was in Sacred Heart Cathedral in Punta Arenas, which was packed with family and friends and with those who knew him through the city's chamber of commerce, of which he was a director, and through his wider business and farming interests. He was also deeply involved in local education and in the hospitality sector. At his funeral, his son Brian spoke, as did two grandchildren, Rodrigo and Julián. Patricio was taken from the cathedral to music played by Aranxante, a local group specialising in Galician and Irish music.

17 JANUARY 2023, SANTA

Leaving Lima, the Panamericana eventually becomes a proper road, not one overrun by market stalls, taxis and buses that stop just about anywhere they like and cause traffic mayhem. In one sense, it's all hilarious and very colourful. But in other ways – like trying to stay upright on a huge motorbike – such a chaotic road is a bit of a nightmare. You have to navigate round vehicles much larger than your own as they flit between lanes without a care as to other road users. There's no point in blowing your horn to warn them that they're about to hit you. Everyone's blowing their horn all the time, and so one more won't make the slightest bit of difference. Instead, I deploy my full repertoire of Anglo-Saxon abuse, which can be extensive, and that usually works. But once past all that, yes, the road shears through flat and well-cultivated countryside, much of it under sugar cane.

And then, quite quickly, you turn off the Panamericana to head inland on Route 16, travelling north-east as it begins to climb. The Andes, and their huge footprint, are never far away. The road to Huaraz, some 200km off, travels the floor of a valley that twists and turns and worms its way upwards, slowly at first with a gentle gradient and then in a more vigorous, more pronounced way. On the way, small communities are eking out a living from the valley floor, which is covered in mango, avocado and trees whose gnarled fruits I didn't recognise. There are some vegetables grown, but it was mainly fruit. I stopped at one of the roadside fruit stalls, bought a mango and ate the whole thing in one go. It was sweet and runny, and there was something deliciously decadent about just sitting there, looking at the lush valley floor and, above it, the arid, desert-like flanks of the mountains on either side, eating this luscious fruit, the juice running down my chin.

There are groups of curvy switchback twists and turns on the road before it joins Route 3N, which travels due north, hugging the flank of the main Andes range all the way to Huaraz. I wanted to stay there as a base for travelling a road right around Nevado Huascarán Sur, at 6,768m above sea level, the highest mountain in all of Peru. Next morning, I awoke to see it in the near distance, a huge mountain of black rock and snow, almost Himalayan in scale and appearance.

I rode Route 3N to Yungay and then turned onto the R106, which loops right around Huascarán Sur and looked like it would be a magnificent road to ride. Immediately, and rather surprisingly, I was onto a dirt road. I thought it would end just as it left the small town and continued upwards. But, no, sadly, it stayed like that the whole way up – for some 25km through scatterings of small holdings where people keep pigs and chickens and grow vegetables in small plots to feed themselves and maybe have a little left over to sell by the roadside. Increasingly, as one rises higher on the single-track dirt road, eucalyptus trees dominate and, with them, logging for fence posts, scaffolding poles and firewood.

At the formal entrance to Huascarán National Park, there's another one of those vistas whose beauty and magnificence stopped me dead in my tracks: huge and almost completely vertical escarpments define the sides of a narrow valley. At the far end of it the view is closed off by a snow-covered Yanarrago, a 'lesser' mountain behind Huascarán Sur, a mere 5,055m. On the right-hand side as I travelled through the valley, the clifftop vertically above me had a castellated and jagged top. So close was I to the cliff face that Huascarán Sur itself couldn't be seen, save when dense, wispy cloud drifted aside for a minute or two, allowing me to catch a glimpse of the enormous mountain.

It all looked vast but calm; the two lakes up there, Chinancocha and Orconcocha, are blue pools of tranquillity and a great photogenic draw for visitors. The wild beauty of the place is captivating, but don't be fooled: this is a place of great instability and hence danger too. In 1970 an earthquake caused by the volcanic mountains sent eighty million tons of ice, rock and mud crashing down the valley at 300km/h, burying Yungay and killing more than 20,000 people in and around the town, as well as 20,000 more in Huaraz. Final estimates were of 67,000 fatalities and 800,000 people made homeless.

On the day of my visit, workers were spilling lorryloads of fresh gravel and mud onto the road as it passed the lakes, and the road beyond and round to the main Route 3N was another 175km. Happy at my distance covered, I turned round, rejoined the road north and headed off again.

Slowly, and then quite quickly, the road north changed character. Initially it was the same two-lane tarmac road I had travelled before and after Huaraz, essentially following the same course as the Río Santa, along a wide valley, with towns and farmland along the way. But then both road and river took a turn west and began their journey to the Pacific through a lengthy and dramatic steep-sided, narrow-valley gorge. The road shrank to a single lane, twisting and turning, hugging a steep cliff face on the left and, on the right, revealing a huge drop, in places hundreds of feet, down to the bottom of the gorge, frequently with no barrier to deter vehicles from plunging into the ravine. The landscape all around was bare rock, was almost nothing growing anywhere except for the bottom of the gorge. The mountainside was extreme shades of brown, rust, red, black and grey – like the minerals are shouting at you. It's a landscape both terrifying and exhilarating to traverse, and such is the dramatic change that you start to wonder, 'Have I taken a wrong turn?' or, 'Did I miss the sign saying R3N this way?' or, 'Am I in the middle of a giant mine?'

Then the road starts entering tunnels – one after another, some short, no more than a few feet, the length of a car, say; but one must have been close to a kilometre long. The tunnels are little more than crude holes knocked through the mountainside as the road plunges down into the ravine. The sides of the tunnels are not encased in concrete but left as they were made, holes smashed through the rock. There are no supports to stop them caving in, and there are no lights. The road surface in many of the tunnels is non-existent, just pounded mud and rubble and potholes. It's pitch-black inside, save for one's own lights, and there are no passing places, just width sufficient for a single vehicle. If you stopped a car, for instance, I'm not sure you'd have room to open the door. And there's no way of telling whether another vehicle has entered the tunnel at the far end, unless the tunnel is straight (which many are not) and you can see their lights. You just enter, sometimes seeing no more than a white dot in the distance – the light, literally, at the end of the tunnel – and you drive cautiously, hoping that nothing is coming at you, especially a lorry. Blow your horn, signs tell you at the entrance, not very helpfully.

And when you exit the tunnel, blinking into the light of day, the gorge and the great plunge to the bottom are right there, a foot or two at most to your right. Truly, this has to be one of those Peruvian *caminos de la muerte* ('roads of death') one reads about. That said, I recall seeing only one roadside cross.

At Cañón del Pato, emerging from a tunnel, suddenly there appears a large dam and hydroelectric plant whose size and noise gave me a jolt and somehow, quite irrationally, frightened me. I stopped. Dug out of the mountain behind me there was, for no obvious reason, a huge hole large enough to fit an articulated lorry into, but it's empty and gaping at you like a cave. I'm not sure how long it went on for. Perhaps 10km. But it is one of the most terrifying and amazing roads I have ever travelled on.

Not once did I meet any of Peru's infamous kamikaze drivers – the ones, and there are many, who overtake on bends and never yield to oncoming vehicles. After the tunnels, the open road resumed, and then more tunnel, open road again, followed by more tunnel ... a pattern that ended at Campamento Hidro Cañon del Pato, a place that exists solely to serve the hydroelectric operation and those who work in it. It's all red roofs and has an institutional look about it, the way military barracks often do – which is why, I suppose, it's called Campamento. Somewhat oddly, a real town, Huallanca, which has shops, hostels, homes and a church, exists a few kilometres down the road but still manages to appear dead.

After Huallanca the road returns to something one would call normal. But it's still hugging the side of a giant gorge, there were lots of potholes and the light was fading. At a tiny place (which still has a police station, mind) the Route 3N resumes its northbound trajectory. I stayed westbound on the R12 and eventually came to the town of Santa. I had little choice but to carry on, even after it got dark, but it was great to get there. Santa really does exist, I promise, and he serves excellent cold beer ...

21 JANUARY 2023, PAITA

On the north coast of Peru, close to the border with Ecuador, is a place easily overlooked. It's small enough not to make much of a dent on most maps – even though it calls itself a city and has a population close to 200,000 – and it's also a little off the Panamericana and therefore likely to be bypassed.

Don't make that mistake.

I wanted to spend a final night in Peru before crossing into Ecuador, and Paita, being on the coast, caught my eye. Getting there turned out to be touch and go. I left Chiclayo for the 200km dash to Piura, with just two fingers of fuel on the tank gauge. 'No problem,' I thought, 'I'll fill up on the way.' The country is awash with petrol stations – I don't quite understand it: you sometimes find six in a row, and they can't all be profitable. It turned out that this particular 200km stretch of the Panamericana is 100 per cent bereft of petrol stations – the only such stretch in the entire country, I suspect.

Hurtling through a landscape of desert dunes, I watched as two fingers became one, and then the fuel light appeared, with that note saying the range left was forty-eight miles, then forty-seven, then forty-six ... I poured my two spare tanks into the bike's tank and carried on. A police patrol car and occupants lounging on the far side of the road said the next station was 80km away ... in Piura. The first person to gouge me – the owner of a dusty, run-down cafe in the middle of nowhere – took twenty soles (about €5) for maybe a single litre. He poured it in so fast that I couldn't tell how much he gave me. The next man, a puncture-repair guy operating from a corrugated shed in the middle of nowhere else, charged €7.50 for what seemed like a small bottleful. Still, between the pair of them, it was enough to get me over the line, as it were.

From Piura, which is inland, to Paita on the coast the road crosses a wide and flat open area of maybe 20km. So bleak and unpromising did it look that, when I hit the outskirts of Paita, I feared the worst. 'Here comes a shambolic dump,' I thought, 'where I'll sleep in my clothes and scarper first thing in the morning before anything else wakes in the bed.' And then the way through the town suddenly plunged to the coast to reveal ... the largest collection of small fishing boats I have seen anywhere, ever. There must have been a thousand of them, bobbing up and down in a natural harbour with a beach. I chatted to someone later who confirmed that estimate as being about right.

The boats were painted all sorts of colours but mainly blues, white, light greens and some yellows and reds. They were heavy timber boats with wheelhouses forward and prows that arched sharply upwards, making them seem to stand out of the sea. They were lined up, each tied securely to the next, making a line across most of the bay. To the right of them was a modern jetty at which huge cranes with buckets were unloading cargo from the Oceanlove, a medium-sized bulk carrier, and pouring the contents into waiting lorries. The fishing boats were moored many lines deep, and the horizon between them and the sky was broken by a forest of masts and aerials and lots of seabirds.

The most engaging of the birds were the magnificent firebirds – hovering and lurking, hoping for the best – but there were pelicans too, gangly birds when they land but aces at flying, which they do just inches above the waves, gliding effortlessly before landing with a great awkward splosh. The firebirds are extraordinary: dark and with wide, angular V-shaped wingspans, they hover and glide at a great height, their tails sometimes splayed open with two sharp points, sometimes closed and looking like a dagger. But they don't seem to swoop: they just glide about in clusters and then suddenly they're gone.

I couldn't believe the number of boats. Surely, they didn't just serve this city. How could they all make money? The road down to the coast took me right to the seafront and, around a corner, a hostel presented itself – sanctuary for the night!

Next day, wandering round, I could see that Paita had a lot of history to it. There was the old semi-derelict customs house just by the hostel – a two-storey building in part propped up by scaffolding poles and with road all around it. It was a beautifully proportioned square building with tall fan-light windows and balconies and must have looked commanding in its prime, now long gone. Behind it was a timber church, with a portico entrance and a spire, which was leaning precariously forward and looking like, with another few inches, it would topple and crash to the ground. A woman in a shop opposite told me it was the Iglesia Antigua de las Mercedes Church but that it hadn't been used for at least thirty years.

All over this part of the town there were dilapidated buildings with first-floor verandas that must have been stylish in their day. One could see families sitting there of an evening, relaxing and chatting, or summer parties taking place, laughter and conversation filling the air along with the chink of glasses.

Perhaps the most interesting building was the one that had certain pretensions and which, rather pathetically, announced itself as the 'Club Liberal'. It fronted onto the busy main street hugging the coast, and part of the ground floor was given over to a downmarket T-shirt and jeans shop. The building ran back from the road right to the edge of the beach and to the sea itself. I doubt that the Club Liberal of Paita today has fraternal relations with its namesake National Liberal Club in Whitehall, London, but I wouldn't be surprised if, back in the day, it had.

Paita used to be a great whaling port. The city was founded by the Spanish in 1532 and was their capital for north Peru before they moved the administrative function inland to Piura because of the activities of English pirates. But its prime was in the nineteenth century, when whaling was big in the Pacific. British and American whalers used it for supplies and repairs and for recruiting seamen as well. The Americans established a consulate and hospital, such was the volume of trade and the numbers of visiting US citizens. The boom years lasted until the 1860s – bad timing for the Club Liberal, founded in 1863.

The building today really is falling down but, reflecting perhaps the spirit of its founding times, it's carrying on gamely. What was once a grand double-door entrance leads via bare wooden stairs that split, fanning to the left and right, to a large first-floor landing that runs the full front of the building. Balcony windows there overlook the street below, and then the landing leads into a huge hall or ballroom (perhaps), which has a long skylight ceiling that looked ready to collapse. Nonetheless, there remains in place hanging brass chandeliers and two large gold-coloured mirrors, the remnants of more gracious times. The wooden floor is half polished, from overuse rather than nurture, I suspect, as it's also host to many bird droppings. This long grand room leads to a balcony restaurant overlooking the beach and harbour, and, in its heyday, it must have been the place to socialise. Today, two young women, Zaida and Zarella, run the bar and restaurant ... which serves surprisingly good food.

But everywhere is peeling paint and rotting timbers. You can wander about the place, poking your nose in here and there, and no one will stop you. There's a sort of sapped spirit, a lack of interest in what anybody might be up to. Plaster on the rear facade that faces the beach is falling off, revealing the wattle-and-daub skeleton of the structure. The entire building rests on foundation poles rammed into the sand. It all looks like one severe sea storm could wash the lot away. And yet it carries on ... in a manner of speaking.

Around the corner at night, back beyond the old customs house, I saw great activity. By then it was dark, and arc lights had lit up a modern quayside and what was obviously something of a fish market and transport depot. Many of the fishing boats were landing their catches, which were being loaded into a posse of lorries and driven off. Down below, inside the fishing boats tied up against the quay, men filled fish boxes from the holds of the trawlers. Other men with grappling hooks then hoicked them onto the quayside, where the contents were weighed and noted. Sometimes the boxes were just stacked; sometimes they were abruptly shoved this way or that, to be dealt with later.

Great drama surrounded one part of the catch – the giant squids, which are enormous animals. Trays of the creatures were emptied into large but shallow stainless steel troughs, into which hoses pumped water, which poured over the sides of the troughs and onto the ground. Men in long plastic aprons and large white wellington boots washed the squids by sloshing them round in water before throwing them individually back into the plastic boxes. Other men, often boys, actually, shovelled ice on top of them. It was then into the lorries – huge, articulated lorries or those rigid flatbed lorries with refrigerators. Men on the back of the lorries stacked the iced-over boxes until they filled the space floor to ceiling, and then, without hesitation, the doors were slammed shut, and they were off – off from the quayside and depot, out through the steel gates and into the clamour and chaos of the night streets and then away ... but to where? I asked one of the men. 'Russia, Japan, Spain,' he replied.

All around, there were pelicans and sea lions waiting for shambles to fall their way. And the noise, the clatter of boxes, of ice shovels and hoses washing down the concrete as the lorries pulled out ... it was a great sight of urgent hard work, of getting the job done in the middle of the night, of colour and drama, of everybody knowing what to do and doing it. I was raging that I didn't have my camera, which had run out of battery. When I returned next night, it was much calmer; but I was unable to slip inside past the security guard. No, I could not go in was the firm response to my pleadings.

That night there was a festival in honour of San Sebastian and the fishing families, who all lived in fairly basic conditions around the harbour. There was much drinking and dancing and ribaldry and letting off of fireworks.

Wandering back to the hostel, I noticed a prostitute in the portico of the long-disused church. The sight of her there, wearing a black Covid facemask, vulnerable in among the mess and debris of the half-wrecked church and its dodgy spire, was just overwhelmingly miserable.

22 JANUARY 2023, CABO BLANCO

There are a couple of ways out of Paita. One is directly back onto the Panamericana. Okay, so we know what that heralds: a flashy dual carriageway north and on into Ecuador. The other is a lesser-travelled local road that hugs the coast and eventually, maybe 80km or 100km later, joins the PanAm and then whooshes on up to the frontier. I knew what the first option would be like and so went with the other, which actually turned out to be a grand road. It wended its way through a series of villages tucked into oasis-like valleys separated by lengthy swathes of dune-desert plateau. At a place named El Alto, which is perched on top of some cliffs – as you'd expect, with that name – there was a suggestion of a beach down below, at Cabo Blanco, which sounded good.

The road started plunging through chunky, bare rubble mountainside, down through twists and turns and switchbacks, none of them with protective walls or crash barriers, but that was fine because the vista beyond was fab – a panorama of wide blue ocean, and this time it was an azure blue, not that muddy brown seen earlier along the north Peruvian coast. This had a Caribbean feel to it.

At the bottom of the road, it becomes a short, simple drag by the beach – a lovely, clean sandy beach of maybe 150m and without a hint of litter anywhere, unlike other parts of Peru. The road goes on but only for a couple of hundred metres before it disappears around a headland. The drag had little on it, but it too was clean, and the promenade was well kept – all freshly painted, with places to sit and beds for small trees and cactus plants.

There was an officious bloke at the start of the drag, manning a barrier preventing vehicles from going any further. He directed me into a car park and wouldn't entertain the notion that I might continue along the road. And so I parked and started walking along the seafront, clunking in my biking gear in the pounding heat. There was a cafe and restaurant named the Black Merlin, which looked like it might do breakfast ... and it did! So, very soon, I was sitting there munching away on bread and jam, coffee and fresh orange juice, looking out at a flotilla of small sailing and fishing boats just off the beach and at an inshore petroleum rig. I started to notice all the marlin fishing photographs on the restaurant walls. Men, with or without parties of admirers, standing beside vast fish, usually three or four times their own height, suspended upside down by their tails, their killers standing proudly beside them, fishing rod in hand. And, I suppose inevitably, there he was: Papa himself, Ernest Hemingway in all his degenerate glory.

Hemingway had a big impact on me in my teenage years. I devoured A Farewell to Arms and still think it's one of the best novels. Ditto For Whom the Bell Tolls, and even a mention of A Moveable Feast has the smell of roasting chestnuts in the Jardin de Luxembourg fill my nostrils. I loved his terse style and the fact that he began his working life as a reporter. I wanted to be a reporter. The macho thing never got to me: I was never that and never felt it was something to emulate. But what did get me was the full-on way Hemingway lived his life. I'd much rather that it had not involved killing animals for sport. That I can't abide, but his zest for life, his lust for living, for food and drink, for adventure – that appealed to me and still does.

Hemingway was only fifty-seven when he came to Cabo Blanco in 1956, and then for only thirty-two days, but he was already in steep decline. At the end of 1955, and before his Peruvian escapade, he had been bedridden and was told by his doctor to lay off the drink – advice he was unable to take. Cabo Blanco has been dining out on this old man and the sea ever since his month-long visit. The sea because this is one of the few places where black merlin live, in large numbers and close to the shore, attracted apparently by two currents, El Niño and the Humboldt, as well as by the mackerel, which themselves come for the anchovy. The merlin were fished easily, according to the restaurant owner, Francisco. And the old man? Well, because that was what Hemingway was by then: thirteen years younger than me now, but in his head an old man who was depressed and aging rapidly, and his body wasn't in good shape either. Within four years, he would shoot himself in his hunting lodge in Ketchum, Idaho. (Across four generations, five Hemingways have taken their own lives.)

Hemingway came to Cabo Blanco because this was where much of the filming of the screen version of his novel The Old Man and The Sea was to be done. Spencer Tracy played the old man. By coincidence, my former reporting colleague Patsy McGarry, whom as *Irish Times* foreign editor I dispatched to Cuba, once returned from Havana with a present for me: a Cuban copy of The Old Man and the Sea signed by Gregorio Fuentes, former captain of Hemingway's boat, the Pilar. Fuentes claimed, and maybe this was his dining-out story, that the character of Santiago, the old man of the novel, was based on him, although Hemingway said he was based on no one in particular. Either way, the little book from Patsy remains greatly treasured.

Hemingway held court at the Cabo Blanco Fishing Club and in local bars, as photos in the restaurant show. He looks – to me, at any rate – a lot older than fifty-seven and – as in some photos in bars and cafes around Estafeta, the famed bull-running street in Pamplona – he cuts a rather pathetic figure. They've put up a bust to him along the seafront, and one of the bars displays a large picture of him behind the counter. The Cabo Blanco Fishing Club was a magnet for rich Americans (not unrelated to the fact that rich Americans ran it: founding membership cost $10,000), and in the 1950s it played host to Marilyn Monroe, Paul Newman, James Stewart, Humphrey Bogart, John Wayne and Nelson Rockefeller. That heyday is long gone now.

'Rich Spanish, Germans and Italians still come here to fish,' says Francisco. But it's not the same: there are fishing restrictions aimed at preserving merlin stocks, and catches are to be returned to the sea, not suspended from a quayside gibbet. So the days of big game fishing are over, even if the memories linger. Cabo Blanco's future may be more in surfing than in macho fishing. Hemingway is said to have fished every day he was here, and of all the famous habitués of the club, his is the image that dominates the restaurant walls and adjoining bar.

In a 215-page history of the club published in 2011, nineteen pages are devoted to Papa. He didn't manage to catch anything weighing over 1,000lb, a trophy known as a 'grander'. The grander record for the largest fish ever caught on a line remains held by the Texas oilman Alfred C. Glassell, Jr, who landed a 1,560-pounder here in 1953. Hemingway's best at the club was a 910-pounder, which ain't half bad either. No grander has been caught for over fifty years.

I ate that night beneath the photos of the man himself. I had plain fish a la plancha, potato and salad. I thought I should have some wine too. Sadly, it would be bloody awful red wine, and dulce at that. I doubted they had Margaux.

ECUADOR

27 JANUARY–4 FEBRUARY 2023, GUAYAQUIL AND THE GALÁPAGOS ISLANDS

I crossed from Peru into Ecuador, which, despite some initial bureaucratic difficulty, went smoothly enough. I spent the night at Machala and then headed for Guayaquil, the largest city in the country. The contrast between Peru and Ecuador was stark and immediate. I haven't written too much about the litter in Peru, but it's pervasive. Vast quantities of domestic waste are dumped almost everywhere but particularly on the ways in and out of towns and cities. The filth is indescribable and the dangers to human health are obvious. Still, neither local nor national government seems willing or able to do anything about it, and so people just keep on dumping.

Once you're over the border into Ecuador, all that changes. The roadsides are clean and largely litter-free, and signs extol environmental responsibility. A sign along the roadside, a small sign maybe half a metre square, says, very simply, Plant a tree. The sign has a photograph of large male hands cupped together protecting a seedling that has just sprouted. A variation of this image occurs a little further on, with the adult hands handing the seedling to a pair of child's hands. The message is clear: Ecuador cares about the environment,

Later, I read that in 2008 Ecuador became the first country to enshrine in its constitution legally enforceable 'rights of nature' – a concept similar to the notion of human rights. In other words, nature and ecosystems have a right to exist and be respected and maintained so that life cycles are regenerated and nature can function properly and evolve accordingly. Much of this was driven by a left-wing president, Rafael Correa, who was in office for ten years from 2007. I suppose some of it is linked also to the fact that the Galápagos Islands are part of Ecuador, and so there's an enhanced appreciation of such matters.

In Guayaquil I found what looked to be a nice hostel, Casa Michael, a small single-storey house near the airport, which turned out to be more than usually interesting. There were books in Hebrew, and the TV, in front of which a young man sat watching what appeared to be a brainless soap of the Neighbours variety, had Hebrew subtitles. The place served falafel and hummus and was run by Michael, a forty-five-year-old Israeli married to an Ecuadorian woman. Michael convinced me that I had to go to the Galápagos, even finding me a safe haven for the bike. After a couple of days secluded in the seaside town of Playas for catch-up writing, on 29 January I flew there for a week.

I knew I was in the Galápagos Islands because, when walking from the plane to the terminal building on Baltra Island, there was an iguana asleep in a flowerbed right by the edge of the footpath. At first I assumed that it was a piece of concrete – a sort of Galápagoan version of a garden gnome, put there as a 'Welcome, tourist!' gesture. But, no, it was real. Next, the bus that takes everyone from the little ferry linking Baltra Island to the much larger Santa Cruz Island had to stop along the way because there was an iguana crossing the road – and rather slowly, at that. Why did the iguana cross the road? I have no idea, because one side looked just the same as the other: a barren mess of half-dead plants, cactus and mangrove, and volcanic lava debris. From Puerto Ayora, the main town on Santa Cruz – in fact the main town in the archipelago – I took a ferry to Puerto Villamil on the neighbouring island of Isabela, a bumpy ride that lasted several hours and that I thought would never end. But it was worth it.

The Galápagos Islands are Ground Zero when it comes to evolution. There are twenty-one islands some 900km out into the Pacific Ocean, and they straddle the equator. A few are little more than rock outcrops, but a dozen or so are sizable. Three – Isabela, Santa Cruz and San Cristóbal – contain almost all of the 33,000 people who live in what is a province of Ecuador. When Charles Darwin came here in 1835 during the second voyage of the Beagle, it had been largely isolated for millions of years. The Spanish arrived in 1535, and various buccaneering British sailors followed suit and mapped the place in 1684. But, for all that, the Galápagos had largely been ignored ... though not by nature.

Darwin was twenty-two when he began his work, spending most of five years observing nature in and around the Pacific and just five weeks in the Galápagos. But it was enough time for him to join a pile of dots suggesting that plants and animals adapted to their environment in order to survive and prosper. Twenty-three years after that voyage, Darwin published *On the Origin of Species by Means of Natural Selection*, and nothing has been quite the same since.

The first thing that strikes the visitor to the Galápagos Islands is that there are animals everywhere. Amazingly, they don't seem afraid of people. In fact, they don't seem the least bit interested in us. Sea lions loll about on seaside footpaths, on boats and on jetties. Some even sleep on benches put there for humans but that have been turned into beds by the sea lions, who contentedly defecate where they flop. There are even notices saying, I'm sleeping, please do not disturb. The animals have taken over ...

On my first morning on Isabela I took a snorkelling tour to the tunnels, a place about an hour west along the southern coast of the island. First stop was Roca Unión, a single rock outcrop maybe two or three kilometres offshore on which sit several boobies. There were two types of the bird there when we visited, the red-footed and blue-footed variety, the first on top of the rock and the other on a ledge below, facing inwards and not at all interested in us. The booby is a strange-looking bird. It has a head and face quite like a gannet and a body about the size of a small goose. But its legs are stumpy, and it waddles, rather than walks, lifting each foot in turn in a rather exaggerated gesture outwards and upwards, and then forwards, as though it has glue on its soles. It was this manner of funny walking that earned it its name: booby means 'silly' in Spanish, said our guide, Diego Rivadeneiva.

Diego took us to the tunnels at Cabo Rosa, which are made of lava and through which liquid volcanic rock flowed into the sea. What's left today is a complex mass of black rocks and broken-open tunnel tubes and arches, perfect cover for sea creatures. On top of the tunnels there are nesting sites used by boobies, and we got close to some that, again like other creatures, seemed almost completely unfazed by our presence.

Snorkelling around the lava tunnels, I saw a wholly different world open up. There were fish everywhere – parrot fish and puffer fish and yellow-tail damsel fish – all of them sporting electric blue, yellow and pink colours. And there were Pacific sea horses. Under one of the arches created by the lava, white-tipped reef sharks were sleeping. They lay in the water, floating just off the bottom, completely still and seemingly unaware of our presence, or at least uninterested in our being there. They're not huge, perhaps a metre and a half in length, and don't look dangerous at all. According to Diego, who led us to them, they sleep during the day and at night will go further out to sea to hunt shellfish and octopus.

The big thrill came when we encountered sea turtles. As we were snorkelling about on the surface, all the time looking down, suddenly one loomed out of the half-light ahead – a big thing, maybe three feet long and a foot and a half wide. A male turtle, he snuffled along the bottom, ripping out greenery and sending clouds of sand into the water. Lots of electric-coloured fish hung round his mouth, feeding off whatever was in the debris from his pulling up and chomping. We saw three or four of them, all lumbering through the water, their flippers active but not flailing, just looking relaxed and going about their feeding. Again, they seemed uninterested in us and not the least bit disturbed. I asked Diego about this. Why aren't the creatures fearful of humans? Because, he said, they're not hunted and it's illegal to touch them, let alone to try to remove them. And so they just get on with whatever it is they're doing, and they're left alone.

The same appears to be true for the iguanas. They're everywhere close to water – on the beach, on rock outcrops along the beach, on boardwalks – big ones up to three feet long and scores of tiny ones. It appears that they breed rather successfully. You can be sitting on a barstool, look down and suddenly notice that the long black shape in the sand by your feet is not a sleeping cat but an iguana! Wherever mangroves-meet-sand-meets-jetties, there you will find these weird, gargoyle-like little fellows. Up close, they look ferocious and medieval or like something out of one of those sci-fi-meets-Vikings nonsense series. You can see where at least some of the inspiration for Gremlins came from.

The next day I went to see the famed Galápagos giant tortoise, which gave the islands their name, again from the Spanish. Darwin noticed small differences between the tortoises on different islands. According to Diego, on Isabela there are five types of tortoise, each differing from the others in small but not unimportant ways because each grew up on the flanks of different volcanoes. The lava flowing from each of Isabela's five main volcanoes cut the tortoises off from each other (they all came originally, millions of years ago, from Peru and Chile), and so they developed – evolved – slightly differently.

At the tortoise sanctuary on Isabela, there are some 900 of the creatures, 800 of them newborn (which means, in tortoise span, anything from two years to about seven). The one I looked at most – named, with stunning lack of imagination, No. 2 – is believed by the sanctuary to be 100 to 120 years old. Despite that, he's nimble enough on those feet that you might think would have evolved better for walking. The tortoises were removed from the south-facing flank of Volcán Sierra Negra in the late 1990s because predators (rats, birds of prey, dogs, cattle) were killing the young or eating eggs.

Adult tortoises mate for up to five hours (it seems like we missed out on that bit of evolution). When the female lays eggs and buries them in a pit 30–40cm deep and then defecates and urinates on top to put predators off, the young hatch after 160 days and have to get on with life on their own. They never know their parents, who have no interest in them after the eggs are laid.

Walking back to my hostel, I found half a dozen flamingos feeding in the lake. They were the pinkest pink I had ever seen. They looked terribly beautiful and fragile, but they too seem to thrive here, despite the annual 270,000 or so tourists – mainly retirees and backpackers – who come to look at them and wonder at all the extraordinary creatures in this most unusual place before flying off to the next stop on that bucket list …

6 FEBRUARY 2023, QUITO

Leaving Guayaquil was a relief. I had done next to no biking in the previous ten days and was beginning to feel guilty. I didn't regret going to the Galápagos – far from it: I would have regretted it forever more had I not gone, and I don't think friends back home would have understood my not going despite being close to such an extraordinary place. But being on the islands made me acutely aware of being on my own – and of not particularly liking it. I missed my wife, Moira, a lot, partly because I knew she would have loved to have been there. The wildlife, the colours and the beautiful beaches would have appealed to the painter in her, and every time I saw them, I was aware that she was not seeing them with me, and I felt bad about that. So after one night back in Guayaquil and a good sleep at Casa Michael's, I was more than ready to hit the road again.

Once outside the city, I decided to head up through the centre of the country, but not on Highway 35, the main route to Quito. I opted instead for the 487, which runs more or less parallel to it and is, as it happens, the

Panamericana, as opposed to the better, more modern 35. The countryside was getting more and more tropical as I moved north, with banana and cacao plantations giving way to greater varieties of vegetables, lush green fields and, upland, dense forests of trees and tall plants, some of them with the sort of giant leaves one associates with the tropics. But it was an uneventful run until the junction at which the two roads converge, a few kilometres south of the city of Riobamba.

Along one side of the road, for perhaps one hundred metres, there were barbecue braziers all in a line, one after the other, each with roasting spit wheels turning above the embers. And on the spits were cuy (pronounced koo-ee), that is, roasted guinea pigs. I have a deep aversion to rejecting any food without trying it at least once. But I had not been able to summon up the courage to order cuy in any restaurant, and I had seen the menu option regularly since southern Peru. In fact, oftentimes one enters a room at the rear of a country hostel or a restaurant, usually the bathroom, only to provoke a chorus of excited squeaking from somewhere further out back – a shed or garden compound. The first time I heard it, I knew immediately it was a small herd of guinea pigs destined one day for the kitchen.

In Quito I headed for the Centro Historico, riding towards the spires of what I assumed was the city's cathedral. It's a strategy that I have found by experience generally brings one to the nicest parts of almost any city and that is especially useful when blundering round on a huge motorcycle and not really knowing where you're going. On a narrow street on a hill leading into Plaza de San Francisco, I noticed a slightly scruffy hotel entrance with a narrow alleyway – somewhere to park the bike, always a major consideration – and so I swung into it. The location was terrific even if the Hotel Boutique Portal de Cantuña didn't look all that promising. But how wrong can you be?

Further on into the plaza is the extraordinary Convento y Iglesia Católica San Francisco, which dominates one whole side of the square. It's an astonishing 40,000m2 (the largest such site in all of South America) and is the most important religious complex in Ecuador. Construction began just three years after the Spanish founded the city, so it dates from the mid-sixteenth to the mid-seventeenth centuries. Walking inside the church is a 'knock you off your feet' moment, such is the opulence of the place. If there is a square inch of wall or ceiling that isn't covered in gold, I missed it. I exaggerate but only slightly. It's astonishing and, despite the vulgarity of such opulence and questions as to where it all came from, it's very beautiful.

Beside the church is the convent, now largely a museum. I was told there were perhaps fifteen residents left in the whole institution – a place that must surely have housed hundreds in its day. Upstairs, a gallery corridor mirrors the cloister below, with cells, now mostly empty, off it. From here, you may also enter the choir room, with its beautifully carved chorister seating and double-organ loft and an elevated view down into the church. The stairway has what is said to be the largest painting in all of Ecuador, an eighteenth-century genealogical representation of the Franciscans. At the bottom of the tree is St Francis himself and then, above him, like an espalier fruit tree, row upon row of various luminaries of the order – 589 in all. They look, I have to say, strange.

At the top of the bell tower, a young woman and I peered out over the city rooftops. She pointed to the cathedral, to which I never got, and then to the vast complex diagonally across the square. 'The Jesuits,' she said. And then, in the near distance, another vast church, that of Santo Domingo, the Dominicans. Between these three huge, sprawling complexes is essentially the entirety of Quito's historic centre. All the streets running between them, now filled mainly with tourist shops and restaurants, were, one imagines, all part of the infrastructure supporting the religious institutions in their heyday.

Just a few feet away from where the Jesuits used to dominate is Plaza Grande – not as grand as Plaza de San Francisco but a lot prettier and beautifully maintained. A troupe of clowns entertained a crowd of onlookers, adults and children alike, with staged idiocies and death-defying antics on unicycles. I sat and watched and had a beer and thought what a wonderful place this was ... but also what awful stories must be hidden in the massive, and at times very beautiful, religious structures all about me.

Next morning I rode the short distance north of the city to Mitad del Mundo, where the equator slices east–west across Ecuador, marked by a 30m obelisk made of volcanic stone holding up a giant stone globe. From the obelisk there comes a thin yellow line painted onto the ground – the equator itself (hence the name Ecuador), which you may straddle, one foot in the Northern Hemisphere, the other in the Southern.

COLOMBIA

TO PEOPLE IN MUCH OF THE REST OF THE WORLD, modern Colombia may bring to mind drugs, drug cartels and maybe FARC guerillas. In fact, I saw no evidence of drugs and only an echo of the other, but two things piqued my interest as I entered the country in early February 2023. One was that Route 25 north towards Popayán and Cali from the border with Ecuador had been engulfed by a huge landslide about a month before and might still be impassable. The other, of much greater interest to me, was that a small town on the Gulf of Darién had become a staging post for undocumented migrants trying to reach North America. I wanted to see both and, having entered Colombia by crossing the border between Tulcán and Ipiales, I set off north via Route 25. It was about 300km before I came to the enormous landslide ...

10 FEBRUARY 2023, ROSAS

'Landslide'. The word seems wholly inadequate for describing what had happened a month before. Essentially, the side of the mountain between Piedra Sentada and Rosas, on which there were four villages – Parraga Viejo, Santa Clara, La Soledad and Chontaduro – began to shift on 6 January after exceptional prolonged rainfall. The initial warning signs allowed for an evacuation and, to the best of my knowledge, no lives were lost in what ultimately happened three days later. But sixty-four homes disappeared as the side of the mountain slipped further, folded in on itself and poured down the valley side, leaving seven hundred people homeless.

I knew I would come across some difficulty on Route 25, but I really didn't expect it to be that bad, not after a month. I spent the night in a hotel in El Pilón, about 70km south-west of Rosas, after which the road wound its way through countryside that was covered by dense tropical vegetation. I had left the hotel so early that some people were walking to work. Women swept the road outside their homes, often making small bonfires of the dry-leaf debris. Schoolgirls in neat plaid skirts and knee-high white socks waited for lifts. For much of the time, the road followed the San Pedro River Valley, always riding high on its shoulder, thereby offering stunning views of down below and beyond. Sometimes the landscape was quite cultivated; other times it was tropical, with incredibly dense growth, including bamboos that appeared to be about 40m tall. The sides of the mountains were often eaten away by steep-sided gullies with pointed ridges, one after another running along the whole flank.

When I came across my first landslide, it lulled me into a false sense of security. The first indication that something wasn't right was the queue of lorries that appeared about 25km south of Rosas. It was a very long line of lorries stopped nose to tail on one side of the road. Bikes could ride past on the wrong side of the road because, with few exceptions, nothing was coming from that direction. The head of the queue was stopped at a toll plaza, 22km south-west of Rosas, and police were everywhere. But it was clear that they had no problem with bikers going up the outside and slipping through the barriers. I asked one of the policemen why the vehicles were stopped. He pulled out his phone and showed me pictures of what was up ahead – bite-sized chunks of collapsed road – but you could see that two wheels could get through easily enough. 'Yes, you can pass,' he said, and so I rode on.

After maybe a kilometre, a tiny mound of clay and rocks, no more than a wheelbarrowful, appeared on the left, and I thought, 'Jaysus, is that what they're worried about!'

But eventually a really big hole did appear: it was like a giant of the mountains had taken a bite, as though out of a slice of cake. The road had simply ceased to be on one side: a whole semicircle was gone. Workers and huge earth-movers were busily creating a new road, one that would itself plunge down into the valley before rising again to reconnect with the existing road. Again, all this was passable, but it was noteworthy that the road builders were all working under military guard. The now largely defunct rebel group FARC used to be active there, but since the 2016 peace agreement they have been replaced by a motley collection of dissident drug gangs. I asked a contractor how long it would take to build the new road. 'Three months,' he said, which made me wonder whether the lorries in the queue were really going to wait that long.

I rode on, thinking again that maybe that was it with landslides. And then, around a corner, a vista opened up revealing the true nature of the problem: the side of an entire mountain had shifted, obliterating settlements and making the Pan-American Highway impassable for what looked like a lot more than half a kilometre. I guessed the only four-wheeled vehicle that could traverse the mess would be a Land Rover and not much else.

People trudged across the gaping, muddy wound, hauling their belongings in plastic bags and shopping bags, in pillowcases and cardboard boxes and in those weekend-break suitcases with little wheels. There was something biblical about the scene: hundreds of thousands of tons of clay, rocks and boulders, smashed trees and shrubs, strewn across an area perhaps the size of six football pitches – a pulverised mountainside that slithered down into the valley below, leaving behind it a gaping scar on the landscape.

And across the debris, like a line of ants on a patio, people made their way as best they could, not on a path – that would be far too grand a description – but on a trail hammered out by the feet of hundreds and by motorbike riders. It wasn't until I turned round to look at the spectacle yet again that I saw just how disruptive the landslide had been to those most affected.

'*Los muertos, los muertos,*' someone shouted, urging those about to cross, including me, to hold back for a moment. And over a dip in the mound came four men carrying a purple wooden coffin that was roped onto a makeshift metal frame a bit like a stretcher. The pallbearers paused briefly above a small cliff within the debris to let some others cross the makeshift bridge below where they stood – six thick poles slung across the small gorge. And when the people passed, the pallbearers resumed their task, walking over the narrow bridge and down onto terra firma. A waiting hearse, which itself had seen better days, reversed and took delivery of the dead.

I stopped, dismounted, looked in some disbelief and thought, 'What do I do now?' At that moment, several young men rushed towards me, offering their services in getting across. I hesitated. The trail across was maybe two feet wide at most but frequently shrank to eight or ten inches. It was anything but smooth: it had rocks, big rocks, jutting up from the mud – no problem if you are on foot and able-bodied or riding a motocross bike, a 125cc or even a 250cc. I was on a 1,200cc fully laden monster that, as a result, was difficult to keep upright except on a reasonably smooth surface.

The lads were pressing. 'We'll help you. Leave your luggage on the bike. That way, we can keep you upright.' That filled me with confidence. 'Go on! Do it!' Seeing my reluctance – my fear – they encouraged and even browbeat me. It was at that moment that the pallbearers appeared, and I had to wait. But once they passed I went for it – partly out of a sense that I had come this far, so I had nothing to lose; partly out of a sense that I couldn't just give in without even trying: and partly, I suppose, out of a sense that I wasn't going to limp off, defeated and with my tail between my legs.

Well, I cannot think of a more arduous, strenuous or testing fifteen or twenty minutes on a motorbike. That I fell once (and thought I had broken my leg, instead of having merely a horrendous bruise) was due entirely to my lack of skill and not to the efforts of the lads, who were heroic. Several times I stalled on really steep inclines, especially where they narrowed to mere inches at the top and I had no sense of which direction the path took after the crest. I screamed curses at myself, but the lads kept me steady ... and upright.

I got to the other side, drenched in sweat from head to toe and barely able to talk, let alone stand. We had agreed no price for their help beforehand, and when I asked what I owed them, they sort of shrugged – a shrug that said, 'Whatever you think yourself.' I opened my wallet, but all I had was 150 pesos (about €30). So, a little more than €5 each – a mean reward, though not intentionally so. It was all I had in the wallet. When I stopped at a roadside cafe a few hundred metres on, I pulled out what coins were in my pocket and asked the woman there for whatever liquid she had, but that was all the money on me. She smiled and gave me a small bottle of water.

11 FEBRUARY 2023, IBAGUÉ

The square at Ibagué is black and filthy and gets to look worse as the dusk turns to night. It's a square that goes nowhere, that is, it leads nowhere. You don't drive or stroll into it to marvel at its beauty or conduct urgent business before passing on out the other side. There's no beauty here, or at least nothing obviously beautiful: it's a dirty hole of a place, and everybody knows it. The square is an afterthought bit of road, a cul-de-sac, the butt end of one of Ibagué's main shopping streets, which is filled with small shops that sell gaudy rubbish and stay open late.

The square was created by another road crossing the shopping street and slicing off the bit left over. Buses use it to swing round the traffic island in the middle so that they can retrace their route. Other vehicles use it similarly. That's part of the reason the concrete surface of the road is so very black. It's from the oil and rubber and filth that stick to both. The concrete is also broken, cracked and pockmarked. During the day, it's home to market stalls, but at night it's a different place.

One side is filled almost entirely with drinking dens ('pub' would be an exaggeration). There are six or eight of them in a row, each one a single void facing onto the footpath and with little inside except for a concrete floor, plastic tables and chairs, a counter by the back wall and a fridge or two stacked with bottles of beer. Each den is full of people, many spilling out onto the footpath and into the square, and each has a loudspeaker pumping out awful sounds: *Dhun, dhun, dhun.*

But there was one other drinking den, diagonally across the square, with only a few people in it. The sound system was turned down low, relatively speaking. As I walked across to it, I saw a man who had almost no clothes on, and those he had were so ripped that he was rendered virtually naked. He looked like Tom Hanks after a decade on that deserted island in Cast Away. He was wandering round the road somewhat aimlessly until he came to a pothole – more of a crack, actually, that had opened up into a long split. From a side street on the other side of the square there was liquid flowing down the gutter, into the square and into the hole. The man lowered himself and knelt down on the road. He arched forward, placing both hands on the ground, until his shoulders were almost touching the road as well. He then drank the liquid, and not in a furtive way: it was a slow, deliberate slurping of the filthy stew.

It's one of the most degrading scenes I have ever witnessed. I felt diminished just watching. That another person could be brought so low as that was shocking, but what must he have felt at that moment?

I sat at the open front of the quiet bar, ordered a beer from the woman who runs the place and watched the square. That was when I noticed the pile of rubbish at the end of the traffic island in the middle of the square – the one the buses swing round and where the man drank the filthy liquid of unknown provenance. Another man was going through the rubbish aggressively. There was a big cardboard box full of stuff that he tipped over and emptied by pulling everything out and throwing it over his shoulder. What looked like a pizza box had discarded food in it, and he ate whatever it was. But otherwise he just seemed to scatter all the rubbish from the box and also from a long white plastic sack, similarly left for the waste collectors, not finding anything of value.

Near my drinking den were several closed premises whose raison d'être was not obvious. But the man who had emptied the box wandered over to their doorways to hang about. I went over to him and gave him money – 5,000 pesos, which is only about €1. He thanked me profusely, and I returned to my veranda seat.

The man had an associate, a fellow with a red baseball cap, jeans and a pink-highlighter vest. The pair of them talked and wandered about the square, to no obvious purpose. The woman in the den came over to me and scolded me. She tapped into a translation app on her phone, and out came *Be very careful they steal it.* I told her that everything was fine, no worries. Another man then appeared. He had a red baseball cap on, black jeans and a brown T-shirt and was carrying a puppy under his arm. I didn't know if he expected to sell it, but he didn't seem to try to. He just wandered about with the dog under his arm. Later, he shouted at an adult dog, which followed him away out of the square.

Across the way from where I was, the drinking dens filled even more. Several police were hanging about on the traffic island, watching and just being there. There was no aggro, just a lot of noise.

At the pile of rubbish, a new searcher appeared. He picked up the cardboard box, and other bits of cardboard, and walked off purposefully into an alleyway with a concrete arch over it and a sign saying *Centro Commercial.* He was not to be seen again.

The first man who rummaged in the rubbish, the one to whom I gave a paltry sum, wandered about with a wooden stick, like a walking staff, and started to dance and balance it on one finger. I took a few pictures of him and asked him his name. 'Alejandro,' he said. He was younger than he looks, I reckoned. His hair was jet black, his face was weathered and his teeth were all gaps and rotting. He had a boxer's flattened nose. I thanked him for the photos, we shook hands and he wandered off again. Later, for no obvious reason, he placed the stick against the kerb and snapped it with his foot. Pink-highlighter vest was with him after the dance and asked me for money. I give him a few notes – again, a paltry sum.

The bar woman was really anxious now. And one of the regulars, a man with a sort of walking cane or swizzle stick tied to his wrist, tried to tell me all sorts of things, one of which seemed to be whether I would like the police to come over. No, I tell him. Everything's fine. '*Tranquillo*,' I said – a great word here which means, essentially, 'It's grand. Relax!'

I asked the woman the name of the square. Plaza 15. I asked her the name of her bar. Planchon 15. Then she asked, via the app, Do you need them to come? meaning the police. No, no, I said. '*No problemo, no problemo*.' A few minutes later, someone – the woman's husband, I think – handed me a phone. 'Talk, talk,' he said.

'Hello,' I said.

'Hello,' said a woman at the other end, in English.

'What can I do for you?'

'My family is very worried about you.'

'I'm fine,' I said. 'Everything is fine. There's no problem.'

'Are you sure?'

'Yes, absolutely. But thank you for asking.'

'Okay.'

Everyone calmed down, more or less. Swizzle stick remained agitated, apparently believing that a mob was about to set upon me. 'Listen,' I tell him, 'I'm fine. There's no problem. But I think really that it's time I went.' He wanted to walk me back to my hotel, which was about two hundred metres away. 'No, thanks, you're grand,' I told him as I left and ambled across the square in the direction of the rubbish and the dens, probably giving swizzle stick a heart attack.

I had a good look at the dens and took photos, some of the cops. Nobody paid a blind bit of notice, and I walked to a petrol station opposite the hotel and got a sandwich, which was surprisingly good.

I never saw again the man who drank from the hole in the road …

19 FEBRUARY 2023, CÚCUTA

After Ibagué I rode north through Bogotá and on to Cúcuta, a city on the border with Venezuela. Well over seven million Venezuelans have fled their homeland in recent years, most of them crossing the frontier into Cúcuta. For a country of thirty million people, that's close to a quarter of the population upping sticks and getting out. In effect, Venezuela is bleeding people, mostly into neighbouring nations and the Caribbean but also further afield – to Spain, for instance, for obvious linguistic and other cultural reasons.

It's almost an entirely self-inflicted wound, starting in 2010 when the government of Hugo Chávez declared an 'economic war' because of various shortages. In the face of fiscal meltdown, the government maintained a high level of spending – mismanagement that continued apace under Chávez's successor, Nicolás Maduro. The country has one of the most substantial reserves of oil in the world, right up there with Saudi Arabia. In fact, according to British Petroleum, it has slightly more than the Saudis – 304 billion barrels against their paltry 298 billion. But who knows for sure because Venezuela has mismanaged itself spectacularly for years, and official figures are somewhat meaningless. For instance, in 2018, inflation peaked at 16,374 per cent, falling back to the more manageable current rate of just 195 per cent, according to Statista, the German-based consumer data company.

When I began my journey through the Americas, I first encountered Venezuelans in the far south – in Punta Arenas in Chile and in El Calafate in Argentina, only marginally less far south. In both instances, they were working in hospitality, just like thousands of Irish people who work abroad, although they're prompted to leave for reasons rather less extreme than those facing Venezuelans.

In snatched conversations in cafes and restaurants, most Venezuelans seemed stoical enough. 'It's just the way it is' was a common refrain, and they simply got on with life as best they could. But one can only guess at the emotional bruising beneath the surface. Many, perhaps most, leave the country by heading west into Colombia, with which Venezuela shares a

Near the end of the most southerly road on continental America: the dirt road leading to Cape Froward in southern Chile.

From Isla Navarino, the crystal waters of the Beagle Channel reflect the mountains of Tierra del Fuego to the north.

A photo portrait of Cristina Calderón Harban, the last full-blooded Yahgan, by her grave on Isla Navarino.

Torres del Paine, Chile.

The Perito Moreno Glacier flows into Lake Argentina, where I scattered the ashes of my geography teacher, Ian Broad.

Andres, the have-a-go puncture repair man of Bahía Murta.

Motorbike enthusiast Francisco Maturana with the rare Ducati Bimota, part of his museum collection of over 130 bikes near Puerto Octay, southern Chile.

Graffiti art in Valparaíso's Concepción district.

The burnt red desert landscape of the Valle de la Luna near San Pedro de Atacama, Northern Chile.

The train cemetery at Uyuni in Bolivia.

The vast Salar de Uyuni in Bolivia, seen from the rocky, cactus-strewn Isla Incahuasi outcrop in the middle of the salt flat.

Sunset on the Salar de Uyuni.

Indigenous Bolivians in Sica Sica mark the ascension to office of new members of indigenous administrative bodies on New Year's Day 2023.

Roadblock protesters on the edge of Juliaca posed for me before letting me through.

Burning tyres and riot debris blocking the Pan Americana at Chao, north of Lima.

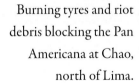

An obliging llama posed for me at Machu Picchu.

A sea lion on the Galápagos Islands snoozes contentedly on a bench, unperturbed by humans.

The huge landslide near Rosas in Colombia.

A coffin is carried across the mud slide wasteland.

A migrant woman and her baby, probably from Haiti, about to board a ferry across the Gulf of Darién and walk through the jungle into Panama.

Two hopeful lads from Shanghai, China, in Capurganá, Colombia, hoping to get to the US.

Near Puente Linda on the gravel road through the jungle between Medellín and Bogotá.

Panama: Restored colonial elegance in the old city.

La Expocisión, the down-at-heel poorer area of Panama City, sandwiched between the restored, tourist-popular old city, and the brash, modern high-rise city.

Quintessential Panama – hats and Cuban cigars.

The F&F Building, known locally as The Corkscrew, emblematic of the bank and law firm that dominate modern Panama City.

Part of Costa Rica's idyllic Caribbean coastline at the Cahuita
National Park. The forest is home to howler monkeys.

A stallholder at the Huembes market in central Managua strikes a
pose for me.

A young man in contemplative mood in Managua's Huembes market.

'Diaphanous Hyacinth' (left) and 'Ferret' from Coyolito on the south
coast of Honduras.

San Salvador's Cumbres del Volcán Flor hostel.

Carriers struggle to hold up one of the huge religious 'paso' floats during Antigua's Easter procession in Guatemala.

border 2,220km long and several official crossing points. One of the largest – the San Antonio crossing – is just outside Cúcuta. The actual frontier is in the middle of a long concrete bridge, the Simón Bolívar Bridge, over the River Táchira, but you can walk across it without anyone checking anything. All that is done on the Venezuelan side. And it's all rather shambolic.

I wandered well inside Venezuela, maybe a kilometre or so, and was taking photos of the constant flow of people, almost all of them going in one direction (into Colombia), when a Venezuelan customs official intervened. What was I doing? I explained that I was a tourist and a journalist and wanted a few photos. 'Oh, no, that isn't allowed,' he said firmly but in a friendly enough manner. He asked for my phone. I gave it to him, and he directed me to stand to one side. A bit left, he indicated. Yes, there. And he took my picture for me, in front of a Venezuelan flag, and handed me back my phone.

The stream of people leaving just didn't ease up – at least not in the few hours I was there. It was a Sunday, so it was difficult to divine exactly why everyone was making the journey, which most were doing on foot. There were family groups with children; groups of teenagers and young adults, all mobile phones and chatter; some single young men; and some quite elderly people too. But no one thing appeared to define them, at least not to me – something that would indicate fleeing, or escaping, from something awful. Many had no bags or suitcases and appeared merely to be crossing from San Antonio (the town on the Venezuelan side) to Villa Rosario (on the Colombian side), perhaps to shop, meet friends or simply have a day out, as it were. But some, maybe a third, did have suitcases and looked to be making a more significant journey.

The Venezuelan checks were random, to put it mildly. The road on the Venezuelan side was wide and laid out a bit like a roadway toll crossing – several channels through which vehicles might be funnelled. Every now and then police would step into the road and stop a vehicle heading into Colombia (almost invariably a taxi) and check the passengers and the boot. At the side of the road, the police had a desk set up in what looked like a garden gazebo. One of the crossers would occasionally be directed to the desk and asked for ID. I hung round there for a while and eventually got talking to a middle-aged man who had walked across from Venezuela with a younger companion. The man had what looked like a weekend-break bag. He also had another black case slung on his back – a violin case. We got chatting.

He was heading for Lima in Peru because life in Venezuela was so difficult. Food, petrol and all services had become too expensive. He mentioned the cost of a bottle of water, which he said was three times more expensive in Venezuela than in Colombia. '*La economía*,' he said – a catch-all explanation as to why, aged forty-six, he was leaving behind his wife and two children, aged ten and twelve.

The police started taking an interest in the two of us. Who was I? asked one. I told him and showed him my press card and passport, which was not stamped for entering Venezuela. 'I'm not entering,' I said. 'I'm just hanging round talking to people.'

'Come with me,' the policeman said, and into the gazebo we went. He wanted to know much more about me, and so I told him. After a while he took out his phone and began showing me photos of his Suzuki 600 racer, his pride and joy. We did selfies. Eventually, I was let go without any fuss. I walked on ahead of Violin Man, fearing I might be causing him anxiety. But we met again on the Colombian side of the Simón Bolívar Bridge, where the activity was frenetic. Fellows on motorbikes, others with taxis, would light on anyone who looked like they might need transport. Taxis coming to the border from the Colombian side were equally lit on by runners offering to carry bags for the occupants. Hawkers flogged drink, food, phone chargers, clothes ... anything you could think of. It was all colourful and crazy at the same time.

'I'm not really going to Lima,' Violin Man said to me, but he didn't want to go into detail. He said that life back home was a disaster and was getting worse by the day. Another man approached Violin Man – we agreed that I would refer to him as 'Juan' in anything I wrote, but I prefer Violin

Man – and directed him to join some others, eight or ten maybe, clustered together, waiting at the end of the bridge. His companion meanwhile had gone off elsewhere. After a little while a fellow on a motorbike came, and Violin Man got onto the back of it. He allowed me to take his picture, with him turning his face away from the camera. And then he was gone.

Seven million plus one.

*

When I was in Bogotá a diplomatic source there told me that if I wanted to see where migrants were trying to get into North America, I should go to Necoclí, a small Colombian town on the southern shore of the Gulf of Darién, part of the Caribbean Sea. I arrived there on 23 February and spent the following days observing an extraordinary drama. As my own Tip2Top journey progressed, I tracked migrants into Panama and on through Central America into Mexico.

23–26 FEBRUARY 2023, NECOCLÍ AND CAPURGANÁ

Every morning, as the sun rises over the Caribbean, hundreds of people gather on the beach at Necoclí, a small town on Colombia's north coast. Surrounded by suitcases and black bin bags containing all they have, or all they can carry, they're pursuing the dream of a new life in North America. In front of them is the Gulf of Urabá, the southernmost part of the Gulf of Darién, which separates northern Colombia and Panama. Most of the isthmus that links South and Central America is impassable swamp and jungle-covered mountain. There's no road. But cross the sea from Necoclí to a small Colombian town named Capurganá, on the extreme northern tip of the Colombian part of the isthmus, and Panama becomes accessible on foot.

From Capurganá a few who travel legally catch a plane to Panama, but most do not. Most are undocumented migrants who hike a mountain pass through the jungle that straddles the frontier between the two countries so they can progress their dream, which for most is to live in the United

States or Canada. In this little-reported drama, tens of thousands of people are making the journey every month. According to Colombian migration officials to whom I spoke in Necoclí, on current numbers, over 360,000 will make the journey this year, up from 200,000 the year before. What is happening is a human drama that is truly epic in scale.

In the middle of the beach at Necoclí, the Colombian Red Cross has set up an outreach station. Local people in need of medical and other advice, mainly women, wait patiently between two portable office cabins that act as surgeries. In a quiet corner in the open between them, there's a gazebo with a table and two chairs. There, Nelson Laverde, a psychologist, offers counselling to anyone seeking it, mainly migrants. 'The migrants often need emotional support,' he told me, 'and we try to prepare them for when they are crossing the jungle.' There's a play area for children, a brief respite in what must be a mystifying and perhaps traumatic experience.

Beside the Red Cross operation, a number of private ferry companies operate from a beach dispatch area and a wooden jetty. A similar but much larger ferrying operation, supported by the UN's International Organization for Migration (IOM), takes place further along the beach. Some notices there are in Spanish, English and Chinese. One huge sign in English advises migrants about the journey they're about to undertake. Never rest on the bank of a river, they're told; never share a tent with strangers; do not walk alone; it is vital to stay hydrated. Tell loved ones what you are doing and where you are going; do not travel at night. Help children memorise their place of origin, parents' names, relatives and contact number.

The warnings, and the implications they contain, seem to deter no one. In both locations, every day from about 6:00, a mass of people gather, all with one aim: to get across the sea to within walking distance of Panama – the gateway, they hope, to a new life further north again.

There are many young men in their late teens or early twenties, individuals, pairs of friends and some in larger groups. There are mothers breastfeeding babies. There are whole families – mothers, fathers and children, often very young, some babies in harnesses strapped to one or other parent, some sitting in buggies, some toddlers playing in the sand, not fully unaware of the drama of which they're a part. And everywhere there are people living off the migrants, in one way or another. There are the black-bag sellers, flogging bin liners in which to keep belongings dry in the rough seas. Hawkers also offer transparent plastic pouches to allow mobile phones to be hung round your neck. There are sellers of fresh fruit, empanadas and juice. Stall holders offer camping cookers, small gas cylinders and tents, though they're hardly better than what you'd buy as a plaything for kiddies in your back garden.

And walking among them are the ticket checkers with their clipboards on which are lists of names given to them by the ticket sellers. A one-way ticket costs 85,000 pesos (about €17) and may be bought on the spot or from nearby ticket offices. Despite the seeming chaos, a certain order is maintained. The migrants appear endlessly patient. Once a ferry is ready, names are called from the clipboard manifests, and the migrants respond. Buoyancy vests are distributed, cases and black bags are thrown on board and the boats speed off.

'*Mil* [one thousand],' said the migration officer to whom I chatted in a nearby cafe.

'*Mil?*' I replied, sounding surprised.

'*Si, mil. Todos los días* [every day]' he said, his two female colleagues nodding in agreement.

Luis (twenty-six), a refugee from Venezuela, had a job in Necoclí. 'I send money to my family,' he told me. Some had died, and the others had no other source of income. He wasn't going further than Necoclí, but 'this is the door of the Darién,' he said, looking at the mass of people on the beach waiting to board the ferries. Conversations with the travelling migrants are snatched. This is due partly, I believe, to the circumstances. While not seeming to be terrified at their situation, most are nonetheless anxious – at exactly what I'm unsure, but fear of damaging their chances of getting into the United States is an obvious surmise; fear of 'minders' and those on whom they depend is another. Language is a huge barrier also, for which

I'm at least partly at fault. But all to whom I spoke and who responded were able to indicate that they wanted to go to the US or Canada for work, for money ... for a better life.

The migrants come from many countries, but overwhelmingly, from what I saw, they're from Haiti and China. Suggestions by sources in Bogotá that Ukrainians had also taken this route to North America were not confirmed by anyone on the ground to whom I spoke. The migration officer listed migrant countries of origin as India, Venezuela, Ecuador, Haiti, Africa (he didn't specify countries) and China. He said some Colombians were also making the journey, but most I encountered were travelling between different parts of Colombia to visit family or friends. The woman at the ticket office by the IOM posters said that 75 per cent of people travelling and who bought tickets from her were Chinese, and the tickets were always one-way only. Most of these had first flown to Ecuador (which offers visa-free entry for Chinese nationals) and then made their way north.

The ferries are long slender boats, each holding about seventy passengers. They're steered from an elevated position high above the deck towards the rear and are powered by four massive 300 horsepower outboard motors. The boat I took was crammed – sixty-six of us and three crew – and the crossing was uneventful at first. But when it turned north-west and headed for Capurganá on the opposite side of the gulf, the waves began hitting side-on because of the prevailing wind. As we got more into the centre of the channel between the two land masses, the rollers got higher. There was maybe 80m between each wave crest, and the trough separating them was perhaps 30m deep. We rode up the side of each wave to its crest, shooting over it and plunging down, slamming onto the side of the trough as if it were a slab of concrete. The crashing sound had some passengers whooping excitedly initially, while others looked worried. Children were frightened and some vomited, but the speed never let up. Huge quantities of spray drenched us all.

After nearly two hours, and to the considerable relief of many on board, the ferry pulled in to Capurganá. Before anyone could get off, men on the pier were shouting out services on offer, but most of the migrants who land here appear to have arrangements already made. The town is tiny, and there are no cars, because there's no road in and no road out. Its perimeters are defined by the sea on one side and the jungle-covered mountain on the other. There's an 800m asphalt airstrip, and a Britten–Norman twin-engine turbo-prop Islander plane, which can seat nine passengers, comes and goes regularly. There's also a small office of the Colombian Ministry of Foreign Affairs, where travellers may get their passports stamped. But few people call there, as far as I could see.

Capurganá used to make all its money from tourism, but now anyone I ask about the local economy says that the flow of migrants, and the money 'earned' from them, if that is the appropriate term, plays a more significant role.

The migrants were directed off the pier and to the left, round the corner and past a hotel and left again into a dusty gravel lane, where they were told to wait. A woman with a clipboard started checking names, and within a few seconds a fleet of what are called motocaros arrived. These are three-wheeled transporters – essentially a motorcycle front and engine and a small two-wheeled pickup-truck rear, with capacity for luggage and about eight passengers. A burly man with an Abe Lincoln beard who was seemingly in charge of the operation didn't like my taking pictures, but I continued because he was also taking shots of the migrants. It's not clear why he did so, but it was possibly proof (for whom?) that they arrived and were dispatched to the next stage. If migrants objected to my taking pictures, I stopped, but most didn't. There were between sixty and eighty in the group I observed – men, women and children – and all appeared to be Asian in origin.

Two young Chinese men told me as much about themselves as our language barrier allowed. They said they were from Shanghai and posed for a picture. They appeared happy, a little giddy even, at the prospect of getting to North America – which was their dream. Squeezed into the back of a *motocaro*, stuffed between black bags, they smiled as I took a picture of them.

No sooner was each motocaro filled with people and luggage than it was off, whizzing round the corner and along a rough gravel track that runs parallel to the airstrip and eventually enters another village, named 15 Mayo (Teacher's Day in Colombia is on 15 May). It's a run-down place, a single street that begins with a filthy plastic-bottle recycling operation and on which most buildings seem half-finished. The motocaros pass through, and gradually the boreen gets stonier and narrower until, quite deep into the jungle, it reaches a river, where the migrants and their belongings were disgorged.

One of them, a man perhaps in his forties, told me as he alighted a motocaro that he was from Brazil and wanted to get to the United States. He had but a few words of English. He was with his wife, their two children, both aged two, and a male friend. They didn't want their photo taken. But another man directing operations didn't like my presence. Who was I? What was I doing? And where's my wrist band? The Brazilian man and his family had wrist tags, indicators, I assume, that they had paid whoever had to be paid. Didn't I know that this is private property? I told him that it's public (which it is) and that I wasn't a migrant but a journalist. The man questioning me was with other men. These, I later learnt, were the *caminandos* ('walkers)', in other words, the guides who will, they promise, show the migrants the way from here through the jungle, over the mountain and into Panama.

A good source, a local hotelier, told me later that the caminandos charge $180–200 for their services (confirming a figure I had heard earlier). He wasn't sure how much is paid to organisers of the sea crossing, and indeed for getting to Necoclí in the first place and for the motocaro lifts in Capurganá, but he thought it was maybe $300.

Capurganá is a little over two kilometres from the border with Panama, as the crow flies. Anyone to whom I spoke and who knew the migrant trail said it took at least three days to get to wherever the end point is inside Panama, presumably a settlement or handover place, possibly somewhere with a bus going north. There were two separate routes, I was told. The longer one, which is 100km, takes up to seven days to trek. The kilometre or so of jungle I walked through was inhospitable, difficult terrain. The jungle is very dense, humid and hot. It's also teeming with insects, especially at night. According to the IOM, thirty-six people are known to have died making the trek last year, but the true figure is believed by the IOM to be much higher. In January 2023 the IOM said that 'anecdotal reports indicate that many migrants die in the Darién Gap and their remains are neither recovered nor reported, so this figure presents only a small fraction of the true number of lives lost.'

At the river, more and more motocaros disgorged their passengers and their flotsam of cases and black plastic bags. Few looked prepared for what they were about to undertake. Almost none had appropriate footwear or rucksacks. Most were in trainers or even flip-flops. It was telling that one of the last shops they would have passed in Capurganá had a large display of wellington boots. No one in the town wears such boots, but the shop owner knows they're needed for a hike through the jungle.

I left the migrants as they began their hike, disappearing across the river and along a dusty brown path into a sea of jungle green, fortified by hope – by a belief that a better life was to be had and that the risks of getting it were worth taking. But I really didn't know what lay ahead for them, along the trail on which they were being led.

And neither did they.

After Capurganá and Necoclí, I made south again, heading back to Bogotá in order to get to Panama.

28 FEBRUARY 2023, PUENTE LINDA

After my few days with the migrants in Necoclí and Capurganá, I made a dash for Bogotá, feeling that it was time to progress my own journey into Central America. The road south from the Gulf of Darién was good and passed through some pleasant lowland countryside – lots of banana and oil palm plantations and quite a bit of cattle ranching – of which there isn't that much in Colombia. After 400km, I leapt at the first Ibis Hotel I saw in Medellín. Fifty euro for a night isn't bad for a clean, modern hotel with a working shower, and it meant that next day I was off early for what should have been the final run of five hours or so to Bogotá.

But it ended up taking two days and nearly broke my spirit. Looking back now though, I wouldn't change a thing about it. Google Maps suggested Highway 56 for a fairly direct run from Medellín to the capital, and so I took it. Somewhere about 100km outside Medellín, the road began to take on the characteristics of a less-used road, and I began to wonder. It had just one lane in either direction and was not at all busy. I had imagined that the main highway between two such important cities would have been bigger than this.

Before Sonsón the road started to rise into mountains – nothing unusual in Colombia – riding up steep valleys with sharp peaks, before plunging down again, and all the time through dense jungle. Several times I came across military patrols – lines of soldiers, armed with rifles, walking on both sides of the road, maybe 100m apart and on the lookout for anything unusual, and nothing in particular. Most soldiers exchanged waves and smiles.

At a small town named Nariño the road disappeared altogether. I rode through the town and out the other side, whereupon a paved road veered left. Straight on, Highway 56 presented itself as a stony, muddy track, the sort you'd see leading from an Irish farmyard off into the fields behind. I wasn't sure whether it was the right road for Bogotá, so I stopped and asked a man walking by. Yes, he said, that's it. 'Directo!'

And so I set off. The road began with a steep hill down and quickly disappeared round a bend. I felt certain that the proper road, the main route to Bogotá, for God's sake, would resume round the next bend. But it didn't, and very quickly Highway 56 became a consistently stony road, sometimes firm and relatively flat but most of the time scored by horrendous gullies on both sides of the median. There were numerous cones of mud and rubble half blocking the way, the result of landslides caused by rain. Sometimes, on acute bends, the outer edge of the road had collapsed, but it carried on, winding its way up and down the increasingly dominant mountain landscape.

I couldn't decide whether to call a halt and turn back (which would have been physically difficult), but, as is the way, each kilometre I progressed, the idea of turning back became less appealing. Carrying on increasingly had little to recommend itself either. In the event, I carried on, my spirit wearing down, and with it a growing sense of alarm: I was getting deeper into mountainous terrain – and I mean the really steep-sided mountains of the Cordillera del Tigre that were all covered in jungle and, initially at least, had few signs of human habitation.

Whenever there was a gap in the vegetation, the views of the mountains and valleys below were spectacular. I stopped to take photos but didn't manage to get good ones of the road because, on the worst stretches, the last thing I'd think of would be stopping to take a picture. I just wanted to get through and remain upright. Biking along tracks that regularly become little more than a dry riverbed requires intense concentration and is hugely stressful, for me, at any rate. You stand on the pegs, lean forward and, crucially, must not lower the revs when coming to a place that looks difficult. The 'road' may have fallen away on one side, there may be a 50m stretch of large boulders, rocks the size of footballs, say, all mixed in with gullies and mud and flowing water. But the only way to get through is to approach it with determination, keep the revs up, stay in first gear and, well, just go for it. Easier said than done ... And despite the narrowness of the road, and the sometimes precarious grip it has on the side of the mountain, occasional buses and lorries lumbered their way along it as well, some with reckless abandon. All a biker can do is stay out of their way!

After 20km of this, the road ballooned into a flat triangle of open space where three small valleys met and a wide, fast-flowing river surged past. On one side of the triangle there was a long colonial-style two-storey building, with ground-floor and first-floor verandas wrapped round it and a large mural running the length of it; on another there was a restaurant and hostel; and on the third, backing onto the river, there was a large hotel. The Santa

Isabel, which has a bamboo construction theme and has two storeys at the front but four at the rear, thanks to the land falling down to the river, boasted a swimming pool and promised food and a bed for the night. I needed no encouragement to call it a day and get myself in there.

The woman who ran it, Diana, was immediately great fun. Warm and slightly flirty, she served me a cold beer and said I could help myself to more from the fridge. She then gave me dinner – a big bowl of hearty bean soup, followed by a steak, tomato, rice and fried banana. There was a Colombian couple staying at the hotel. The woman and her husband spent most of their time playing cards. There was another man staying there too, but he just wandered about offering huge avocados to anyone who wanted one. (They were delicious.) The dining area overlooked the pool – three pools, in fact, connected and well up to large hotel standards – set back from the river, a raging torrent after a night of thunder and downpour. Its muddy waters crashed around large boulders and tumbled under a steel bridge – the Puente Linda, from which the place took its name.

That night, and the following morning, I had long conversations with Diana and her husband, Alcibiades, a similarly warm fellow. It turned out that, all around Puente Linda, the land was littered with anti-personnel landmines. The mural on the long building opposite included an image of someone with a mine detector and, separately, contained a reference to the Halo Trust, the Scottish demining NGO, which was patronised by Princess Diana and is funded today by, among others, the US, Canadian, Norwegian and New Zealand governments, as well as by Irish Aid, the government's international development aid programme. Earlier, as I was leaving Nariño, I had passed a large complex of low buildings and a sign that announced the Halo Trust. To be honest, though I had noted it, I didn't think much about it, so concentrated was I on the damn road!

Were there mines around here? I asked Alcibiades. Yes, he said, lots – about 2,000, in fact. It turns out that this area was a hotbed of guerrilla activity by FARC, the Revolutionary Armed Forces of Colombia, which dissolved in 2017 following a peace agreement with the Colombian government. Over 260,000 people died in the five-decade-long conflict, and seven million were displaced.

FARC, which professed itself to be Marxist–Leninist, financed its operations by taxing Colombia's drug gangs and engaging in kidnappings, bank robberies and extortion. It had long-standing links with Sinn Féin and the IRA, as established in 2002 by US congressional investigators. They found that the IRA had received at least $2 million in drug money from FARC, allegedly for training members in bomb making. In August 2001 two IRA explosives experts, Jim Monaghan and Martin McCauley, were arrested in Bogotá, along with Niall Connolly, Sinn Fein's representative in Cuba. Convicted of travelling on false passports but on bail while the authorities appealed their acquittal on FARC training charges, the three fled the country. A former police inspector alleged that he had seen McCauley with FARC members in 1998. If true, perhaps some of the IRA's 'expertise' was used by FARC in an atrocity committed in Nariño that Alcibiades told me about. (His account is supported by a journalistic history of the conflict, rutasdelconflicto.com.)

In July 1999 300 FARC guerrillas, led by Elda Neyis Mosquera García, known as Karina, attacked the town. During a thirty-hour assault, sixteen people, including four children, were murdered, and another sixteen were kidnapped, including eight police, seven of whom were held captive for two years. The town's police commander was executed in the town plaza. Using car bombs, gas cylinder bombs and mortars, the guerrillas demolished the town hall, a number of shops and houses and the police station – a total of four blocks. After the massacre, half the people left the town, reducing its population to 9,000.

All these years later, Alcibiades said it still wasn't safe to walk freely through the jungle, though many of the mines placed there by FARC, often crude homemade devices, had been cleared. I asked him about another panel of the mural, one showing men panning at the river. Was there silver there? I asked. 'No,' he said, 'oro' – gold! And with that he rushed into his and Diana's bedroom and rummaged through a bedside chest of drawers, returning with four small plastic vials, their lids taped shut. He placed two sheets of white paper on the table and turned the contents of the vials onto them. And there it was, pure gold – some specks not much more than dust, really, but several small nuggets, each about the size of a lentil or split pea. Alcibiades also had a tiny weighing scales, and he put the contents of one vial onto it. It read 3.3 grams. I asked how much that was worth, and he said about 660,000 pesos, or $120. We both stared at the gold in wonderment and laughed.

*

Soon I was off again, over the bridge and up the rocky road for more energy-sapping thrills – but no spills, thankfully. Somewhere along the way, however, I lost one of my spare two-litre plastic petrol cannisters. A pair had been mounted on the back of my panniers, one on each side, held in place by straps. As my fuel got worryingly low, I had decanted them into my tank to be sure I could keep going. But with the bike jolting over extremely rough ground, one had evidently been bumped out, never to be seen again, as I discovered later. I had been promised that the paved road resumed at Norcasia, but in fact it reappeared just before then, at a village named (like several others in these parts) Berlin. And was I glad for it! By that stage I was running out of cash and petrol, but in Norcasia I stocked up on both and made the final dash for Bogotá.

CENTRAL AMERICA

ALL TRAVELLERS WISHING TO TRAVEL OVERLAND between South
and Central America face a problem: there's no road linking the two.
The tongue of Colombian land that joins modern day Panama to form
that twisty, snake-like neck that is the Panamanian isthmus is a swampy
mess of rivers, lakes and jungle, some of it mountainous, though
the mountains are not themselves very high. However, the terrain is
inhospitable and humid and full of mosquitoes that can transmit yellow
fever to the unvaccinated and other diseases such as dengue. And then
there are the gun-toting bandits and drug traffickers.

The highest mountain in the region is Cerro Tacarcuna and it's only 1,875m.
The mountains immediately south of Yaviza, the first village in Panama,
coming from Colombia, are much smaller. There isn't even a half-decent
track that might be ridden by a motocross motorbike, though a few have
tried, and a small number have succeeded. One such was in 1960, when
a Land Rover and Jeep got through ... travelling about 200m an hour
and taking five months! A handful of bikers have also done it, but for all
practical purposes, the area is impassable.

From Yaviza to the border with Colombia is about 80km, as the crow
flies, and from there to existing roads in Colombia is another 100km or so.
I don't know why there's no road, but I suspect that governments on both
sides believe, wrongly, in my view, that a direct, well-maintained road linking
the Americas would create more problems than benefits. A well-built and
well-maintained roadway, and a properly operated border crossing, with
all the security necessary, is not, surely, unachievable. Panama's southern
province bordering Colombia is Darién. The absence of a route through it
explains why the area is known to travellers as the Darién Gap.

This awkward hole on the Pan-American Highway has an interesting
historical link to Scotland. The story goes back to the late seventeenth
and early eighteenth centuries and involves a group of Scottish investors.
They set up a company, the Scottish Darien Company, with the aim of
establishing a colony in the southern part of the Panamanian isthmus. There

was no Panama Canal at that time, and the investors reckoned they could create an overland route, in effect linking the Atlantic and Pacific Oceans and capitalising on trade between the two – doing in other words what the canal would achieve many years later.

The Company lasted just twelve years, from 1695 to 1707, but in that short time it managed to crash the Scottish economy. When investors were sought there was something of a stampede: between February and April 1696 the funding target of £400,000 (about €60 million in today's money) was reached through investments of between £100 and £3,000 – all of the money coming from Scotland itself and most of it from ordinary residents of the Scottish Lowlands. The ill-fated scheme sucked in approximately 20 per cent of all the money in Scotland.

Two separate expeditions sailed to Darién and set up the colony that would operate the overland trading route, but both ended in disaster. Some 80 per cent of those involved (a total of 2,400 people) died within a year of arriving in the isthmus. The causes were many. Yellow fever and other diseases from unsanitary conditions played a part, but so too did trade blockades (engineered by the English government and the rival East India Company) and a similar siege by the Spanish.

When the company collapsed, the Scottish economy went with it, leaving the Lowlands (the southern heart of the country) in financial ruin. There was uproar, not surprisingly, accompanied by riots, including the lynching of three innocent English sailors. The more lasting effect was that resistance ended in Scotland to the idea that it should merge politically and economically with England. This led directly to the 1707 Act of Union, creating the constitutional marriage we know today as Great Britain. (The Act of Union that created the United Kingdom of Great Britain and Ireland came a century later.) So much for the Scottish Darien Company and its lasting impact on the history of these islands ...

You would think that getting from Colombia to Panama today by sea would be routine enough. This used to be the case for bikers. A German sailor, Capt. Ludwig Hoffmann, used to sail a former fishing vessel between

Cartagena on Colombia's Caribbean coast and the Panamanian port of Colón, at the eastern end of the Panama Canal. Capt. Ludwig was well known to adventure bikers and ran a good business ferrying them and their bikes around the Darién Gap while serving lobster and pausing for a few days' R&R snorkelling on Panama's San Blas Islands. But Covid put an end to his business. Now, there's no regular passenger or vehicle ferry between Colombia and Panama, so bikers face the prospect of renting a shipping container in either Cartagena or Colón and assembling enough bikes and bikers to make the exercise financially viable ... and waiting for the container to travel between the two, all of which can take weeks. The only other surefire way is to go by air freight.

To get my bike from Colombia to Panama City, I used the excellent Air Cargo Pack, a Bogotá-based airfreighting company well known to bikers. It cost me $1,200 in cash (€1,100), plus a $65 cargo handling fee at the Panama end, and a further $100 for my own, separate, one-way flight. There was also a $3 decontamination fee payable in Panama, where the bike gets sprayed as it leaves the airport cargo area.

Luckily, I was warned by a fellow traveller in Bogotá that landing in Panama City on a commercial flight and without an onward departure ticket could prove problematic. The Panamanian authorities like to know that, if they let you in, you will leave on a given date, and they want to see proof of that. Seeing as I would be collecting my bike separately and leaving the country on a date unknown, after riding through it, I could get into difficulty at the airport if I didn't have an onward ticket and may be refused entry. The solution, as I learnt, was to use a website named onwardticket.com. Through it, you can book a flight, a reservation for which is confirmed by email, allowing you to download a proof-of-purchase ticket, which has yet to be paid for. Of course, you will not be able to board the flight until it's paid for. But in the meantime you have secured, for about $20, a seat on a scheduled flight, which will be cancelled automatically in forty-eight hours if you don't pay the rest. However, by that time you will have flown to Panama, shown the official the supposedly onward ticket (mine was to Miami on 10 March) and been waved through! I did this without a hitch, and the next day I collected my bike from the cargo area of Panama City's airport – also without a hitch – and rode into my first city in Central America.

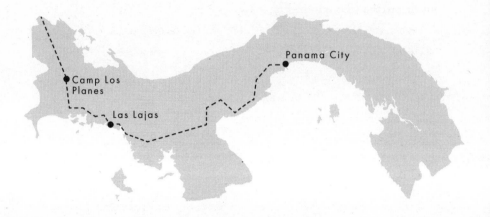

PANAMA

7 MARCH 2023, PANAMA CITY

In the core of inner-city Panama City there are at least three distinct cities. The first is the big, brash, reaching-for-the-skies modern city, with its gleaming, glass-facade skyscrapers mirroring everything around them. The second is the old city, with its fortified promenade jutting into the sea, all narrow streets, cathedral and older government buildings, many dating from the nineteenth century and some from before that. And the third is what's between them: the inner-city poor and the buildings in which they live. A taxi driver told me that the average take-home pay in Panama was about $600 a month and that most people, whether better off or less so, were actually close to that average.

But it's clear from simply wandering about that there are also people who are much better off than just being a bit above the average. Michael, a travelling retiree from Rhode Island, said that Panama is now favoured by a lot of elderly American men, many of whom, he said, have young local partners. 'It's not yet like the Philippines, but it's getting that way.' I didn't notice, but that was certainly his reading of the situation.

The materialism is undeniable, however. The place is awash with large four-wheel crossover cars – Mercs, Lexus, Jags, Porsches and the like. It's also awash with banks and other financial services companies – and the lawyers who facilitate them. Skyscrapers sixty to seventy storeys tall are huddled together in downtown clumps, with inner-city freeways swishing this way and that between them. The place has a Dubai feel to it. It's no surprise that one of the tallest buildings bears the name Trump – a sixty-eight-storey 'ocean club international hotel and tower'.

The hostel in which I stayed, a hippyish kind of place named CulturaHumana Living and Guesthouse, did me fine, thanks. Beside it was a most extraordinary green-glass skyscraper, the fifty-two-storey, 243m F&F Tower. Imagine a stack of books laid flat, one on top of the other, each one twisted an inch or so in the same direction, creating a sort of spiral stairs effect. Known locally as the Corkscrew, it's the ninth-tallest building in the city. It's quite beautiful – eye-catching, for sure. The shape of the Corkscrew marks it out for special attention, but in its size and modern feel it's not the least bit unusual: all around it are other glass-wall skyscrapers and similarly tall residential apartment blocks.

Most of the office buildings are local outposts for international banks or other corporate entities or multiple-occupancy buildings, the occupants in many cases being linked to the legal profession, smaller financial institutions or shipping. And all around them are shopping malls, replete with shouty chic brand names: Gucci, Hermès, Rolex, Tommy Hilfiger, Dolce & Gabbana, Chanel and Louis Vuitton. There are more than a few large poster ads displaying beautiful people whose single message is, 'You want to be like me.'

The malls are air-conditioned and soulless places. Something inside you dies when you walk into them. I guess what was exposed by the Panama Papers – millions of leaked documents exposing the practices of offshore financial entities – explains some of this. The place is a haven for dodgy stuff – stuff that may not be illegal here but probably is back home, wherever home is for the principals behind the dodginess. Banks are notoriously reluctant, unless under threat of dire consequences, to turn money away, whatever the source. And with Colombia next door, all the loot related to its most notorious 'business' has to end up somewhere. Many of the well-off are from other banjaxed economies in the region (Venezuela and Argentina, for example – or so one of them, an Argentine, told me; he washed his money through Switzerland, London and Panama while continuing to live very well in Argentina, untouched by the wreckage all about him).

Panama's old city is what you'd expect: a grid pattern of narrow streets and squares with mainly three- and four-storey buildings that have a nineteenth century or vaguely colonial feel to them. The area is defined by a promontory that in recent years has been embraced by a ring-road bypass built on stilts in the sea, compromising the view from the promontory. Despite that, the area is a delight of cafes, restaurants, tourist shops, Panama hat shops (of course!) and stylish independent fashion outlets. And there's the cathedral (an architectural disappointment and surprisingly plain inside) and official buildings and museums (the Panama Canal Museum is definitely worth a visit). Many of the buildings have been done up in recent years and look superb, while quite a few others remain derelict. But local tensions are also evident: in one rectangular open space where development plans are clearly afoot, large posters say *No to building and No to gentrification*.

Between the new and old Panama City is an area named La Exposición, a residential and shopping area for those Panamanians whose fortunes have not been lifted by the rising tide of prosperity. Street after street is grubby and lined with broken-down retail buildings and apartment blocks that look like tenements. Garbage is strewn everywhere; facades are dingy, cracked, stained and peeling; and the streets are filled with discarded broken things. Many of the people look broken too.

But what really dominates Panama is, of course, the Panama Canal.

There's a huge bridge, the Bridge of the Americas, that spans the estuary beside Panama City, which is the start of the canal route from the Pacific end. I got a great kick from riding across it several times. One side affords a panoramic view onto the Pacific, the other inland towards the Miraflores Locks. There was so much about the canal that I didn't know before getting there that I felt ashamed by my erstwhile ignorance. Without going down a rabbit hole on the subject, world powers, including Britain, France and Spain, had for centuries dreamt of linking the Atlantic and Pacific oceans through what is now Panama, thereby vastly shortening the trade route around Cape Horn and Tierra del Fuego. But it wasn't until Theodore Roosevelt took the notion by the scruff of its neck that anything really happened. In 1903 he supported what is now Panama in breaking away from Colombia, which then ruled the area, despite local opposition. It did so, and immediately Panama created itself as a separate state. The US got a lease on land through which it would build the canal.

The Americans succeeded where others (notably the French) had failed, for two reasons. The first was that two medics, Carlos Finlay, a Cuban epidemiologist of Scots heritage, and Walter Reed, of the US Army Medical Corps, discovered separately, and some years apart, that yellow fever was spread by mosquitoes. Malaria and yellow fever had killed thousands of workers during previous efforts to build a canal, but because of what Finlay discovered, and Reed brought to fruition, it became possible to control the diseases and therefore protect workers.

The second was the genius of the US canal project's unqualified but self-taught engineer, John Stevens. He adapted, and used as a solution, what others had seen as a problem. Previous efforts to build a canal along the valley of a river, the Chagres, became a nightmare in the rainy season, when it became a raging torrent, impossible to control, impossible to work with. Instead of fighting it, Stevens decided to dam the river, thereby creating a huge lake that itself became part of the canal. In effect, Stevens made an inland sea between the two oceans. It's known now as Gatun Lake, and the Atlantic and Pacific are linked by two short canals and locks at each end.

Locks lift and lower ships to and from sea level, which then sail across the lake and, yes, through some traditional canal waterway as well. This, rather than a single, linear artificial waterway, is the Panama Canal.

'A human triumph and one of the great stories of all time,' Morgan Freeman tells audiences at the IMAX cinema in the visitor centre at the Miraflores Locks at the Panama City end of the canal. And I guess it is. Creating the lake didn't solve everything, of course: some traditional canal had to be carved out of the landscape. They had to dig – and blast their way – to create a mile-long trench that was 107m deep through the most challenging part of the terrain. George Washington Goethals, who succeeded Stevens as chief engineer, used thirty million kilos of dynamite (more than that used by the US Army in any conflicts by that time) to create the Galliard Cut (now the Culebra Cut), slicing through the Continental Divide, the mountain range extending the length of the Americas and from which rain waters drain into the oceans on either side. When creating it, workers christened it Hell's Throat.

Workers on the canal were discriminated against according to race. On what was known as the Silver Roll, black West Indians received the lowest pay: 10 cents an hour, with a maximum possible income of $30 a month. Panamanians, Colombians and Indians got 13 cents an hour, while Europeans (i.e., white people), other Caucasian ethnicities and (oddly, given the treatment of black West Indians) black Africans, all got 16 cents an hour – even though everyone on the Silver Roll did exactly the same work. At least none of this is hidden today – it's all explained in the museum.

Today, the canal carries 300 million tons of goods a year. It's been expanded and widened, and parallel channels have been added in recent years, but the fundamental structure remains much as it was created more than a century ago. The 82km waterway knocks 15,000km, and three weeks, off the east–west, west–east trade route, and it takes just ten hours to pass through. Amazingly, there are no pumps involved in filling and emptying the locks at each end – it's all done by gravity – and hydroelectricity from the dam generates all electricity needed.

After the IMAX presentation, as I was walking out onto the Miraflores Locks viewing area, the ticket inspector asked where I was from. 'Ireland,' I said, without dallying, as there were others in the queue behind me. But before I could exit, she burst into 'Molly Malone', singing, 'Alive, alive, oh! Alive, alive, oh!' – and suggested a selfie. Out on the viewing area, the Antwerp-registered *Warisoulx,* a 28,000-ton liquid petroleum tanker, carrying 38,000m3 of gas, was inching its way into the lock, the first of that afternoon's east–west traffic. The ship was tethered on each side, forward and aft, to little trains, called 'mules', that seem to haul it along the towpath but that are just steering it, keeping it straight while it's in the locks and not touching the side walls. The ship is actually moving forward on its own engine power. It takes just eight minutes to empty the lock and allow it to enter the next lock on the lower level – one stage closer to the Pacific. It's quite a spectacle seeing something that enormous moving across the landscape, as it were. What a clever fellow John Stevens was, and I just love the idea that he was a self-taught engineer.

The Americans held on to the canal for a century, ceding control back to Panama only under a 1978 treaty, negotiated by President Jimmy Carter but not implemented until 1999, after the US invaded and deposed Panama's drug-trafficking dictator General Manuel Noriega.

Panama is now a fairly healthy democracy but with a lot of poor, and poorly educated, people, with about 15 per cent of people living on $5.50 a day.

11 MARCH 2023, PLAYA LAS LAJAS

I had my first shakedown after I left Panama City. It was the real deal but was done so nicely that I hardly even felt it. I was riding west, along Panama's Highway 1, the Pan-American Highway, heading towards the border with Costa Rica, though still a long way off my destination. In between, there would be a few stops, but the journey itself was back on track. The road was good: a dual carriageway with two lanes in each direction and a central median ditch. The traffic was light. I was taking it easy: 100–120km/h – a steady pace. And then, just as I was passing a lorry and a couple of cars, I saw two motorcycle policemen on the hard shoulder flagging traffic over. They were standing in the shade of a tree and at a point where the road, which was completely straight, was sweeping down from the crest of a hill. I thought they were indicating one of the others, but I wasn't sure, so I pulled over as well.

I was later than the others in reacting and so I stopped maybe a hundred metres past the policemen. I switched off the engine and, still sitting on the bike, began to walk and roll myself back towards them, noting as I did so that the other vehicles were already leaving the scene and carrying on their journeys. The policemen walked towards me too. When they got to me, I put down the side stand, got off the bike, removed my helmet and went through the routine: hand out in greeting, saying hello.

'Where are you from?' one asked.

'Ireland.'

He looked at the registration plate. 'Passport.'

I handed him my passport, at which point he showed me the radar gun in his left hand. It said 112, my speed.

'*Sí,*' I said, not challenging the clock.

He agreed: it was indeed reading 112km/h, and he was indicating that this was not good, not good at all. I asked what the speed limit was on the road.

'Eighty,' he said.

Oh, I thought. So I was going 40 per cent above the limit – a significant breach in percentage terms but, given the size and condition of the road, not fast at all. But clearly I hadn't a leg to stand on, and I didn't attempt to argue otherwise. Why would I?

The first policeman asked me where I was going. I told him Alaska but first to a nearby Panamanian city named David and then on to Costa Rica. He seemed quite interested in this.

At that point, policeman 2 joined the scene. He was very friendly. '*Cómo estás?*' he asked.

'*Bueno,*' I replied.

Policeman 1 told him that I was going to Alaska, and I chipped in that I had come from Tierra del Fuego. Policeman 2 responded with a sort of 'Respect' reaction. It was all very chatty, very friendly – no coming the heavy or anything like that.

I took some stickers from my jacket pocket – the shamrock Ireland ones given to me by two Irish biker pals, John O'Kelly and Ken McGreevy (a garda whose biker moniker is Adventure Detective), and the Tip2Top sticker. I gave them a pair each. '*Este es mi país*' ('This is my country'), I said, handing them the shamrock sticker, adding, '*Y este mi viaje*' ('And this is my trip'), as I gave them the Tip2Top Chile to Alaska sticker. They seemed pleased. Policeman 2 said he would put his on his motorbike.

'*Ah, tu moto?*' I said to him.

'*Sí,*' he replied, indicating that his was smaller than mine and that he liked mine.

Policeman 1 took out his fines book, a sheaf of pages each with lots of sections to be filled in – name, address, location of incident and so on – and started to fill it out. The fine was $75, he said. I said okay and asked where to pay. He went into a rigmarole about paying either in Santiago, the next town, or in David, which was notionally where I thought I'd stay the night. So I said I'd pay in David. He nodded and continued filling in the form. I asked where to pay in David, and this was where I lost him. I think he was telling me the name of the office and the street it was in and when it was open, but I really don't know. Because then he said, 'Or you can pay here.' This sounded like a good solution because I also got the impression (though I didn't realise it fully at the time) that if I wanted to pay the fine at the office, wherever it was, I would have to get the bus there because they would be confiscating the bike until I sorted things out. Policeman 1 repeated the amount of the fine but added that if I paid here it would be reduced to $40. This immediately struck me as an offer I shouldn't pass up.

I took out my wallet and extracted two $20 bills. Policeman 1 opened the fine book and, rather than take the cash in his hand, closed the book over the notes. He thanked me, said that was the end of it and started to walk away, back to his original position down the hard shoulder. I asked if I could take their photo, a selfie maybe with the bike. Policeman 1 laughed, a nervous 'You must be joking' giggle, and indicated no, thanks. Policeman 2 seemed initially more willing, partly I think because of the biking connection. But then he saw the implications.

As they walked off together, I saw policeman 1 hand one of my dollar bills to his partner. Did I get a receipt? To paraphrase the developer Michael Bailey, did I fuck!

But I rode off to a surfer hostel by the Pacific, where the young Italian woman in charge told me of her earlier life working on a yacht owned by a Russian oligarch, which seemed like it could have been fun ...

12 MARCH 2023, CAMP LOS PLANES

After I left the migrants with whom I crossed the Gulf of Darién at the edge of the jungle near Capurganá for their hike through it and into Panama, I wanted to see what awaited them at reception centres in that country. One such was in the mountains of western Panama.

The defunct army camp at Los Planes, some 460km west of Panama City, has had a new lease of life. Although many of its timber-clad buildings were falling apart, the former base in the middle of a small, isolated pine forest in the mountains had been turned into a reception and processing centre for thousands of refugees and migrants who cross into Central America from Colombia and places further afield. It's the final such centre in Panama for them. Some will stay a while in the old camp as others make their way, as soon as they can, to the frontier with Costa Rica, about 90km away, and from there, they hope, to the US or Canada.

Busload after busload of people came to the camp every day. On 15 February a bus missed the slip road into it and plunged down a steep bank, killing forty people. Each of the eight or so double-decker Volvo and Mercedes buses I saw arrive had a passenger capacity of eighty, according to their drivers, and each appeared to be full. A Panamanian migration official said that about 1,000 people a day were arriving at the centre – a number that chimed with an estimate given to me about the numbers leaving Colombia to hike across the Darién Gap.

The buses queued on the slip road, their passengers mostly waiting on board. But, in turn, each eventually drove sufficiently past the entrance gate for their doors to be opened to disgorge passengers inside the camp. It was an extraordinary sight. A procession of men, women, children and, in a few cases, family pets held in arms, disembarked. They lugged their possessions in plastic bags, small rucksacks and, in a few instances, suitcases.

Once off the buses, they formed a line across part of the camp, through pine trees and along a gravel path leading to an open-sided building where, it appeared, someone was taking their details. On the public side of the chain-link fence surrounding the camp, a man sold sweets and other food – fruit and polystyrene containers with dinners inside. Occasionally someone would leave the queue and buy food through the fence. As the processing of arrivals continued, most of those whose buses had yet to cross the threshold of the camp stayed on board. But some of the passengers on one got out to stretch their legs or have a smoke.

One man managed to tell me that he was from Beijing, despite having no English. His right ankle was badly swollen and had a reddish bruise. I asked whether he had walked from Colombia, making a walking sign with my fingers. He said he had, across the Darién, and he indicated that he fell and injured his ankle. He was unable to tell me his name or age because of the language barrier. His friend, also from China, was unable to help.

Another man, who spoke English, said he was from Lebanon, via Ecuador. I asked how he got into Panama. 'Like everyone else,' he said, 'I walked it.' He wanted to get to the US. 'I have some friends there. I don't know exactly where, but I have some directions.'

Just then, the bus driver announced that everyone had to get back on board as they were going to enter the camp. On the steps of the bus the Lebanese man said he was sixty-seven and had been in Ecuador for three years – but life there was not good. He had a wife in Lebanon. 'The situation is very bad. I need to help them. What can I do?' It wasn't a question – more an explanation.

He said he would not have made it through the jungle of the Darién had it not been for a new friend, the man standing beside him by the step of the bus. That man said that his name was Calib, that he was twenty-seven and that he was from Venezuela. The Lebanese man said, 'He's a good guy. He help me till now. I tell him, "You are my son now."'

As the buses were arriving, a heated discussion was taking place immediately outside the camp in what appeared to be a small bus shelter. The dispute was between migration officials who run the camp and some local people. The local people said they were unhappy about the lack of onward transport for the migrants and about facilities at the camp. Despite officials engaging with them, voices were raised frequently in apparent exasperation.

After the conversation ended, one of the local people, Anayansi de Miranda, who lives nearby, spoke to me. 'If they [the migrants] no have money, they stay here until their family send them money,' she said.

She said the migrants paid $40 to get to the camp from Panama City. Taxi drivers at Los Planes charged $5 to take them to David, the nearest city, from where they would go to the frontier, 270km away. She said the usual fare for that journey was $2. Anayansi said the migrants were being ripped off and that some had to stay at the camp until relatives could get more money to them, presumably via internet banking, which migrants could access on mobile phones. There were no proper facilities at the camp, she maintained. 'No installations have for the migrants.' There was a very bad kitchen.

It was not at all clear from outside the camp where migrants staying at the camp would sleep. Most buildings that could be seen were in an advanced state of disrepair and partial collapse. At one open-sided timber building, clothes were hanging out to dry, suggesting that people were sleeping inside. Several rows of portable toilets could also be seen. It's understood that one of the services given to migrants when they arrive is a medical check. On my way up the mountain to the camp, two ambulances passed me on the way down and, given the paucity of homes or anything else near the camp, I suspect both were taking unwell or injured migrants to hospital.

The Panamanian government runs several *Estación de Recepción Migratoria*, as they're known. Two are in the Darién, close to the border with Colombia, and the third is at Los Planes. Officials at Los Planes were extremely reluctant to talk about their work, even to disclose seemingly uncontentious information, including the number of people helped and the services offered, such as medical assistance. 'We have about 1,000 per day,' a government official, Derek Onavis, said, adding, 'We are working right now.' In other words, go away. He said further information could be had only from the migration office in the town of David, between 8:00 and 16:00.

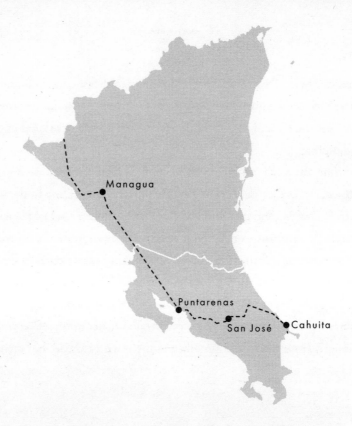

COSTA RICA AND NICARAGUA

I DIDN'T BACKTRACK TO DAVID BUT PRESSED ON, crossing the border into Costa Rica, where I was able to buy roadside insurance and find an inexpensive hostel in Cahuita, a small resort town on the Caribbean coast.

13 MARCH 2023, CAHUITA, COSTA RICA

Cahuita, whose population can't be more than a couple of thousand, is a mecca for backpackers. There's the usual collection of colourful hostels and equally colourful bars and restaurants, whose wide-open fronts blur the distinction between inside and outside. A lovely crescent-shaped sandy beach curls out into the sea, behind which is flat land and a mass of jungle with a walking trail through it. Out to sea, the coral reef is the best preserved in Costa Rica and the tropical rainforest hugs the back of the beach, which curls around the turquoise bay in a semi-circle of Costa Rican Caribbean picture postcard beauty, with palm trees draped over the sand as if trying to dip into the water. The beach carries on out along the shoreline to Punta Cahuita, the outer reach of a small, north coast peninsula that is now one of Costa Rica's many national parks.

As the evening faded and I sat by the beach, drinking a beer, a strange noise echoed through the forest, a sort of primal scream, like something from one of those old black and white horror movies. I thought it might be a recording – some sort of animal grunting through loudspeakers laid on by the authorities, part of what one friend called Costa Rica's tendency to the Disneyesque in terms of its ecotourism offering.

Early the next morning, a small clutch of tourists, mostly middle-aged retirees but a few also in their twenties and thirties, were waiting for it to open. This wasn't strictly necessary, as you could just walk onto the beach and then into the forest, if you wished. The sun was barely up and there was almost no wind but still there was a rustle of leaves from the light breeze that blew through the very tall trees. A boardwalk path from the entrance soon gave way to a much more pleasant sandy path that ran parallel to the beach but stayed within the forest. Every now and then, something scampered along the ground, which was covered with dead leaves and other natural debris of the forest. But I never saw what it was.

There were lots of birds but they were mostly too deep in the forest for me to see them, though I could hear their calls well enough. The great-tailed grackle is common here, a black bird about the size of a magpie, with very long tail feathers. They make a lot of clatter (like magpies) but also whistle. There were also many black vultures, ugly things that are about the size of a large chicken. Ungainly on the ground, they grace the sky, sweeping with elan through great arcs, looking down for something dead to eat.

Gradually, the sound from the night before re-established itself. Up ahead of me, the deep growling, which sounded like something heralding the arrival of a great evil, echoed through the dense forest and soon dominated.

Back on the boardwalk, on either side of it high up in the trees, two sets of monkeys appeared to be having a go at each other. I learn later that they are called howler monkeys, for obvious reasons. There were maybe half a dozen on either side of the boardwalk, adults and juveniles, and they seemed to be in two distinct groupings because the calling started with one group and then the other seemed to respond. In general, there wasn't a huge amount of movement, just noise. And, looking up trying (and mostly failing) to take pictures, I caught hold of the boardwalk rail for balance ... and found my palm deep in monkey shit. They just do it whenever and wherever they fancy. Entirely sensible of course, from their point of view.

A little further on, a German couple were looking up at something else. A sloth, the woman told me without taking her eyes away from the object. Sure enough, there it was, hanging upside-down on a tree branch underneath the canopy of a palm – light tan with a slight brindle and a youngster clutching on to its tummy. Well, the woman said she could see that but I wasn't so lucky. When the animal moved, which was not a lot, it was with such deliberation that it looked like a slow-motion manoeuvre. There was a sloth sanctuary nearby and the animal is something of a mascot for the whole country.

People walking the trail become very respectful of where they are. They whisper, as though not wanting to disturb the residents, and absolutely no one leaves any litter. Signs tell you not to feed the monkeys, or anything else, especially with yourself. Don't swim in the creeks, say signs, as there are crocodiles about. I didn't see any and I didn't swim either.

After Cahuita I rode north and west, through the centre of Costa Rica and into the capital, San José. It was a bit of a disappointment because, unlike almost every other Latin city centre, there was no pretty square replete with well-kept churches and shaded restaurants and cafes.

So I rode on, south to Puntarenas, a seaside town on what looked on maps like a sandspit jutting into the Pacific – which is what it was. With the exception of El Salvador and Belize, the other countries of the region – Panama, Costa Rica, Nicaragua, Honduras, Guatemala and Mexico – have both Atlantic and Pacific coastlines. And there's a big contrast between the two sides: the Caribbean side is generally attractive, with clean, sandy beaches and thriving tourism. The Pacific side, however, tends to be somewhat grey – the beaches at least – and certainly less picturesque. Puntarenas (which means 'Sandy Point') was similar: a long sandy beach bashed by the ocean on one side and with a working port on the other.

I stayed in Pura Vida, a hostel on the oceanside but that was in fact a seafood restaurant with some accommodation in another street about a kilometre away. The restaurant was fine – friendly staff and great food, beers and wine – and the somewhat detached nearby room was clean and safe. I couldn't ask for more, and it was a good jumping-off point for the ride next day into Nicaragua.

16 MARCH 2023, ENTERING NICARAGUA

Nicaraguan officials do not like journalists. Or, to put it more neutrally, a journalist presenting themselves at the border seems to send them into a tizzy. The first thing I encountered was a surly attitude at passport control.

'Occupation?' asked the woman behind the counter.

'*Periodista*,' I replied.

'*¡Periodista!*' she said, clearly alarmed.

'*Sí*. Retired,' I added, giving her the travel spiel and also my press card. There was no point trying to conceal my erstwhile occupation, seeing as it was written on my US visa, which was in my passport. To hide what I was and what I was doing, only for it to be discovered, would create greater problems.

'Wait here,' she said, clearly unhappy. And then she vanished with my passport and press card, leaving me at the glass screen.

After about half an hour, a Nurse Ratched–type appeared and told me to move back and sit over there, pointing to an open space in the passport hall that had no chairs. After an hour, Ratched returned with a slew of questions – about my career, what I wrote, whether I was still a reporter, why I was entering Nicaragua, where I was staying, when I would be leaving and by what border crossing. I answered them as best I could, saying I could not answer everything because I was travelling day by day and going where the journey took me. I'm not sure she could quite handle this concept, and she kept on seeking cast-iron answers.

'You know, this is the first country where I have been asked such questions. Why are you asking them?' I said, exasperated at her approach.

She looked at me in silence and walked away. After an hour and a half I was called to the screen again, but this time my passport was stamped and I was free to enter the country. No explanation was offered.

Next stop, Nicaraguan customs, which was hilarious ... in a sort of Keystone Cops kind of way. Outside in the car park, there were two sentry-box cubicles that had no significant identifying signs. I went to one first and got a form checked and was then dispatched to the other. There the man wanted a photocopy of my bike's Irish registration document and a photocopy of my driving licence. 'Do you have a photocopier?' I asked. He didn't. But he suggested riding out of the gate over there, where I'd find a photocopying place down the road.

Over at the gate, they were having none of that. Leave the bike here and walk, they said. I walked. I got the copies. The humidity must have been well over 90 per cent.

Back at sentry box 2, he asked for all the forms again. I handed them over. Where was the blah-blah form? he asked. 'You have it,' I suggested. We went through my folder of forms, and no, I didn't have it, and I was certain that he, or sentry box 1, was the last one to have it. He said I would have to go back to the beginning and get a new one ...

And so it went on until, finally, sentry box 1 and 2 were happy. Now all I had to do was go back into the main hall – not to Nurse Ratched, thankfully – but to another bank of desks and screens. There an entirely new person took all the papers and finally issued me with the customs permit to import the bike temporarily and therefore (hopefully) leave the country in due course without a hitch.

Immediately inside Nicaragua, the road was lined with stalls, mostly selling soft drinks, fruit and suchlike. But the first stall sold insurance. Two middle-aged women sitting at a desk in an open-air stall surrounded by corrugated iron sheeting sold me third-party cover for a month for $12, backed up by an appropriately officious-looking sheet of paper, replete with rubber stamp markings. A little down the road, I was so glad I had it.

My first impressions of Nicaragua after the border crossing were good. The road north–west, Highway 1 and part of the Pan-American Highway, was just two lanes, one in each direction, but was in a reasonable state of repair. It was tree-lined, many of the trees being cherry blossom in full bloom, and the road hugged the shore of Lago Cocibolca, which has an island in the middle that is home to two beautifully shaped volcanoes. It was a picturesque scene, and I was already thinking to myself, 'Well, whatever they say about Nicaragua, this is all rather pleasant.'

After about 10km along this very straight road, a static police patrol of two young policemen, supported by a paramilitary police colleague holding an automatic rifle, pulled me over. No other vehicles from the line of, I think, four vehicles were ordered to stop. The conversation was curt: passport, licence and *otros documentos para moto* were demanded. I handed everything over, especially the insurance cover, and they were examined in detail. The policeman leading matters handed them back, except for the licence. He said I had committed an *infracción*, an infringement, and he would be issuing me a ticket and retaining my licence. I said there had not been an infringement, that I was in a line of vehicles and was the only one stopped. Why was that? Surprise, surprise, he wasn't interested. But – surprise, surprise again – I could pay the fine now. And how much might that be? I asked. 'Twenty dollars,' he said.

I took out my wallet and immediately he moved close to me, shielding the view of me from passing motorists. I counted out the money – some fives and a lot of ones – and kept moving so everyone passing could see what was happening. Each time I did, he moved close to me until I put my arms over his right shoulders and counted the money behind his back, as it were, in full view of the passing cars. He didn't like that.

'*Cuál es el problema?*' I asked, as he snatched the money and walked back across the road. Asking for a receipt, I shouted at him, '*Un recibo, por favor.*'

At that point, the other policeman, not the one with the gun, who remained lounging against their patrol car on the far side of the road, crossed over towards me. I'm not sure exactly what he said, but it was related to my request for a receipt. He showed me the yellow ticket book and envelope into which, had they taken it, my licence would have been placed. He indicated that not taking the licence was, in effect, the receipt, but I suspect it was closer to, 'Now fuck off out of here or we'll take your licence.' It had that sort of feel to it. I shouted thank yous at them with dripping disdain, which I hope they recognised, and rode away.

Half an hour down the road, a new patrol and another pull over. Again, I had committed an *infracción*, allegedly, and again, oddly enough, I was the only one singled out from a long line of vehicles, all proceeding at the same speed, which was 80km/h. No money was sought or suggested on this occasion, but the policeman rang a pal, Mike, who could speak English and who mediated.

At that stage, I had had enough. I told Mike about the earlier encounter and its outcome. I asked him if this was what I had to expect in Nicaragua, four hours into the country and during every encounter with the police. Mike, who sounded like a very decent bloke, was upset at this suggestion. It was a beautiful country, he said. It didn't seem very beautiful to me, I countered. The phone, which was the policeman's, went back and forth between the three of us, Mike translating. My licence would be taken, and I would be issued with a fine. I could pay it next day at a bank and collect the licence on Friday, maybe Monday or Tuesday, from police headquarters in Managua, to where they would send it. I told Mike that this was outrageous, that I was leaving the country on Sunday or Monday and that the Nicaraguan police appeared to be a bunch of crooks in uniform. I gave the phone back to the policeman.

After a few minutes, Mike was back to me. 'He's going to give you a break,' he said of the policeman. I thanked him for that and for his translating, and I thanked the policeman for the break. He gave me back my licence, and I rode off to the nearest hotel, which was a grim-looking joint in El Crucero, a linear strip town about 15km short of Managua, and had quite a few beers.

18 MARCH 2023, MANAGUA, NICARAGUA

I was stopped once more by the police in Nicaragua and, on that occasion, they could not have been more pleasant, friendly and professional. I'm happy to be able to write that because it proves, again, that even in a society in which something is clearly rotten, individuals can and do act with integrity, if they so choose.

It was just before the city of León on the road NIC-12A, the main route from Managua to the frontier with Honduras. Two uniformed police with two back-up paramilitary-style colleagues were operating a static roadside inspection of vehicles. The road was straight, and I was sticking rigidly within the speed limit. They flagged me over and I obeyed, turning off the engine and removing my sunglasses as I did, greeting them with a smile and a big hello. I showed them my papers, and soon the conversation relaxed into friendly banter about the bike and what I was at. They accused me of nothing (and had no grounds to) and made no demands. I gave them some of my journey stickers, they posed for a photo (one of them was busy and so is not in the shot) and then they waved me on my way, with their good wishes. Such an incident should not be worthy of comment but, sadly, this was Nicaragua.

I stayed at a hostel in central Managua, catching up on rest and writing in the main. I visited just two areas in the city. The first was the Huembes Market, which is bang in the centre. I have a thing for markets, mainly because of their colour and energy. They're full of people (if they're any good), and usually there's a lot of banter and leg-pulling, especially when, as a foreign visitor, you stick out like a sore thumb. I can honestly say that I have never been in a market with as diverse a range of items on sale as the Huembes. It's a vast covered market hall that spills out onto the surrounding streets and footpaths and, while it's shambolic and run-down, it works.

There was everything you'd expect to be able to buy in a hardware store – everything for the home or workshop. There were cobblers and guys operating sewing machines to repair your clothes. There were nail bars and hairdressers, shoe shops, watch shops, jewellery shops and clothing outlets with colourful walls of T-shirts, blouses and trousers all suspended from elevated positions to catch the eye of would-be buyers. There were stalls selling pulses, rice, seeds, spices and oils, baskets and coloured rope, threads and yarns. There were areas for meat and fish and, of course, fruit and veg. And here too were the underdogs' underdogs – the lottery-ticket hawkers, the beggars and those living out of the mounds of rotten fruit and veg that pile up as the day wears on.

Outside a nail bar, a woman gave her caged parrots a shower ... There were ramshackle restaurants ready to serve the thirsty and the hungry. In the meat and fish area, there was also a woman selling live iguanas, their legs tied to stop them escaping. Two had lost the tips of their tails, why, or rather how, I'm not sure. The wretched animals were on an aluminium tray, looking warily at anyone paying them any attention. And why wouldn't they? They were about to be sold onto a dinner plate.

'¿Cuanto?' I asked the woman, curious about the price.

'Doscientos cincuenta,' she replied. It was 250 córdoba, about €7.

'¿Es bueno?'

'Sí, sí,' she said emphatically, 'es muy bueno.'

I decided to take her at her word and leave it at that.

What endeared the place to me, as much as the colour and clamour, was the reaction of stall holders when I engaged with them, often wanting to take their picture. Almost all said yes and smiled or acted up in some playful way. There was an unforced happiness and it was lovely to see it at work.

The following day I went downtown, towards the lake, on the shore of which the city sits, without taking full advantage of it, at least not in this location. There's a grand avenue leading there, Avenida Bolívar, a huge road such as many cities have, a thoroughfare that bisects the city and that becomes a sort of display case for much that is important to the inhabitants. About half way along the avenue, towards the lakeshore end, there's a major roundabout dominated by a 10m representation of Hugo Chávez, the late Venezuelan leader whose policies, and their vigorous pursuit by his successor, have wrecked his country and sparked the largest mass exodus of people in modern Latin American history. Here, it seems, he's a hero.

Towards the bottom of the avenue, in an area called La Bolsa ('The Bag'), one finds a cluster of the sort of statement national buildings one would expect to find, for example the National Theatre, named after the poet Rubén Darío, and the Palacio Nacional, the national museum. Facing the museum is the House of People, built with a donation from the government of Taiwan and used as a presidential palace until 2000 and thereafter for government functions. It's closed now, allegedly because of high running costs.

And here too, completing three sides of a quad, is the forlorn spectacle of a ruined cathedral, the Catedral de Santiago Apóstol, wrecked by an earthquake in 1972 that killed 10,000 people. It's modest by cathedral standards but pretty, even in its broken-down state, and must have looked lovely when whole. The face has a giant slogan across it – *Todo con amor todo por amor* ('Everything with love, everything for love'). On the facade of the museum are two giant posters. One shows a man on a horse, with the words Sandino and the slogan *Estamos cumpliendo!* ('We are fulfilling'). The other poster shows a picture of a man and proclaims *Carlos: Avanzamos en la Revolución!* ('Carlos: We advance the Revolution!'). Both posters are signed Daniel '07.

'Sandino' refers to Augusto César Sandino, a revolutionary opponent of the US occupation of Nicaragua, who was assassinated in 1934. He's the inspiration behind the Sandinista guerrilla movement, the Frente Sandinista de Liberación Nacional (FSLN), that today rules Nicaragua. 'Carlos' refers to Comandante Carlos Fonseca, former secretary-general of the Sandinistas, who was killed in 1976 fighting the family dictatorship of Anastasio Somoza Debayle. The Somozas ruled Nicaragua with an iron fist, and strong US support, from 1936 to 1979. 'Daniel' is Daniel Ortega, the increasingly autocratic and repressive president of Nicaragua, who rules alongside his wife (who has the title vice-president) and who claims to be the successor to Sandino. Ortega is president of the political party the FSLN has become.

The final side of this quad, facing both the square and Avenida Bolívar, is Parque Central, a well-maintained public open space in which the heroes of Nicaragua's political establishment are honoured. The setting includes the mausoleum of Comandante Carlos, with an eternal flame and surrounded by the red-and-black flag of the Sandinistas. The little park is an attractive knot of pathways lined with privet hedging and flowers in bloom. But, after a while there, what was most striking was the absence of people. It was a Saturday afternoon, a time for shopping and strolling, a time for sitting on benches in the shade of a tree and eating ice cream, for chatting with friends or cuddling a partner. A time for relaxing and enjoying one's surroundings in an agreeable setting. And yet there was almost no one there.

When I asked people in Managua how things were, the most common one-word answer, after a little thought and some apparent hesitation, was *'Regular'*. The context of my question was invariably related to the political climate and the economy – in other words, the state of the country. *Regular* used in this context translates roughly as 'Okay ...' That is, things have been worse, and they certainly could be better, but I'm doing the best I can. So things are not great here for many people, but they're wary of talking openly about it.

A youngish Norwegian woman I met in a hostel, and who was about to do voluntary work on a farm, said that on a previous visit to Nicaragua she met older men who, probably reflecting their politics and Nicaragua's revolutionary sympathies with the former Soviet Union, wanted to go to Ukraine to fight with, and not against, the Russians, and also younger people who were reluctant to talk openly about politics, except from the safety of their own homes

In my hostel in Managua, they didn't have water during the day, just a piddling trickle from one kitchen tap. 'You better take a shower now,' said Michael of the hostel as he checked me in when I arrived early one morning, 'because the water will be off soon.' A day or two later I watched as they tried to hook hose pipes onto the water circulating in their small swimming pool, directing it to an elevated tank that fed the hostel's shower system. The operation was not entirely successful. 'The aquifers are drying up,' Michael added.

Nicaragua has a severe water-supply problem. Because of climate change, the water table has been lowering, which means that tapping the aquifers for supply, which feed the cities, has to be rationed. The story is slightly different in rural areas, where people rely on surface water – that is, rivers and lakes – for domestic use such as washing clothes and drinking. But surface water has become severely polluted, due in large measure to there being no proper sewerage system. Rural people defecate into holes in the ground, and the deposit is allowed simply to soak away, leeching into the soil and ultimately into rivers and lakes. Over twenty years ago, the US Army Corps of Engineers surveyed the situation and concluded: 'Given the rainfall and abundant water resources, there is adequate water to meet the water demands, but proper management to develop and maintain the water supply requirements is lacking.' Not enough has changed since then, it would seem. The provision of clean water must surely be one of the imperatives for any government, but in this the Sandinistas have been less than successful.

When Daniel Ortega emerged as an international figure in 1979 after the last of the Somozas fled the country, he was lionised by many on the left. He was young and handsome, and there was a whiff of the Che magic about him. Ortega was the leader of the provisional government in 1979–85 and the President of Nicaragua in 1985–90. He was elected again in 2006 and has been president since, winning elections whose fairness has been challenged by the opposition and, increasingly, by foreign observers. Despite retaining power at the polls, Ortega has become increasingly autocratic and thuggish, cracking down on anti-government protests, particularly in 2018, when 360 people were killed by security forces in a series of incidents collated by rights groups.

Perceived and actual opponents are stripped of their citizenship and cast into exile. In February, 222 political prisoners were deported, and 94 people, including some of the country's best-known writers and journalists, were stripped of their citizenship. Two of the 222 were past presidents of the country's business association, which in March 2023 was shut by the government. Eight of Nicaragua's nine TV channels are owned or controlled by Ortega's family and supporters, some of them external, including the Miami-based Mexican oligarch Ángel González. At Ortega's behest, constitutional term limits on the presidency have been abolished. When I was there the US State Department said there were now credible reports about arbitrary killings and torture. The department's human rights report for 2022 pointed to 'numerous reports that the government or its agents committed arbitrary or unlawful killings'.

For much of its existence, Nicaragua has been plagued by meddling by the US, behaviour that inspired Sandino, emboldened the loathsome Somozas and is now used by Ortega to justify his own anti-democratic behaviour. It struck me as odd, therefore, to see so much of Managua looking like a giant American mall. The lifestyle, retail and architectural influence of the US is striking – whether it's the malls and their car parks, the style of the hotels or the type of outlets that flourish. There are signs of it everywhere, in the branch of Walmart near my hostel and in the profusion of American fast food outlets. And amid them all, one sees people regularly travelling the city by horse and cart ... something not uncommon in Dublin well into the 1960s.

It's no surprise, then, that the place is in a bit of a state. Today, Ortega looks like just another second-rate despot, clinging to power through nepotism and the support of cronies – a man doomed to fail his country and, ultimately, to go the way of the Somozas.

HONDURAS AND EL SALVADOR

21 MARCH 2023, COYOLITO, HONDURAS

Leaving Nicaragua was not as difficult as I feared it might be. The officials at the frontier were polite and efficient in their work, and so I and the bike passed through their hands without incident – a far cry from my arrival into the country.

When I came to leave, I gave in when approached by a frontier fixer and went along with his instructions, contrary to how I usually do these things. I have an instinctive reaction to people who swarm round me when I arrive at a border crossing, telling me (without having been asked for help) to do this and that, to park here, not there, and to 'Come, come, this way ...' But this man was less pushy than others, and my resistance was low. He was also good. He led me to the photocopy guy – a sweet huckster shop at the side of the road with, yes, a photocopying machine behind the counter. He was doing a roaring trade, too, as border crossers got their documents copied, which the officials would soon demand. For me, it was the driving licence, passport and bike's Irish registration form.

Then it was into immigration and customs, copies taken, originals examined and – whoosh! – '*Pasar*'. I was cleared to proceed. On the other side of the bridge, Honduran police had a first look at everything before I got off the bridge itself. This is when you fear the worst – what if something is not right and I'm turned back and have to go through the whole rigmarole again? But all was well: he waved me on.

Next, the immigration woman was charm herself, and then customs went smoothly as well. The setting was slightly odd: an ugly building straddled the road right at the end of the bridge on the Honduran side. It was a long building, creating a tunnel effect. Customs was at the far end of the tunnel, after immigration, and there were several people hanging about – the usual freelance currency traders (the US dollar is the currency in Honduras, something I hadn't realised), a few people who appeared to be fruit or fish traders and a couple of women with an empty Slingsby trolley – what it carried or was about to carry remained a mystery.

As we all waited, one of the trolley women made great fun of me and my bike and, when the customs guy said that all was in order and gave me the crucial papers that would allow me leave Nicaragua, I said goodbye to her with a full embrace and a big hug. That got whoops and jeers from the others. And she loved it!

The first thing that hit me about Honduras was, 'Oh, God, I'm back in Peru!' The dumping and filth at the roadside were incredible – as bad in many instances as Peru was. Great heaps of rubbish – plastic bags, bottles, paper, nappies and organic matter – in huge mounds lined the roadsides. The second thing that hit me was its solar energy farms. There were quite a few of them west of a place named Nacaome, where I biked past big spreads of solar panels all feeding electricity into the national grid. Why there are not more in the whole region I don't know, because there's a hell of a lot of sun going to waste. In 2015 Honduras was the second-biggest producer of solar electricity in Latin America, the largest output coming from the

Nacaome region. In fairness to Nicaragua, they too have invested heavily in renewals, which now account for about 60 per cent of energy produced, and the country is exporting to its neighbours. Renewals account for 98 per cent of Costa Rica's electricity needs – also pretty impressive.

Honduras is a narrow country on its southern flank by the Pacific – just 130km border to border. The coast is wrapped round a bay named the Gulf of Fonseca. I decided to head in that direction and get a seaside perch for the night. I ended up in a place named Coyolito, a jumping-off point for Isla Tigre, a visually striking volcanic island maybe a kilometre offshore, that looked beautiful as the sun began to sink below the horizon. Coyolito was in a bad way, however. Sitting on the edge of the bay and looking across to Isla Tigre – it did its level best to make the least of its setting. The backs of the houses were facing the water, and there was rubbish everywhere, especially along the tidal high-water mark. An open drain, a channel maybe a foot wide and with a dangerously buckled grill, missing parts, looked like it carried much more than just water. Still, it was getting late, and I asked a man at the slipway for the small ferries to the island whether there was a hostel. Yes, he said, pointing to a place in the middle of the huddle of buildings. I could see a first-floor patio and, on its side, the word Hotel. That would do nicely, I thought.

The entrance to the hotel was through a garage protected by a wide metal-bar gate. A young boy opened it for me, and I was soon greeted by a middle-aged man who was evidently drunk. As he was telling me that, yes, he had a room, a striking middle-aged woman rushed forward, eclipsing your man. She had a great mop of hair, all curls and plumped up. She was in beach wear, a bikini of sorts, as far as I could make out, and had over her shoulders and wrapped round her one of those bright, multicoloured diaphanous flowing throws that failed to conceal entirely. Her shoes were peep-toe wedge heels that looked as though they were missing a couple of feathery pom-poms.

She sailed towards me and swatted your man aside and showed me the room. It was, well, basic, but it would do. Yes, they had beer – served on the terrace above – and there were indications of food. I was in like a shot.

After a shower and securing the bike, I went up to the terrace and met the other members of staff – a man, in his late thirties perhaps, who wore a baseball cap back to front, a T-shirt and jeans that looked as though they had not seen a washing machine since about 1957; and a woman in her late forties who seemed to actually run the place. She busied herself ferreting around here and there and, if not, giving directions to Baseball Cap – usually to bring more beer. I was the only hotel guest.

Diaphanous Hyacinth, she of the peepy toes, was in a hammock, where she stayed for most of the following five or six hours, tap-tapping on her phone or chatting excitedly. She had a big gold Coco Chanel chain and a padded latex handbag that appeared to be stuffed with money. She directed the man and woman from the terrace on beer and food runs as she and I chatted. She had a big personality, and there were lots of interesting aspects to her life and background, but, ultimately, I think she was sad inside. Despite her charm and good looks, there was also a big emptiness. She owned the hotel but was about to lose it. She had a business in the capital and three grown-up children, but her marriage was kaput after twenty-six years.

We chatted, drank lots of beer, and then I went to bed around midnight, getting up next morning at seven. When I went to check the bike, the woman who ran the place was at the iron gates, on the outside, blind drunk, evidently having been up all night, God knows where. Wherever it was, there had been drink involved. Hyacinth emerged from her room and got back into a hammock. Baseball Cap, who had slept fully clothed in the upper terrace hammock, was roused to unlock the gates so I could escape. But this had the complicating effect of letting the drunk woman back into the compound, where relations with Hyacinth deteriorated rapidly.

I hit the road ...

22 MARCH 2023, SAN SALVADOR, EL SALVADOR

Crossing into El Salvador, I headed straight for the capital, San Salvador, and a hostel named Cumbres del Volcán Flor Blanca. It was hard to find because Google Maps was not precise and the place didn't exactly advertise itself with a big sign. Still, it was everything I could want. It's managed by two pleasant young people, Andrés and his assistant, Saraí. The thing about travel is the stuff you don't know but find out along the way. I knew, of course, about El Salvador's appalling civil war from 1979 to 1992. A colleague and friend from the Sunday Times, David Blundy, was killed here in 1989. But I had no idea, for instance, that Salvadoran architects were significant design pioneers throughout Central America and had a major impact on their own capital city.

Hostal Cumbres del Volcán Flor Blanca is an example. It was built in 1950 but has a 1930s art deco feel. The first owner, for whom it was built, was a man named Carlos Dordelly. He sold it immediately to a Dr César Emilio Lopez, an obstetrician, and it was known thereafter as the Lopez Mansion. The doctor died in 1958, and for the next forty years the place was home to his widow, Lola, and a number of other women, the last of whom died in 1997, aged one hundred. The current owners bought it for $160,000 from the estate of the doctor and Lola's daughter, Bertha Lopez, and had to do a lot of work on it because of the effects of what is described, rather quaintly, as 'deferred maintenance', that is, jobs that weren't done when they should have been. These included a new roof, new plumbing and wiring and a new kitchen.

The place had to be completely redecorated and furnished, but in some instances they used old Lopez family pieces, including two distinctive wooden rocking chairs, plus a timber dining table and matching chairs and wicker seating for the hall. The whole place has a light, airy feel to it, with a gentle and welcome breeze flowing into a plant-filled atrium and out again. There's a photo of the widow, Lola, in the hall reception area and also a painting of Bertha. There's a tiny bit of Frida Kahlo intensity about Bertha's appearance. She never wanted to leave the house, apparently, repelling family efforts to get her to sell. It still feels homely, in part due to the furniture and, I think, a sense that the Lopez family influence endures.

The current owners are Malcolm Collins and his wife, Gladys Hernandez. Malcolm's a bit of a character. For a start, he's seventy-seven but looks like he's in his early sixties. Like most of his hostel guests, he lives in jeans and T-shirts and spends much of his time sitting at an elevated desk (an old bar from the Lopez family era, he tells me) in a corner of the hall, beavering away online. Malcolm is from the US. 'I grew up in LA but had my teens on an alfalfa and cattle farm near Mexicala, about five miles from the Mexican border,' he said. Gladys, to whom he has been married for forty-four years, is originally from El Salvador but spends most of her time at their other home in Los Angeles, while Malcolm oscillates between there and El Salvador. He's a retired maintenance engineer for an LA corporation and bank that ran data centres. Despite his surname, he doesn't think there's an Irish connection.

'My family came to America in 1632, from Maidstone to Virginia,' he said. 'Collins is an odd name. The English Collins is derived from Nicholas.' I tell him I didn't know that.

'El Salvador was a very prosperous country right up until the 1970s, when the wheels came off,' he explained. 'Only now is it beginning to get back on its feet.' The source of wealth was coffee, the price of which exploded, said Malcolm, when the US entered the Second World War and coffee consumption went through the roof. The oil crisis of the 1970s saw a fall in prices, with economic consequences for El Salvador, and then there was the collapse of centrist politics.

Malcolm told me that Dr Lopez had been married once before he met Lola. Newly qualified, he and his new wife, who was pregnant, went for a break in the mountains, where she, then in her early twenties, began haemorrhaging. Inexperienced, he was unable to prevent her death, but he vowed never again to be so impotent as a doctor. He went to France to train as an obstetrician and became the most renowned in El Salvador, founding a maternity hospital that continues to this day.

I love the way old houses are full of stories, and Malcolm is a diligent curator of the story behind San Salvador's Lopez Mansion.

*

After San Salvador, I rode south to the Pacific coast and then west, staying for a night in El Tunco, a surfer's paradise. After a while I swung off the road to find a hostel, stopping more or less at the first one. The woman there said a room was $55 for a night, which I thought was a bit steep and declined. 'Okay,' she said immediately, 'how about $40?' I accepted. There was a small pool, and I was sweaty and tired.

After a bit of exploring (actually foraging to acquire beer) I returned to find that another bike had appeared, a KTM with an Argentine plate. The rider introduced himself as Fernando de Rosas from Mendoza, the Andean city that is Argentina's wine capital – and we got chatting. He was fifty-five and had several businesses, including one making pallets for vineyards. I told him I had been to Mendoza some years before and visited the Uco Valley and several Doña Paula vineyards. He asked where I was going and said he was going to Alaska too, but tomorrow he would be heading for Antigua in Guatemala. I was too, so I suggested we ride together, and so we did – my first time on this long journey (about 14,000km so far) with a biking buddy.

We set off just before 8:00, and the road west hugged the coast for perhaps 20km. It's a jagged coast because of numerous small valleys that flow off mountains running parallel with it and then dip into the sea, creating a string of inlets. And so the road fell with the valley sides and rose again out of them, delivering wonderful panoramas round almost every corner. I was riding in front and felt awkward about stopping to take photos, and so I didn't. You know the way it is with a new friend you don't really know. Is he going to be really ticked off if I stop to take pictures? I didn't even know whether I was going at a speed that suited him. When I did pull over, Fernando was first to speak. 'You know, if you want to stop for photos, just go ahead. It's fine with me!' Of course, the best scenery was already behind us by then!

The road soon went inland, making its way to the frontier with Guatemala. It was sugarcane harvest time, and there were lots of huge lorries on the road, pulling two and three open-top container-sized trailers laden with sugarcane stalks. The harvesting is done by machine now, but I still associate the crop with slavery and the brutal way in which the canes used to be hand cut by men wielding machetes.

At the frontier, the Salvadoran passport man indicated that I was to lean down to the tiny opening in the glass screen hatch, behind which he sat. A colleague was beside him. 'My friend has a question for you,' the official said in English. 'He wants to know which is the best Irish whiskey.'

'Well,' I answered, 'it will either be Bushmills or Jameson.'

'Yes!' he responded almost triumphantly. 'Jameson – is the best, no?'

'Well, I like it,' I said, and with that, he waved me through with a smile.

Before parting ways with Fernando, we had some beer in Antigua that night and talked biking and Argentina. 'What's the problem?' I asked him, referring to the miserable state of his country. 'Populist politics,' he answered, the umpteenth Argentine to come up with that diagnosis. But he still loves it and the life it has given him.

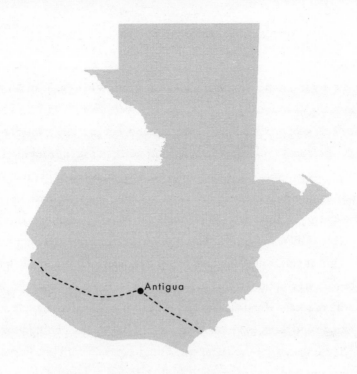

Antigua

GUATEMALA

26 MARCH 2023, ANTIGUA

The gods have blessed Antigua, once the capital of Guatemala. They may have wrecked it with earthquakes in the late eighteenth century, but in doing so they almost certainly stopped it turning into just another sprawling Latin American city, choking with people, traffic and new buildings surrounding a historic centre. Today it's probably Guatemala's major tourist attraction, along with Mayan ruins, many of them concentrated in the northern parts of the country. Antigua is home to about 60,000 people, quite a few of them British or American migrants (though the British for some reason always refer to themselves as 'expats'). It's visited annually by over a million tourists, many of them backpackers.

And while it's in the Tropics, being 1,500m above sea level, it's cool, in every sense of the word. It's also surrounded by volcanoes, including Acatenango, at 3,976m the third-tallest mountain in Central America. I had climbed it a few years before with my daughter, Natasha, who was working as a volcano guide, leading parties to the summit, camping for the night to see the dawn and then leading them down again. When you're in Antigua, Acatenango has a really big presence. It towers over the city, and yet it doesn't seem oppressive. It has a sister volcano, Fuego ('Fire'), which is one of the most active volcanoes in Central America and sits just 16km west of Antigua. When you're at the summit of Acatenango, it feels like it's within touching distance. Fuego erupts daily, belching smoke and ash upwards every twenty minutes or so. In December 2018 a major eruption killed 215 people, and there was another big eruption in 2022. From Acatenango you can watch it puff away, sometimes spewing enough for it to rain ash. It used to be that the eruptions from Fuego came out of its top, but since the major activity of recent years, the lava and fire exit has moved to the side of the mountain and is not so visible from the city. But it's still puffing away ...

In the shadow of the volcanoes, Antigua gets on with life. Its narrow cobblestone grid-pattern streets are full of clothes and trinket shops, cafes, restaurants, bars, hostels and cute posadas whose internal courtyards are full of plants and dappled light. Indigenous women are everywhere, their arms laden with brightly coloured woven fabrics they sell to tourists. And everywhere, too, are the ruins of huge buildings, most of them churches or structures related in some way to the church, such as convents. One whole side of the Plaza Mayor – central fountain, shrubs and flowering trees – is taken up by the Catedral San José. But what one sees today as a grand statement church, dominating the city's main square, is but a fraction – about a sixth by my estimate – of the original sixteenth-century complex. This took up an entire quad of the city and included all the buildings associated with ecclesiastical learning, great power and dominance. But today it's a ruin, frozen in time, not restored to its former glory and made safe only as a living wreck for tourists. Pigeons swoop in and out where the dome's ceilings once were. The place has an 'Ozymandias' quality to it:

> *Round the decay*
> *Of that colossal wreck, boundless and bare*
> *The lone and level sands stretch far away.*

NORTH AMERICA

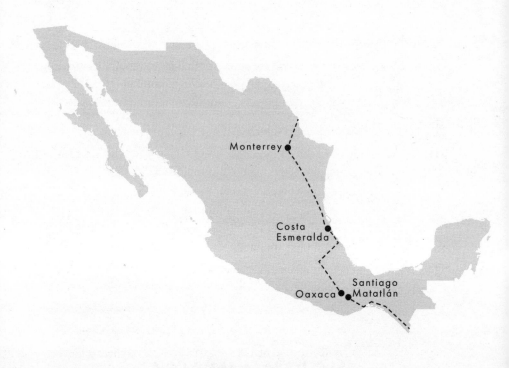

MEXICO

IN LATE MARCH I ENTERED MEXICO and decided to travel north through the country by staying east of Mexico City, which I decided to avoid. I had no wish to ride through a city of some ten million people (the largest in North America), and I had planned also to enter the United States at the far eastern end of the US–Mexico border, at a place named Matamoros on the Mexico side and Brownsville on the Texas side. For that reason, I didn't see western Mexico, which I believe is beautiful, or the Baja California peninsula, which is a favourite among bikers. In retrospect, I regret that, because I don't think I saw the best of the country. But I had my reasons for staying east ...

31 MARCH 2023, SANTIAGO MATATLÁN

Not long after I crossed the border from Guatemala into Mexico, it began to dawn on me that Mexico is a huge – a massive – country. No great revelation there, but I just hadn't dwelt on its size before arriving. At two million square kilometres, Mexico is more than double the size of France and Germany combined. It has a population of 130 million.

Where I crossed from Guatemala brought me into Chiapas, one of the thirty-one states that make up what is officially known as the United Mexican States, and I headed for the capital, Tuxtla Gutiérrez. The elevated view of the city came from heading into the mountain that forms one side of Cañón del Sumidero, Tuxtla's main visitor attraction. When one heads out of the city into the foothills, the urban area comes to a sudden halt with the entrance to what is a national park. The road zigzags its way up, pausing regularly at viewing points. Soon one is standing on the lip of one side of a canyon that is 1,000m high, with near-vertical sheer rockface sides.

A river, the Grijalva, flows through it for 17km like a giant snake. It's 80m deep in places and, from above, looks about 100m. The canyon is about the same age as the Grand Canyon in the US – that is, about thirty-five million years old – and is essentially a tear in the Earth's crust that has been deepened by river erosion. At the northern end of the canyon there's a hydroelectric dam. The river is heavily polluted from the wastewater from over half a million upstream inhabitants getting into it, along with rubbish, mainly plastic. Every year some 5,000 tons of garbage is fished out of the river, the fourth most polluted in Mexico. Thankfully, one doesn't see it from 1,000m above.

I peered over the edge along with Mark and Odette Nolan from Southampton and Paul and Charlotte Reisch from Los Angeles. At one of the viewing stops, they told me about a tightrope walker who traversed the gorge, apparently successfully, but a parachutist wasn't so fortunate when his chute failed to open and he plunged to his death. It's easy to see the attraction for daredevils: the rockface sides are extraordinary – fossil-laden limestone walls, buckled out of shape by movements in the Earth's crust and stained orange in places by leaching.

Next day, I rode on, heading towards Oaxaca, capital city of the state of the same name. The road from Tuxtla soon enters a large plain between encircling mountains. The air was extremely hot – in the high thirties – and the land was bone dry, with quite a lot of sand. Some cattle, scrawny-looking beasts, were snuffling in the dust and eating dried grass that looked about as nutritious as cardboard. There was some evidence of crops, but the whole place had the look of somewhere just about hanging on ... I wondered how much of a temperature rise, with maybe a decade of drought, would be needed to turn it into desert. Not much, I suspected.

On the road into a place named Cintalapa de Figueroa there was the arresting sight of a large sculpture of a traditional Mexican horseman riding a horse rampant. He is wearing chaps and a big sombrero and very much looks the part. Further on, a one-legged man was standing on a traffic-calming hump in the middle of the road, holding out a plastic beaker in the hope that drivers would slow down and drop money into it. He told me his name was Eri, and I suppose that he was in his mid-forties. His left leg had been amputated high above his knee. Most cars drove past, but some lowered their windows and dropped coins into his beaker. I put some money in and chatted briefly with him. He was incredibly smiley – a warm and cheerful man standing there hopping continually to keep upright. Could I take his picture? I asked. 'Of course,' he said, laughing.

At the side of the road, under the shade of a bush, his pal and accomplice, Gabriel, banged out tunes on an electric piano, aided by a loudspeaker and microphone. Between the pair of them, they were quite an act. I rode on, passing a vast prison near Lázaro Cárdenas. It was in the middle of nowhere – nothing immediately around it but scrub and land that was, as far as I could tell, largely unused for agriculture. There were lookout towers and chain-link fencing topped with razor wire and various buildings that appeared to be courts or tribunals of some sort. There was the usual collection of visiting families one finds outside prisons everywhere – people who have made often long journeys to visit an incarcerated loved one. 'How many are inside?' I asked the fellow at the gate. 'There are 1,472,' he answered. Nothing is small in Mexico.

I rode along Mexico 190, the federal highway that slices through the mountains south-east of Oaxaca. The heat was intense and the landscape arid. The mountainsides were covered in dead grass and shrubs and in trees stunted by the conditions and apparently unable to grow more than 10m. Fires were commonplace, evidenced by swathes of the landscape being blackened and struggling to recover from something that had happened maybe the year before. But every now and then there would be a clearing where spiky plants were planted in neat parallel rows, a bit like aloe vera plants. These were, as I learnt later, agave plants, probably somehow connected with the making of mezcal.

I suspect that Emelio Mato was catching forty winks somewhere out back when I called in to his roadside mezcal distillery on the edge of Santiago Matatlán. The distillery, a ramshackle affair, was set back from the road by about 50m of sand and gravel and was inside a long, open-sided lean-to shed. I rode across the gravel forecourt, and no one was about, so I began poking around, taking a few photos, expecting someone to appear any second. Mezcal, or mescal (it's mezcal with a 'z' in Mexico, and with an 's' outside), is a sort of Mexican hooch. In fairness, it's a bit more than that and is now marketed slickly and backed by brand names and classy displays in upmarket shops. Nonetheless, most of what I saw was at the hooch end of the market.

'¡Hola, hola!' I shouted as I poked my way round, and soon enough there was the sound of movement out back. Eventually, a man named Emelio emerged, slightly bleary-eyed. I told him who I was and what I was interested in and asked if it was okay to look around.

'No, no, no!' was the quick answer. 'Away with you!'

'Fine,' I said, and apologised, making to leave.

All of this was in Spanish. And just then, in English, Emelio said, 'You pay me? What you pay me?'

'Yes, of course I'll pay.' I had no problem with that and fished a one hundred peso note (about €5) from my wallet.

Emelio's eyes lit up. He took the money and said, 'Come, come. You have camera?'

And with that he took me over to the pile of what I would call agave hearts – the core of the plant, after the leaves have been sliced off to reveal something a little like a pineapple, though perhaps ten times the size. This, Emelio explained, was the start of making mezcal.

'You drink mezcal?' he asked.

'Not yet,' I said. He smiled, and I thought he was warming to me.

The agave hearts had been sliced two or three times into pieces. Next to them was a large circular fire pit – perhaps two or three metres across. In it were logs carefully arranged so that they rested to form a small dome. Emelio explained that on Monday he would set the logs on fire. On top of them would be placed the split agave hearts, and then everything would be covered with stones. Essentially, the hearts would be slow roasted and the wood would turn to charcoal, as I could see from the debris of a recent fire.

'How long will the fire burn?' I asked.

'*Quatro días*,' said Emelio.

'And what then after the four days?' I asked.

He ushered me towards what looked like a pile of browned and rotting agave hearts – some so much so that, sitting there for a week, they had blue mould on them. He picked up a machete and went at one of them, slicing off bits about the size of orange quarters. He threw them into the next stage of the process – an ancient-looking circular-stone crushing trough. A large stone wheel, maybe a metre and a half across, was set on an axle and, when pulled by a donkey, went round the inside of the trough. There was a hole in the centre, down which the liquid went to a tank underneath. The puller of the wheel was at that moment resting in a small shed across the lot, munching away and happy, one imagines, for the break.

The result of all this, apart from the liquid, is a mass of pulped agave hearts, though they now looked like matted hair more than anything else. The whole lot – liquid and pulped hearts – is decanted into large wooden vats. Emelio had three vats on the go, each quietly fermenting away during my visit.

'Dip your finger in and taste,' he urged.

I did. The first one – that is, the newest fermentation – was quite sweet, and the next one was much more so. But the third was a little bitter and tended towards something alcoholic. After several days' fermenting, the liquid is drawn off and distilled. The pulped hearts are thrown away.

Behind us as we spoke, a log fire was roaring away underneath a copper vat encased in concrete, just in front of the fermentation vats. A copper pipe came out of the top of the distilling vat and crossed over to a cooling tank beside it, spiralling into a worm as it entered the cold water. From out of the bottom of the cooler, a small white pipe delivered into a twenty litre container a constant trickle of liquid – mezcal!

Emelio stored the distilled liquor in a black plastic drum at the back of the distillers. Just like one of those experts one sees in whiskey distilleries, he lowered a pipe into the drum and sucked up some of the mezcal, holding it in the pipe with his mouth before allowing it to decant with a flourish into what looked like half a coconut shell.

'Taste, taste,' he urged me.

I did and, yes, it was liquor for sure. The nearest thing to it I had tasted was grappa, the Italian brandy made from grape skin, seeds, pulp and vine twigs. 'And what do you do with it?' I asked him, wondering if there was some bottled Emelio hooch out the back that I might buy.

He told me that he sold to one of the big distilleries, which in turn markets it as Fandango, premium mezcal. He was much too cute to tell me what a full drum was worth. At that point I could see that Emelio had a pleased air about him, the sort that said, 'There you are, now. What do you think of that?'

I told him it was all fascinating and thanked him for showing it to me. We chatted about me – where I was from, what I was doing, my wife and children. I asked him about his. His wife's name was Sinara, but she had died two years before, he said, pointing to a little photographic shrine to her on the wall. He has two grown children – a son and daughter – who help in the distilling. 'How long?' I asked, indicating his work.

'*Cuarenta y siete años,*' he said – forty-seven years.

'And how old are you?'

'Sesenta y siete.' Sixty-seven, and that made me feel terrible. Almost his entire working life had been at this, and a lot of it is physical. He looked ten years older than he was, aging that I can attribute only to his having lived a hard life, and I suspect that he was clinically blind, such was the state of his eyes.

He asked me how old I was – seventy, in a few days, I said – and that seemed to shock him, I suppose because he couldn't quite believe it, judging maybe that I didn't look that age – a difference attributable to our having been born in different countries and into different circumstances, mine more advantageous than his. The world isn't fair.

We parted with a couple of big hugs, and I felt better for having spent an hour or so with such a lovely, obliging man – despite his initial grumpiness!

9 APRIL 2023, OAXACA AND MONTE ALBÁN

Easter Week in Mexico is a bit of a riot: loud, long, brash and noisy, reflecting, I suppose, the character of the country and its people. It's known here as Semana Santa, and while it starts on Palm Sunday, it doesn't necessarily come to an end seven days later on Easter Sunday, the day of the Resurrection. It can go on for another full week of religious ceremonies.

I came across the start of it all when I arrived in Oaxaca. I got a pretty good hostel in the historic old town, with secure parking nearby, and headed quickly to Plaza de la Constitución. I was immediately relieved that I was in a real city. There was a big square with an impressive and well-maintained Victorian bandstand, mature trees and beds, the Metropolitan Cathedral, dating back to 1535, and colonnades along two sides of the square, one length of which was home to restaurants and cafes. It was early evening, and the square was full of people strolling, meeting friends for a chat, allowing children to run a little wild with toys. And, of course, there were sellers of everything imaginable but mainly balloons and hats, tourist tat and traditional throws.

But what made the place really hop was the music. Several mariachi groups were playing and singing for diners. They wear large wide-brimmed sombreros, very tight trousers (the outside legs of which are covered in silver studs) and a waistcoat-type jacket that seems several sizes too small. They're a wonderful sight and are quintessentially Mexican. While Oaxaca gets most of its income these days from tourism (or so I read), these fellows were local and doing their thing for audiences who were also overwhelmingly local, though not all from the city, certainly.

Competing with them, if at another level in style, were two musicians playing marimbas, xylophone-like instruments popular in Mexico and Central America. As soon as the mariachi groups finished with one set of diners, the marimba fellows moved in and began their serenading. And all the time children were running about. During lulls in the music, chatter, laughter and the sound of dining – cutlery being used, glasses being clinked – filled the silence. It was wonderful; it was life.

The next day I went to Monte Albán, an ancient city on a hill above Oaxaca and the reason the modern city will always have visitors. Monte Albán goes back to 500 BC and thrived until AD 850, when it ceased to be, for reasons not entirely known. The city was built by the Zapotec people, Indigenous Mexicans that at one time dominated the Oaxaca Valley. Today, there are about half a million Zapotec people, most of them in this region. Monte Albán was created as a ceremonial centre so that the Zapotec ruling elite – economic and religious – might consolidate their position. The city dominates the highest position above the plain that was farmed and on which people depended for food.

The city, as it looks today, is not dissimilar to other ancient settlements of religious significance in the region, be they Mayan or Inca. It's rectangular and is, by my estimation, about 1,000m long by 400m wide. Many of the buildings look like decapitated pyramids – shallow-sided, with steps leading to large flat areas that were, in some cases, altars or stages for religious ceremonies. The choice of such a high location for the city, also the focal point for religious ceremonies, was because the Zapotecs thought it brought them closer to god. On dying, one attained immortality, which seems like a fairly good arrangement, and one's remains were delivered immediately to the gods, who accompanied them in their tombs ... of which there are a fair few on Monte Albán.

Speaking of matters ancient, I turned seventy on that day, 9 April 2023, staying the night at a grotty campsite on the Costa Esmeralda. I had never been seventy before, so I wasn't sure what to make of it. I was well aware that it had happened to others, but just not to me. When I turned sixty I hated it. None of the previous fifty-nine birthdays affected me in the way that one did, and so I expected I should feel everything I felt then, plus a bit more. I should really be writing something about how lucky I am. And I am fortunate: I'm in good health – so far as I know – and am reasonably fit, though a lot less so than a few years back. I can still hop over a wall, vault a five-bar gate and shin up most mountains in Ireland without much bother. Getting dressed in the morning, I practise standing on one foot to put my socks on and can still do it without falling. Such small triumphs are not to be sniffed at when you're seventy. And here I was riding an enormous motorbike through the Americas, seeing wonderful places and meeting interesting people.

But it was the realisation that – if I'm as lucky as my dad, who lived into his ninety-first year – what awaits me, sooner rather than later, is inexorable decline. The night before leaving the hostel in Antigua, Guatemala, I sat up for a time chatting to two young women from Israel. They were lovely people – full of vigour and enthusiasm, interested in the world and not slow to say what they thought, especially about the current Israeli prime minister, Benjamin Netanyahu. (Answer: not a lot – in fact, they loathed him.) Next morning, when I was leaving, I sought them out to say goodbye and wish them well (they were about to return home to begin third-level). We hugged, and one of them said to me, 'Stay young.'

I took it to mean that she thought I was young for my age, and so, yes, that's what I'll do: carry on, grateful for having a wonderful, kind, talented and tolerant wife whom I love and two healthy children fashioning their own futures. I'll press on ... if I can remember where I left the bike keys and the map.

14 APRIL 2023, MONTERREY

Keysí Lano Rivera was sitting in a wheelchair chatting to another man lying on a bottom bunk when Yoennis González brought me over to introduce

Eri, the cheerful one-legged, middle-of-the-road beggar in Cintalapa de
Figueroa, southern Mexico.

Mezcal maker Emelio Mato from Santiago Matatlán, Mexico.

Platforma Norte (the North Platform), part of the complex of Monte Alban near Oaxaca in southern Mexico, built by the Zapotec people between 500BC and 850AD.

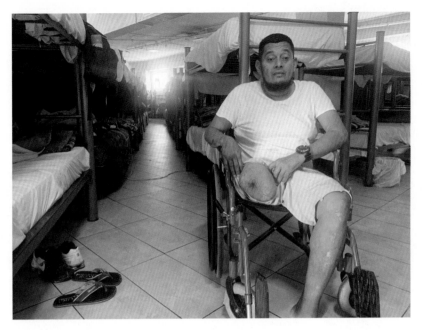

Keysí Lano Rivera, a would-be migrant from Honduras, who lost his leg when a train ran over him as he tried to make his way north to a better life in the US. Keysí was stranded in the Casa Indi, a church-run migrant centre in Monterrey, north-eastern Mexico.

Migrants catch some shade at the Casa Indi centre in Monterrey, north-eastern Mexico, before heading north to cross the Rio Grande into Texas, they hope.

The infamous US border 'wall' separating it from Mexico, actually made up of metal staves closely packed into concrete, near El Paso in western Texas.

Trump supporters in Bandera, Texas.

The odd, DIY graveyard at Study Butte in southwestern Texas.

A young boy examines a gun display at the Tuscon gun show. Note the weapon with the name Trump on the pistol grip and handguard. It was selling for $1,195.

Gun lovers Kylen and Cody with their new AR-10 – Kylen's fifth weapon –
at the Tuscon gun show, before they headed off to hunt Mule Deer.

'Batman' and 'Wonder Woman' strike a pose for me on Hollywood's Walk
of Fame.

The Golden Gate Bridge shrouded in the fog named Karl, with San Francisco in the distance.

The essence of cool: a San Francisco cable car grip man relaxes with his cigar.

Jessica Quinlan has a champagne breakfast at Mel's.

Northern California's stunning Pacific coastline, as seen from Highway 1.

Redwoods in northern California's Humboldt State Park on the Avenue of the Giants.

The North Umpqua River near Indian Creek, exemplifying the Oregon of my youthful memory from the pages of National Geographic.

Astoria Bridge over the Columbia River, linking Oregon and Washington State.

Vernon and Benita: still in love after 70 years together.

Waterfowl Lake and White Pyramid Mountain, from the Icefields Parkway, Alberta, Canada.

A random and nameless pond beside British Columbia's Highway 37 near Lake Meziadin epitomising BC's natural beauty.

Dawson City streetscape – timber buildings, boardwalks and mud streets.

Dawson City's kissing houses, leaning into each other because melted permafrost has weakened their foundations.

Sourdough Saloon's impresario Terry Lee showing a tourist an alcohol-pickled toe before dropping it into her Sourtoe Cocktail - a Dawson City tradition.

Typical Alaskan landscape – the Robertson River and the Mount Kimball range in the distance.

The Trans-Alaska oil pipeline.

At the top of the Atigun Pass (1,444m) through the Brooks Range, before descending onto the Northern Slope down to Prudhoe Bay and Deadhorse.

One of Prudhoe Bay's many oil rigs, all of them land based.

The end of the road – the Deadhorse sign, festooned with stickers from bikers who have made the trek.

us. I was slightly embarrassed to be intruding on their chat, but no, no, Keysí and Yoennis both insisted, it's okay. Keysí spun himself round in his wheelchair, and we had a brief conversation. I explained that I was a journalist, mentioned what I was doing and asked whether he was okay with that. He was. Keysí and I were both in Monterrey, Mexico's second-largest city, for a connected reason. I came here because of 'the Beast'. So did he.

The Beast is an infamous freight train that begins its journey northwards in southern Mexico, close to Guatemala. It's one of those long freight trains common enough in northern America – a moving sausage of carriages filled with goods, or, at times, empty ones being shunted round for reloading. Some of the carriages are like shipping containers, sealed steel boxes; others are petroleum, acid or liquid gas tankers; and others still are like flatbed trucks onto which goods are loaded and strapped down. The train lumbers through the countryside and arrives eventually in Mexico City, where many of the carriages are dispersed to other engines that carry on to different parts of the country. One such destination is Monterrey, about 200km from the frontier with Texas.

Why is the Beast infamous? Because it has become a means by which migrants can traverse Mexico in their quest to get to the United States and Canada. Ride the Beast across Mexico and you're almost there … and so the train is frequently festooned with people as it moves along its track. They jump on board and find whatever flat surface they can – which might be between the carriages, along the side of them or on the roofs – and stay there until they get as close to the border as they can. The risks are many, real and obvious. Sometimes they fall asleep and roll off the train; sometimes they're attacked by thieves who steal and kill without a second thought, snuffing out a life in circumstances few notice or seem to care about. And if eventually they get to the border, to cross the Rio Grande at night, more dangers lurk.

Keysí, who is from Honduras, was on the Beast the previous November. He was now forty-two. His dream, like all the other dreamers, was to get to the US and build a new life for himself. But something happened: he fell off the train, and as it continued along the track, its wheels sliced off his right leg above his knee and mangled some of the toes of his left foot. Keysí told me all this in a matter-of-fact way, a blank expression on his face throughout. I asked to take his picture. Yes, of course, he said, and he immediately rolled up his left trouser leg to show me his severed limb. The skin of his thigh was folded down and under itself to create an almost pillow-like appearance. It was neat and tidy and horrible all at the same time.

We tried – I tried – to have something approaching a normal conversation with him (I think he said he had a family of one back in Honduras), but I felt overwhelmingly inadequate because there was nothing, absolutely nothing, I could say or do to fix Keysí's life. He had lost a leg and was now wheelchair-bound. Whatever life he imagined for himself in the US was no longer available, and whatever life he left behind in Honduras, however inadequate it was to prompt him to leave in the first place, was also gone.

I met Keysí at Casa Indi, one of the most difficult, one of the most draining, places I have ever been to in some forty years' reporting. And yet if there are saints on Earth, this is where they are. Casa Indi is a one-night-only stopover and provider of food to migrants and to this city's destitute, and it's part of the parish of Santa Maria Goretti. It was founded in 2014 by Fr Felipe de Jesús Sánchez Gallegos to help the city's poor, but, three years later, it witnessed an avalanche of migrants from Central America – an avalanche that has not stopped since.

The north city centre location is a bit odd – a triangular wedge created by two busy and fast-moving inner-city highways crossing each other, which is itself then sliced in half by a short road linking the highways. The short road isn't used much and so has become almost a plaza between the two parts of Casa Indi's operations. On one side, donations – food, clothes, bedding, anything that might help – are received. There's regular toing and froing as modest donations, including non-perishable food, are delivered. One of the vans has a UNHCR logo on the side. There's also an ambulance bay. And on this side, too, there's the communal dining hall with, at a quick glance, seating for about a hundred people. There are four sittings a day.

On the other side of the short dividing road is what looks like a repurposed post-industrial building that is in fact the parish of Santa Maria Goretti. The area used to be heavily industrialised, and many of the roads have embedded in them what are now disused train tracks. But the main railway line is only a few metres away, and slow-moving freight trains pass every few minutes, heralded by that mournful hooter sound used on North American railways. The Maria Goretti building includes a one hundred bed hostel for migrants.

At the time of my visit, it was run by Yoennis, who was thirty-nine. He's from Cuba and told me that he left the country for both political and religious reasons. The politics are simply bad, he says, and while he may practise his religion there now, he doesn't trust the government that it will always be so. He wanted a future elsewhere. For now, however, he was running the bunk-bed hostel for migrants. It's a low-ceilinged cavernous place, crammed tight with bunks, some of them with makeshift side drapes, where the occupants have attempted to secure a modicum of privacy.

Yoennis showed me the logbook. The previous night, there were seventy-three men, three women, seven older children and four babies. Their home countries were given as Venezuela, Honduras, El Salvador and Guatemala. The children included a seven-year-old, a six-year-old, two five-year-olds and a four-year-old. The seven-year-old might have been Elbe, a cheeky boy hanging round the bunk beds who was from Honduras and was with his father. Yoennis had photos on his phone of many of those who passed through. They were almost all police station IDs, the subject holding up a large card with information about themselves on it. I almost couldn't bear to look at them: they betrayed no hint of what was to come next – the journey to the frontier; the furtive crossing, during which they're vulnerable to attack and worse; the likelihood of arrest and return; or the incredibly hard life, illegal and permanently under all official radars, if they're lucky.

Guests pay nothing but must sign a form accepting that they can stay only one night. For that they get a safe bed – a luxury for many, surely – and a meal, and they can take any of the donated clothes that are available from plastic bags behind Yoennis's desk.

On the short road there was a half-wrecked caravan-type trailer with, bizarrely, an image of a smiling and waving Pope Francis mounted on the side in such a way that his face straddled the bars of a window, as if he were in prison. Not the intention, I'm certain. Underneath the front of the trailer, where a tractor would connect to it for towing, a few young men appeared to be bartering furtively.

Over by the hostel, and shaded by an awning, young men (and some not so young) were lounging about, waiting for a bed and a meal, I suspected. They appeared almost lifeless and drained, worn out from their journey so far. Did their hope of a better life outweigh any anxiety they may have had about the illegal frontier crossing they were about to attempt?

One of the senior people running Casa Indi was an accountant, José Jaime Salinas Flores – the first person I approached, unannounced and without warning, by wandering into his office on the donations side. It turned out that he was in charge of all that, and despite initial, and understandable, caution about me, he was extremely helpful, showing me round and introducing me to Yoennis. His office was gloriously cluttered: a plastic Santa vied for attention with rubber stamps, stacks of paper, a teddy, an Eiffel Tower, packets of biscuits and jars of sweets. But José's focus stays on fundraising: $200,000 is needed every year.

I told him at the end of my visit that I didn't know how he could come every day to such an upsetting place. His non-spoken answer suggested that this was just how it was, and we must do what we can.

Just before I left, I sat for a while on a stump of concrete on the short street, surveying the scene. A young woman – she couldn't have been more than twenty-four – with a boy who looked about five or six walked past me. The boy was wearing an oversized football strip. She asked whether I had any trousers for him. I hadn't noticed that the shirt was the only stitch of clothing on him: no pants, no trousers, no shoes.

There are saints at work here, for sure. I just hope there are no monsters.

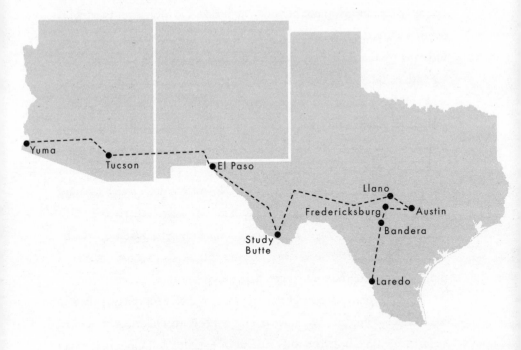

UNITED STATES

TEXAS AND ARIZONA

BY THE TIME I ENTERED THE US, I was ready to leave Latin America behind. People along the way had generally been great, and I never really felt unsafe or threatened. But except for Chile, Ecuador and Colombia's major cities, the level of chaos, of functional disorder in everyday matters — the constant, visible presence of grinding poverty and inequalities, especially in large urban areas — had a wearying effect on the spirit. There comes a time when you just want to get away from it, and that moment had arrived for me. I longed for a few simple things: clean toilets and bathrooms; a shower that had a showerhead and was not just a cold-water pipe sticking out of a cement-plastered wall; towns and the roads into and out of them that weren't chocked by small mountains of litter and roadside filth.

I suppose my mood was not helped by an incident in Monterrey two nights before I left there. I was walking in a street, and a young woman spat at me, full force, so that I felt her spittle hit the back of my neck and head. I can say with certainty that this had never happened to me before. It was about seven in the evening, and she had approached me from the rear on a busy pedestrian street, a nice street with trees and seating, goods shops and a pleasant atmosphere. She touched my lower arm and lower back. I turned round. She was not obviously poverty-stricken. I felt immediately that she was trying to steal my wallet. I said, 'No, no, no, don't touch me,' and turned away, and she just spat at me and ran off. I can only assume that I represented, or she thought I represented, something she hated. So, yes, by the time I was ready to leave Mexico, I was truly ready to leave. I'm sorry I didn't see more of the country; perhaps I'll get another chance.

I had one practical matter to deal with: insurance for the bike. Before my return to Chile in November 2022, I got cover for biking there as well as for Argentina, Bolivia and Peru. But in Ecuador and Colombia I had no cover. In Panama I paid $65 for cover and, on entering Costa Rica, I bought cover from a border huckster for €36 for a month. I did the same on entering Nicaragua (a paltry $12 for one month!) but was without cover in Honduras, El Salvador and Guatemala. In Mexico a premium of $87 kept me on the right side of the law. There was no way I was going to bike through the US and Canada without insurance – even when the best online quote I could find was $400 for one month! I felt I had no option but to pay and, when in Texas, call in to some insurance companies in person and see if I could do better.

People had advised against riding east and entering Texas at Matamoros, which was my original plan. However, when I entered Mexico from Guatemala, the Mexican authorities put a hold of 8,573 Mexican pesos (€435) on my credit card, which they said would be released when I left the country. When I crossed out of the country again, they said, the money would be released and be back on my card after a few days. It was their insurance against my not leaving the country; but what it also meant was that, for me to nip in and out of the country between Matamoros and Tijuana, I would have needed to have several thousand dollars that I could afford to get tied up in this way. And I hadn't.

So I headed north out of Monterrey along Highway 85D towards the border with Texas at Laredo. About 100km outside Monterrey, at a huge roadside restaurant and shop named El Rancho, I pulled in. The place was a hoot – full of Tex-Mex tourist trash, including Stetson hats and other cowboy gear, jeans and T-shirts ... and vehicle insurance. National Unity of San Antonio would cover me in the US and Canada for three months for all of $125. Best of all, cover would start from the day my $400 policy ran out in mid-May.

I bought the policy and paid at the checkout, also paying for a couple of eggs over easy, bacon, hash browns and coffee. The National Unity cover would take me to the end of the trip, I reckoned.

At the border, true to their word, the Mexican authorities released the €435 hold on my credit card. Well, most of it: three days later, €378 was returned to the card. Who knows what happened to the missing €57!

15 APRIL 2023, BANDERA, TEXAS

The frontier crossing at Laredo was the busiest I had seen at the innumerable frontiers I had crossed since beginning this odyssey, but it was run efficiently – on both the Mexican and the US sides. Six or eight lanes of cars and lorries merged inch by inch into two lanes that eventually crawled across a bridge over the Rio Grande. Somehow I expected the river that separated much of south-western Texas from Mexico to be more dramatic. But, no, it was just a muddy brown river, maybe 50m wide, with an attractive linear park on both sides. You could easily swim across it, I'd say.

The border crossing was efficient. On the Mexican side, the bike and I were inspected and waved through. On the other side of the bridge, the two lanes fanned out onto a crescent-shaped forecourt faced by about a dozen individual booths, ten of them manned by US Customs and Border Protection officers questioning drivers and checking vehicles. When my turn came, the officer was friendly but probing. There was some inspecting of the bike, but eventually he said, 'Your visa is in order. But you also need an i94, so if you come with me, we can get that sorted.' What fresh hell is this? I wondered as he walked, and I rode, to the main building and another queue.

Eventually, Officer Rudi Bowles ('It's Rudolph, but everyone calls me Rudi') dealt with me, and what a thoroughly pleasant and friendly guy he turned out to be. We must have chatted for an hour, and while the conversation began as a subtle probing of my story, I think he quickly accepted who I was and what I was doing, and he was fascinated by it. He was fifty-nine and going to retire the following year. He was blown away both by my age and by the journey I was on. After a while he called over a colleague, Tiffaney Santoa, who was a Harley rider, and soon the pair of them were recommending routes through Texas. They said I had to go to Fredericksburg and try some of the wine there. When he eventually got round to stamping my passport, he squeezed his hand out under the glass screen to shake mine and wish me well. Just as I was riding out of the complex, two other officers flagged me down. Officer Rudi was running across the car park trying to catch me. Panting, he said, 'I forgot to give you this, the i94. Keep it with your passport!' And that was it. I was in the States, free to go wherever I wanted, and legal too.

I headed up Interstate 35 in the direction of San Antonio and spent the night in a very ordinary motel in Devine. It cost $75, and I resolved there and then to camp every night thereafter, if I could. The price shocked me but was actually comparatively cheap – $150 a night for bare-minimum hotel accommodation is common in the US, but were I to spend that every day, I'd be broke long before I got to Alaska.

Next day I set off towards Fredericksburg, and in no time at all I was in Bandera. Cowboy Capital of the World read a sign with typical Texan exuberance. And, in fairness, it may well be. I asked several people about the claim, and they all said the same. Bandera (population 839) is surrounded by ranches that are home to, well, cowboys. 'Y'all as likely to see horses tied up here on Main as cars,' as one young woman put it to me.

There were no horses when I was there, but there were plenty of Harleys. In fact, there were dozens of them. It was Saturday morning, and every Harley owner for miles around appeared to be out on the road showing off their chrome and garishly coloured over-the-top bikes. I think of them more as flying armchairs than as motorbikes. One of the riders was a fellow named Stan, whom I met outside a timber-clad diner named Busbee's BBQ and Catering. 'Alaska?' he said. 'Awesome!'

And just then, as we were chatting, right on cue, around the corner came a convoy of up to fifteen big pickup trucks and jeeps, all festooned with Trump flags. The flags had two messages: (1) Trump won the last presidential election, but Biden stole it; and (2) Vote Trump 2024! And while their outsized flags fluttered from long poles at the rear of their vehicles, and you couldn't but notice them as they drove slowly down Main Street, no one walking on the footpaths lined with cute tourist shops seemed in any way interested. A sign, maybe, that despite the brouhaha and shouty flags and posters, Trump may not be as popular as the noise suggested.

Outside of town, further along 173 towards Kerrville, a big sign outside a huge warehouse-type building caught my eye. Connecting Cowboys to Christ, it said. Well, I just had to stop there. A gravel drive led to a large car park in front of a hangar-like building that was – what else? – a church. The Ridin' the River Cowboy Fellowship is run by some of the nicest people you could meet anywhere. There when I breezed in were a former San Antonio police patrol officer, Randy Tucker; his wife, Linda; and her pal Marian Earnest. As I rode across the car park beside the church building, Randy came to greet me and insisted that I come on inside. 'We're a Bible-based church,' he explained, and when I met her a few minutes later, Lynda elaborated. 'If it's not in the Bible, we're not talking about it, we're not preaching it,' she said firmly.

Inside, there was a large reception and dining area, the original space for worshipping, I was told. And beyond it, maybe four or five times larger, perhaps the size of a rugby pitch, was the new church – equally cavernous but nicely done, with lots of timber and a galvanised metal cattle drinking trough doubling as a full-immersion baptismal font. About 550 local people, most of them ranch owners or employees and hence cowboys, come every Sunday for scripture-centric worship, led by their pastor, Jeremy Levi. But the core of the congregation is the 150 or so who come every Wednesday evening for Bible study. 'We've got millionaires in this church, and we got drunks from Bandera,' Randy said, by which he meant that everyone was welcome. And I have no doubt but that they were. He and his wife, and their fellow church worker Marian, were lovely people – full of warmth and with a big-hearted welcome. I don't share their faith, but that's neither here nor there, and I didn't say any of that to them. Why would I?

So far, Texas was more than living up to its stereotype – cowboys and ten-gallon hats; Harleys and churches everywhere, and every type imaginable; barbecue restaurants serving vast helpings of meat. And while Texas is an 'open carry' state, which means it's legal for over twenty-ones to carry a handgun in a holster without any special permit, I hadn't seen that yet. But ask anyone and they'll tell you that almost everyone in a vehicle has a gun with them inside.

18 APRIL 2023, AUSTIN

While I was sitting at a set of traffic lights in Fredericksburg, another biker pulled up alongside me, and we had the 'conversation' – where from, where going and so on. 'I'm going for a coffee,' said the other guy. 'Can I join you?' said I, and with that, Mario Werner (fifty-three) from Heuston, Texas, via the Black Forest and Hamburg, was parking his Honda Africa Twin on Fredericksburg's Main Street, and I was doing the same.

Fredericksburg is right in the middle of what Texans call their Hill Country, a slightly upland region west of Austin, though we're not talking the Andes here: these hills range from 700m to 750m. But the region is topographically pleasing, a mixture of rolling hills covered in small trees or scrub and also farmland, much of it given over to vines producing grapes for Gewürtzraminer and Albariño wines, as well as some reds. Fredericksburg was founded in 1846 by 120 Germans who named their settlement after Prince Frederick of Prussia. In all, some 28,000 Germans would settle in the Hill Country about that time, and the German influence is pronounced even today. The word haus is used frequently by the upmarket tourist shops that line Main Street, where Mario and I stopped for coffee in a cafe festooned with German memorabilia and specialising in those cinnamon pastries Germans love. The fact that Mario is originally from Germany is just by the by. He first came to America as a student and later settled in Atlanta, then Miami and then Texas, working in logistics for a shipping forwarding company before defecting to one of their customers based in Heuston. He's married to a local woman and has a sixteen-year-old daughter. He wouldn't dream of returning to Germany. 'I just love their friendliness,' he said of the Americans. 'People are always welcoming you.'

The whole German thing came as a complete surprise to me. But then so too did the other major feature of this part of Texas – the legacy of President Lyndon B. Johnson and his wife, Claudia 'Lady Bird' Johnson. I knew Johnson was Texan but hadn't realised he was from the Hill Country. Riding through it, one is immediately struck by the wildflowers lining just about every road. There are great big drifts of them – blues, yellows, whites and reds – on the sides of the roads and in the medians separating lanes. And because they are there, so too are flocks of butterflies. The visual effect is striking and quite lovely. This is not the first thing one thinks of when one thinks Texas, and it's all down to Lady Bird. She was passionate about wildflowers and loved seeing them in drifts on her and President Johnson's farm near Fredericksburg, which was left to the state after they died. (The president died in 1973 at the relatively young age of sixty-four, and Lady Bird died in July 2007 aged ninety-four.) Her lasting legacy is the Highway Beautification Act, which her husband signed into law in October 1965. But Lady Bird was the driving force behind its passage through Congress, cajoling and browbeating Congress members and senators to support it. Her belief in nature was total: 'Where there are flowers, there is hope,' she once said. Many American highways were previously lined with grotesquely outsized advertising hoardings that blocked out the surrounding countryside. The act banned them and promoted the planting of wildflowers along the sides of the highways.

For many non-Americans of my generation, President Johnson is associated with one thing above all else: the ghastly error that was America's involvement in the Vietnam War, with its carpet bombing, its Agent Orange chemical warfare and the wasted lives, in Vietnam and in the States. But it's not until one visits the LBJ Presidential Library in downtown Austin that the scale of his legislative legacy is really brought home. Well, to me, at any rate. It's not just the Civil Rights Act of 1964 ('America must overcome the crippling legacy of bigotry and injustice,' he said of ending segregation. 'Justice and morality demand it') or the ensuing Voting Rights Act of 1965 ('It is wrong – deadly wrong – to deny any of your fellow Americans the right to vote', he told Congress, appealing to them to support a ban on all literacy tests and other restrictions used to deny black Americans the vote). Both acts helped transform US society.

Johnson used the assassination of Martin Luther King, Jr, to ram through legislation banning discrimination in the allocation of housing on the grounds of race, colour, religion or national origin. He got a law passed banning racial discrimination in jury selection. He introduced Medicare and food stamps for the destitute and launched what he called an 'unconditional war on poverty', overseeing the largest fall in poverty – from 20 per cent to 12 per cent – of any American president.

Some of the most moving exhibits at the library are recordings of phone conversations, including with King and Jackie Kennedy, the slain president's widow. In one Johnson talks to her after the November 1963 assassination that propelled him into the presidency. You stand there, phone cupped to your ear, listening to Johnson trying to comfort her, telling her she's welcome to come to the White House any time, and her almost girly, high-pitched voice thanking him.

I stopped in to a garden centre to buy wildflower seeds for two friends I was visiting in Austin, Paul and Melissa Vlek. They spend their time between there and Louisburgh in Co. Mayo, and a few days' rest with them was a real battery recharger. In the garden centre four middle-aged women behind the counter got chatting to me. 'I just love your accent!' said one. I explained where it was from and what I was doing. 'Ireland is on my bucket list,' said one of them. 'Well,' I said, 'your president, Joe Biden, has just been with us for four days.' But my remark was about as welcome to them as stepping in dog dirt. Boy, they sure don't like Joe Biden down there, or indeed the Democratic Party as a whole.

Which left me wondering: how in God's name did this place produce a man like LBJ, with such a reforming zeal and a list of legislative achievements, so many of them designed to redistribute wealth and help the less well off? Johnson's politics came from a political ethic that would seem to be anathema to how many of his fellow Texans see the world now. Today in Texas I couldn't see them going 'all the way with LBJ' ... or even a small part of the way.

20 APRIL 2023, LLANO, TEXAS

Almost everything you need to know about Llano can be found in Fuel Cafe on East Main Street – what is seen and unseen, what is spoken about and what is left unsaid. The cafe's motto – 'Coffee + music + community' – sums up how it, and indeed much of Llano, sees itself. But probably more than anything else, it's about community. This is small-town America, big time. It's small-town Texas Hill Country.

Llano is a county and town about an hour and a half north-west of Austin, the university city and, increasingly, the IT heart of Texas, growing ever more so as tech companies invest in the city. Typical of many small towns across the United States, Llano regards itself as a city, and indeed calls itself one. 'City of Llano' says the town's official website. Welcome to Llano, road signs say. Population 3,232.

Fuel Cafe used to be a grocery store, and the tall glass-panelled entrance door still has what looks like its original well-worn thumb latch to open it. Inside, the floor is rough pine. It's easy to imagine when there were open wooden boxes of seeds and pulses, displays of vegetables and shelves stacked high with tinned goods. The walls are exposed stone rubble, and the ceiling is high and also timber-clad. A small handmade sign hangs on one of several timber-clad pillars in the centre of the cafe. God Bless Our Llano, it says. God and simple, feel-good philosophy are never far away in Llano. Today Is a Good Day says another sign in the cafe. And indeed it was.

On the left as one enters there's a day-by-day noticeboard detailing in chalk the activities to which Fuel Cafe plays host. The Knitting Group has Mondays sewn up. Other days promise music, and there's mention also of jam and 'puddles', about which I can tell you no more. Music is a major part of life at the Fuel café, and when I entered, there on stage, over to the right, were Emmet and Debbie McPherson, gently singing soothing middle-of-the-road Country and Western songs. Both were in later middle age but were full of life and charm. Debbie, in blue jeans and a blouse, smiled easily and exuded great warmth. Emmet, equally well preserved and also with a welcoming personality, wore a casual shirt and shorts and strummed the guitar. They interrupted their singing to say hi to everyone who entered, often by name. Their songs included lots of John Prine and old-time C&W favourites, frequently mournful ballads lamenting loves lost or never won, thwarted by insurmountable obstacles, like prior marriage to another. They sang the Jim Reeves song *Don't Let Me Cross Over*, but love's cheating line was nowhere to be seen.

I'd say everyone in the cafe knew every word of every song Emmet and Debbie sang. The listeners certainly all knew each other. A middle-aged woman in a white blouse bounced in through the latch door and threw her arms round a woman of the same age in a tie-dyed blouse. 'Well, girl! How you doin'?' she asked in a voice loud enough for everyone to hear. The other woman was sitting at a long table with six other women – and with one Stetson-wearing feller with a walking stick and lumbar pain. The scene had all the hallmarks of a regular morning coffee get-together where family and community news was swapped eagerly and where ne'er a harsh word was spoken about anyone absent.

I was wearing one of my Tip2Top trophy T-shirts. 'Galápagos!' exclaimed one of the ladies. 'You been to the Galápagos?' I said I had. 'Oh, I so wanted to go there,' she replied. 'I was in Peru, but we never got to the Galápagos.' One of the ladies had relatives in Co. Antrim, another in Cork. Family members had been to Ireland.

On the other side of the cafe, between the stage and the window, were two old armchairs, the type that embrace you as you sink into them, and soon you don't want to leave. An older mother, her daughter and the daughter's toddler were there chatting easily, just as if they were at home. Several other people were reading newspapers. No one was on a mobile phone. It was all coffee, music and community, just like the sign said.

But beneath the surface, something had been stirring in Llano that was far from harmonious, and it was this that drew me initially to the place. This small town was at the centre of a dispute that had split the community and was emblematic of the so-called 'culture wars' that have broken out all over the US and that are tearing at the fabric of social cohesion. At issue in this instance was seventeen books that staff members in the local library – just round another corner from Fuel Cafe – say they removed from shelves because no one was reading them and they needed to free up space. However, opponents claim that the books were removed in an act of censorship and at the behest of conservative forces operating increasingly at almost every level in US society – across government, in national and local politics, in community organisations, in schools and in the judiciary, from Washington all the way to the small-town library board.

Library staff in Llano found themselves caught in the middle of a horrible war that has now reached the federal courts and could well go all the way to the Supreme Court. 'It's been brutal,' says Richard Lelle, a mild-mannered member of Llano's library staff. 'Guy the other day called me "Adolf".'

The precise origins of the conflict are difficult to discern, but here's what I know. Last spring, library staff working under the director, Amber Milum, removed seventeen books from the open shelves. The books in question are the following. *Caste: The Origins of Our Discontent,* by the journalist Isabel Wilkerson, examines the origins of racism in the US and argues that American society is, essentially, a caste system. *They Call Themselves the KKK: The Birth of an American Terrorist Group* by the children's author Susan Campbell Bartoletti has won an award for excellence in non-fiction for young adults. Another is *Being Jazz: My Life as a (Transgender) Teen* by Jazz Jennings. *Spinning* by Tillie Walden is a novel–memoir in which the ten-year-old protagonist describes a regime of romance, bullying and trauma as they try to become a figure skater.

In the Night Kitchen by Maurice Sendak is about a young boy's dream journey, during which he falls into a giant pot filled with cake mix. Critics claim there's undue attention to the child's nakedness and allege sexual innuendo. *It's Perfectly Normal: Changing Bodies, Growing Up, Sex, and Sexual Health* by Robie H. Harris aims to inform pre-adolescent children about puberty, but it has been attacked for allegedly giving age-inappropriate information about homosexuality and abortion, among other matters. *Shine* by Lauren Myracle is about a teenage girl investigating a hate crime. Previous books by Myracle have been banned, notably in Utah, for their alleged prurient interest in sex. *Under the Moon: A Catwoman Tale*, also by Lauren Myracle, is a graphic novel involving domestic violence. In *Gabi, A Girl in Pieces* by Isabel Quintero the protagonist writes a diary about her last year in high school, during which Cindy becomes pregnant, Sebastian comes out and the protagonist dwells on her father's methamphetamine habit. *Freakboy* by Kristin Elizabeth Clark is a novel in verse about a genderqueer teenager, the teen's girlfriend and a trans woman.

The final seven books are ones I imagine would have pre-teens giggling at the naughtiness of it all. They are *My Butt Is So Noisy!, I Broke My Butt and I Need a New Butt*, all by Dawn McMillan. And then there's *Larry the Farting Leprechaun, Gary the Goose and His Gas on the Loose, Freddie the Farting Snowman* and *Harvey the Heart Had Too Many Farts*, all by Jane Bexley.

One doesn't have to be Sherlock Holmes to see a pattern in that list. Could this really be a random selection, the aim of which was to free up shelf space? The library director, Amber Milum, insists that this is exactly what happened. 'At the beginning,' she told me after I dropped in to the library, 'we did it because some books weren't being checked out [borrowed]. If they aren't getting checked out, it's a normal process we keep doing. We didn't think anything about it.'

Could it really be coincidental that, excluding the seven farting books, all but two (*In the Night Kitchen* and *Under the Moon*) were also on a list of no fewer than 850 books compiled by a Texas lawmaker, Republican Matt Krause? In October 2021 he sent the list to the Texas Education Agency, which oversees primary and secondary public schools throughout the state, asking them to check whether the titles 'might make students feel discomfort, guilt, anguish, or any other form of psychological distress because of their race or sex'. Critics, of which there are many, accuse Krause of seeking to ban books that offend conservative sensibilities.

Milum was sent the Krause list. 'I pulled them [the books on the list], and out of, like, sixty books, I only weeded a handful because they weren't being checked out. The people say I was censoring or banning books, which isn't true,' she said.

In April 2022 seven local people reacted to Milum's action by initiating a legal action, at the federal as opposed to the state level, against the library and the authorities that administer all branches in the county. The lead plaintiff is Leila Green Little, a speech and language psychologist who lives in the countryside about five miles outside Llano. She was out when I called in the hope of hearing, first hand, of her concerns, and she didn't respond to a message left on her phone.

However, her and her co-plaintiffs' case – that the weeding out of books based on their content or points of view (which Milum denies) is contrary to the US Constitution's First Amendment concerning free speech – has so far found favour with the judiciary. In March 2023 a federal judge in Austin directed, in a preliminary ruling, that all seventeen books be placed back on the shelves – together with every other book that has ever been removed because of its content. The library authorities are miffed that, despite this preliminary ruling (which is being appealed), the main action by Little et al. remains in play.

Llano County's annual library budget is $450,000, and so far the litigation has cost the county $100,000. The county faces the prospect, it says, of having to close all its libraries if staff members cannot weed out books, as they always have.

In April 2023 the County Commissioners, who oversee the running of the libraries, met to decide whether they had any option but to close them. In the event, and after submissions from local people appealing for the libraries to stay open, they simply took the item off the agenda, following legal advice. But in an angry statement afterwards they hit out at the plaintiffs ('Who is funding this civil litigation?' they asked) and the media. They wondered aloud how long they could continue to fund the libraries and also pay staff members. 'A public library simply cannot function if its librarians, county judge, commissioners, and even volunteers who serve out of the goodness of their heart can be sued every time a library patron disagrees with a librarian's weeding decisions,' said the statement.

And that will be central to the case when it goes to full hearing. Was the weeding done at the behest of State Congressman Krause and his community-based supporters, who are foot soldiers in America's cultural war on 'woke'? Or was it carried out, unprompted and according to the weeding criteria of the American Library Association, merely to free up shelf space, as the County Commissioners claim? The US has a long record of steering clear of censorship, of anything that smacks of the government trying to control what people read and hence think.

Amber Milum comes across as someone who loves her job. Llano Library is in an old single-storey red-brick building that used to house the County Clerk's office. The open-plan library is modern and friendly, with pods of armchairs and tables, a screen for watching videos, internet access and rows of bookshelves. It's a place where book clubs meet and is very much rooted in the community – as is Ms Milum.

'I want people to come in here. I love my job and want everybody to find a book they like,' she said. Did she lose sleep over what was going on? 'Oh, yeah,' she replied, 'the whole thing is so upsetting. It's not what our town is about – being mad at each other. Everybody should be able to have their opinions, their views and morals. Libraries can't parent other people's kids.'

Perhaps not surprisingly, but sadly, nonetheless, Ms Milum didn't want to have her picture taken, lest publication draw further unwelcome attention on her and her colleagues.

Back at Fuel Cafe, a young woman was rushed over to me by the woman in the tie-dyed T-shirt, who knew I was interested in the library dispute. The woman, who didn't want her name used, let alone have her photo taken, was involved in the controversy in a volunteering or advisory capacity. We chatted amiably about many things, but she couldn't really talk about the library controversy, especially not when I took out my notebook! Despite that, she, and everyone else involved or interested in the situation, was politeness itself.

But behind the aura of charm and community chumminess, make no mistake: there's a seething anger over what looks from the outside like a battle of wills over what people should be allowed to read. A tiny library in a small town in Texas may yet find a place in the legal annals of the US when it comes to free speech, free access to information and the role of public employees.

*

Continuing on my journey, I rode west from Llano and soon joined Interstate 10, an amazingly long road that goes all the way across the southern US from Jacksonville in northern Florida to Los Angeles in southern California.

I was urged by friends and other travellers to head south to Big Bend National Park, which I did, but only to ride through it to Study Butte (pronounced locally as Stoody Be-oot), where I camped overnight in a run-down, dusty RV park with a strange, and seemingly DIY, graveyard, the last resting place, apparently, of a Ron Willard (1929–2002). There was what appeared to be a memorial grave to Lawrence P. Harris, Jr, a US Marine Corps sergeant missing in action in Korea since 27 November 1950. The plots were marked by stones and plastic flowers, and beside them, sitting in two camping chairs, were a set of plastic skeletons and a skeleton dog.

Big Bend is real Wild West country: flat land, at times pure desert, at other times just parched landscape with some shrubs and stunted trees hanging on for dear life. And then, very regularly, rising from the plain are tabletop mountains, just like the ones in the Western movies. You expect at any moment any number of characters, but chiefly John Wayne or Clint Eastwood, to appear at the head of a straight line of dust thrown up as they ride across the landscape.

I rode on towards Marfa, an art deco gem in the desert. There, I linked up with another biker, and we paced ourselves until we got to Alpine, where we stopped for breakfast in Magoo's Place. The biker was Jason Espinosa (fifty-two) from San Antonio, a lone rider on his Suzuki V-Strom 650, taking a few days out from his life as a malware problem-solver, a job that helps with his great love: playing guitar with his C&W band, Wild Country.

After a good chat, lots of coffee and eggs, we went our separate ways. Just before we parted in the car park, we spoke about guns (I can't remember what got us onto the subject). To my surprise, Jason was carrying one, a handgun packed into his tank bag. I told him I didn't have one, and in all the time from Tierra del Fuego to here, right through South and Central America, I had never felt the need for one. I'm not sure he understood, because guns really are a part of life here, as I would soon find in Arizona.

29 APRIL 2023, TUCSON, ARIZONA

Between eighty and one hundred gun dealers, gun makers and sellers of anything and everything associated with guns, old and new, laid out their wares inside Tucson's Expo Centre at the weekend for Arizona City's annual Expo Gun Show 2023. Gun enthusiasts turned up in numbers, undeterred by the incongruous signs on the entrance doors saying No guns allowed inside. This wasn't exactly true, either, as several attendees brought weapons to sell, although they were inspected at the entrance for reassurance that they were not loaded or capable of being fired at that instant. And inside there were, literally, thousands of guns.

I parked my bike by a car with a windscreen heatshield that said Biden Senile Idiot. There was little overt politics at the event, however, except for the Libertarian Party stall opposite the entrance, proffering views that are in many instances too far off the scale for even the current iteration of the Republican Party. It claims, for instance, that Covid vaccines being distributed in Arizona are 'experimental' and therefore a 'crime against humanity ... to the magnitude that inspired the Nuremberg trials'.

As we queued to enter, the guy in front of me had a pump-action shotgun slung over his shoulder with a $450 price tag displayed prominently on it. Not much of a bargain, really, as they sell online new for $484 (according to TrueGunValue.com). It was a Remington 870 Wingmaster 12-gauge. Chatting to him later inside, I asked whether he had had any interest from buyers. He hadn't. I checked (not being an expert) that it was a pump-action gun. 'Sure is,' he replied. 'Takes five [cartridges], and if you need more than five, you're in trouble.'

Most of the gun enthusiasts were middle-aged white men, though there was a fair smattering of men in their twenties and thirties as well, and some women. A lot of the men looked the part: big beards, T-shirts with words like Freedom and the American flag emblazoned on them. Many appeared to be hunters and, as I had found since Texas, and all the way there across New Mexico, everyone was unfailingly polite and courteous.

'Where are you from?' asked Lonnie, who manned a stall of attractively laid out holsters I wanted to photograph. He had made them himself. I said I was from Ireland. 'Well, that's okay,' he replied. 'I was a cop in Dallas, and we had plenty of Irish there.'

Nearby, Adrian had an impressive display of what looked like second-hand guns from an earlier era. They were underfolder rifles, he said, showing me how the shoulder piece folded forward and tucked up under the rest of the weapon, making it more compact. They were Romanian and were designed originally for tank crews and paratroopers. His cache came from the Yugoslav Wars of the 1990s. The United Nations had apparently collected the weapons and stored them for eventual destruction, 'but something happened along the way', as he put it, and they reached the open market.

Adrian bought a container load of about 3,000, had them reassembled and made usable again and was selling them now for $1,249 apiece. 'Here in Arizona, people like them as truck guns, so if you're on your ranch and there's a coyote, this is real easy to grab,' he explained.

Mike from Arizona Arms was doing well with an AR semi-automatic pistol known as the Radical, which had, in filigree on the barrel, the words *Trump and MAGA* (Trumps's political slogan, 'Make America great again'). The gun on display was a striking gold colour.

'We have 'em in gold, blue, red, purple, green and dark earth. I think that's about all we have,' said Mike.

'Is it a good seller?' I asked.

'Absolutely,' he said ... $1,195 a pop.

The rifle most on display was, by a long measure, the AR-15. The 'AR' refers to Armalite, the US company that first made the gun in the 1950s and not (as is sometimes stated) 'assault rifle'. Known sometimes as 'America's rifle' because of its popularity (tens of millions are in circulation), it's hated by gun opponents, not least because it has been used in many mass shootings. These include the May 2022 murder of nineteen students and two teachers at a school in Uvalde, Texas; the murder, in March 2023, of three adults and three students in a school in Nashville, Tennessee; and the April shooting of five bank employees by a disgruntled member of staff in Louisville, Kentucky.

There were numerous displays of these rifles – sometimes set out on tables, with military precision, in neat rows, either lying flat or pointing upwards. The gunmakers Lifetime Precision of Arizona have their own versions of the AR-15 – the LPC-15 and the LPA-15 – selling for $1,399 and $899, respectively. As coincidence would have it, the company's Lee Dayley has a strong connection to Ireland, having lived in Rathmines in Dublin from 1989 to 1991. He worked with the Church of Jesus Christ of Latter-Day Saints (the Mormons) on Bushy Park Road in Terenure, proselytising for them on Grafton Street and outside Trinity College. 'What was the reception like?' I asked about his proselytising. 'Pretty good. Super nice,' he said, adding, however, that a lot of people were 'set in their ways'.

We chatted amiably about biking and what to see in Arizona before I asked him whether he felt there was any conflict between his business and his faith, between guns and God.

'I think that depends on how you utilise [the gun],' he replied. 'If it's defence for your family, it's okay. If it's for offensive [purposes], it's not compatible.' He also felt that there was a problem with how a 'mass shooting' was defined. 'They define mass shootings in a way that makes it look worse than it is,' he suggested. 'They define mass shootings as more than three dead.'

He felt mass shootings of students and teachers could be stopped if schools were treated like other government buildings, in which security staff manned entrances and people and bags were X-ray screened before being allowed in. 'That would fix it,' he said. Most people he knew bought AR rifles, and his own rival models, for target practice. 'And we in Arizona have a coyote problem,' he added.

Around the display tables, the array of weapons and paraphernalia on sale was extraordinary. There was a huge variety of handguns, for example, including Glocks (a Dublin gangland favourite); hunting shotguns; knuckle dusters; samurai swords; pen knives, with a concealed blade (Sometimes you just need to make a point, and these Pen Knives can SAVE your Life! said the sign); spare parts and repair tools; military-style clothing and camo gear; and ammunition – mountains of it. Steve had a display of knives the like of which I'd never seen. Joni and James had an impressive display of second-hand sights and holsters. Three fellows were making a detailed examination of a 1960s AR-15 SP1 for $3,000. 'I really want one of them,' said the younger of the three.

And there were the inevitable T-shirt and other souvenir offerings, with pro-gun messages, such as 'God Family Guns & Freedom'; 'In 1776 the British demanded our guns. We shot them'; 'The People will Protect the 2nd Amendment'; and 'The Right to Bear Arms – Your Approval is not Required'.

I spoke to one enthusiast and told him that no other country in the world had the same problem of mass shootings in shopping malls and schools. He responded, 'That's because we have more freedom in America.' At which point you realise – or at least I do – that there's really no point in continuing the conversation. So unhinged and irrational, and so devoid of an evidential base, is the pro-gun case as currently put that discussion is useless.

Two young men, Kylen and Cody, were buying an AR-10, a weapon that began life as a standard-issue NATO rifle. Kylen wanted it for hunting. 'It's, like, my fifth [gun],' he said. Why did he have any guns? I wondered. 'I work in a park store, on the south side of Tucson, and there's always people on drugs,' he said. Cody added, 'A couple of years ago, they did, like, a survey of south Tucson, and it was one of the most dangerous places in America to live. Neither man thought banning guns was a solution. 'They'd just come across the border,' said Cody, as Kylen filled out his background check form. Once they had the AR-10 (which they did less than ten minutes later), they were heading out to hunt mule deer.

At the stand of Distinctive Defence Strategy, I was looking at a handgun, a Masterpiece Mac II, with what appeared to be a silencer. The owner, James Gray, bounded over and pointed enthusiastically at various parts of the weapon and said, 'This, this, this and the case! Nine millimetres, thirty-two rounds – $599!'

'How could I buy?' I asked.

'Say you're from here. Show me your ID. I do a background check. It takes about five minutes, and you walk out with the gun,' he said.

Everyone I asked said much the same. The Firearms Transaction Record form has thirty-six questions, most of them tick-box answerable. Questions include: 'Are you a fugitive from justice?'; 'Have you ever been adjudicated as a mental defective?'; and 'Are you the subject of a court order [...] restraining you from harassing, stalking, or threatening your child or an intimate partner?' The applicant answers and, according to stall holders at the gun fair, approval from the FBI usually comes back in a matter of minutes.

You have to be twenty-one years old to buy beer in Arizona. I'm seventy, and every time I go to buy a beer in a shop, I'm asked to produce my ID.

30 APRIL 2023, TUCSON, ARIZONA

There is another Tucson, and I liked it. Mount Lemmon rises above the city, a little to the north-east. On the way up the mountain – I needed some wild scenery to clear my head after the gun show – I stopped at Windy Point, a beauty spot. It wasn't windy at all, but what a view! From Windy Point the mountain falls suddenly and steeply to the plain below where sits the city. The granite rock is bare at Windy Point and there are great big boulders, some of which appear as though they have been piled one on top of the other to create a sort of sea stack effect. Round here, they call them 'hoodoos', a word that must have been adapted from somewhere, or something, else. Anyway, there were a couple of guys getting ready to abseil down the sheer granite face of Windy Point, and I was trying to position myself to get a good photo of them when I came upon this other guy who seemed a bit anxious.

'I got a proposal going on here,' he blurted out to me, as though that was the most natural thing to say to a stranger navigating his way across a large spread of granite with a steep fall just inches away.

'Oh,' I think I said as the penny dropped.

The young man had spread out on the rock a white tablecloth on which he had placed a cooler box, with its lid open to show a display of bubbly bottles, flowers and a retro radio set playing a carefully chosen song. He also had a friend with him, who was on lookout duty. 'She's coming, she's coming,' I think the friend said as he, and I, withdrew into some bushes.

Down the gravel path came a young woman in a white knee-length flouncy dress and cowboy boots, directed by another friend, a female accomplice. She rounded the corner, saw her boyfriend and the spread he had laid on, heard the music and immediately started to cry. He pulled a green ring box from his back pocket, got down on one knee and said what had to be said. They hugged, and some family members nearby, his mum and dad, I think, maybe a brother or sister as well, cheered and applauded.

'I had my suspicions,' said the bride to be, 'but I didn't dare hope.'

It was a lovely scene and really hit me because it was so normal, so natural and so in contrast with a lot of what I'd been seeing and thinking about here, as well as in Texas, since arriving in the United States from Mexico two weeks before. It set firm in my mind something I'd begun to think about earlier in the day: I wanted to write about the other Tucson ... the one that is calm, normal, caring and concerned about the sort of things people ought to be concerned about.

It began when I returned for the second day to the Five Points Market and Restaurant, a place I had stumbled upon the day before. So named because it's on one of the corners where five roads intersect, the restaurant has a nice industrial chic feel. There's a small patio out front with trees to give shade and, inside, there's lots of space in a large, completely open-plan spread of tables and chairs, with coffee bar on one side and open kitchen behind. And all round are displays of wholesome food.

Five Points also has something of a mission: it seeks, as it says on its website, to 'challenge the idea that profitability in the service industry necessitates the exploitation of labor, resources and agriculture'. To that end, it pays employees a living wage (as opposed to having them depend on discretionary tips). It pays for their health insurance as well and sources products locally. I immediately felt comfortable there, in part, in suppose, because the other early-morning breakfasters seemed to be 'people like me', as the saying goes. They spoke, dressed and behaved in a way that seemed normal to me. Reflecting my own prejudices, everything about the place and the customers said 'liberal', whereas so many other places said 'conservative' or 'Trump' or 'angry', or all three.

There's a bit of gentrification going on in this area, certainly ... Starting my second day's visit, I was sitting at the service counter, waiting for my coffee and eggs, when the guy next to me started to chat. He was Jamie Beatty and turned out to be the general sales manager for Pacific Edge, wine and spirit distributers based in Phoenix, the state capital. He was in Tucson for a mezcal festival, and we got on famously swapping mezcal stories. Jamie invited me to come later in the day to the industry show at Maynards, the best restaurant in town, according to what I had read earlier.

Just then, another fellow joined us. 'Is that your bike outside?' he asked. I said it was, and he was amazed. 'I couldn't believe it when I saw the IRL plate,' he said. He was Martin Coll, a Scotsman now living in Sierra Vista in southern Arizona, right down close to the border, and he had a big connection with Ireland. He co-owns M&M Cycling and is a retired professional racer. 'I used to race with Stephen Roche and Paul Kimmage,' he told me. I said I knew of them both, of course, and that Kimmage, being a journalist, probably knows my name, as I do his. Martin is Glaswegian, but his family have strong connections with Co. Donegal. And so we chatted about cycling and Ireland and places to see and things to do in Arizona.

A while later, Kevin, the barista, started chatting to me. 'We're a little oasis,' he said when I asked him about Five Points. Like the restaurant, there was a bit more to Kevin than making coffee. He spends one day a week helping No More Deaths, a group that places water bottles in the desert on the Arizona side of the border with Mexico so that undocumented migrants don't die of thirst. They also put out beans, socks and blankets (the desert can be ferociously cold at night). It's literally a random act of kindness. Much of the work of No More Deaths is done at Arivaca, a village about 18km from the border, Kevin said, where the people 'don't want to be calling Border Patrol, and there's also a lot of gun-toting libertarian types there, and they don't want them either. So we go.' Before speaking with Kevin, I had watched a local TV news report about another group that leaves barrels of water out for migrants but has to contend with anti-migrant vandals who puncture them so the water drains out.

A safe place for nature is the goal of Russ McSpadden, an environmental activist I met the day before. I got to know Russ on social media about three years before when researching this trip, and I really wanted to meet him. He works for the Center for Biological Diversity, a conservation organisation founded in Arizona in 1989, and spends much of his time monitoring the well-being of various species, large and small, and guarding public lands in the border region.

'The place has been under attack for a very long time,' he said of the border lands. 'The [border] wall is going to rewrite evolutionary history.' He pointed out that animals on different sides of the border 'aren't separate populations [but] we have separated them.' The authorities 'do a lot of damage just in the construction process. This is one holistic landscape, and it is just cut in half.' The wall, which the centre has fought 'tooth and nail since the Bush era', he said, cost between $20 million and $40 million a mile to build. 'It's utterly ineffective – people come through it [by cutting the posts] and come over it. It's just a wall, and it addresses nothing, in my opinion.'

Animal movement corridors have been interrupted by the wall. All species have been affected, including the black bear, the Mexican grey wolf, mule deer, jaguars, mountain lions, snails and waterborne organisms. The concrete footings of the fence extend some five feet into the ground. Because of human activity, aquifers have been damaged, to the extent that 'springs are now on life support', Kevin said.

Later, I heard another environmentalist say that water used to be reached at a ground depth of 120m, but now there's no water until 304m down – an effect, I understand, of climate change. Russ told me that, on one stretch of the border, shipping containers were used to construct a solid metal 'wall' 3.5 miles long that prevented the cross-border movement of jaguars roaming on more than 800,000 acres of habitat critical to their survival. The containers have since been removed.

The Centre uses the law – the Endangered Species Act and the Clean Water Act – to fight its cases. But Russ said that the Real ID Act, emergency legislation introduced after the terrorist attacks in New York in 2001, 'allows the Department of Homeland Security to waive all federal and state laws to push through wall/fence construction. In other cases, they would have to research and make decisions [taking into account the effect] on water, species and Indigenous peoples, [but] all public safety laws you can imagine are waived.'

I asked Russ whether he was optimistic. 'When I get out into the wild, I'm optimistic,' he said. 'I have cameras, and in one canyon I can identify twelve individual mountain lions over several months. I'm optimistic because I have to be.'

*

Unexpectedly, the mezcal fair – the 18th Annual Agave Heritage Festival, to give it its proper name – turned out to have a mission as well. There were maybe a dozen stalls at Maynards on what used to be a train station platform. At one stall were the agricultural ecologist Gary Paul Nabhan and David Suro Piñera, joint authors of *Agave Spirits: The Past, Present and Future of Mezcals* (2023). Nabhan is also a Franciscan brother. Piñera, who was born in Mexico, is a restaurateur and founder of the Tequila Interchange Project.

I had a tiny sip of a Rancho Tepúa spirit, offered to me by Jamie, who had invited me to the fair, but, riding a motorbike, I sadly had to decline any more. He, like everyone else there, was full of enthusiasm for the Mexican spirit and its export potential. Near his Pacific Edge stall, the family behind the Los Cantiles 1905 bacanora (like mezcal, also distilled from the agave plant) were on a mission.

'We're trying to rescue our culture,' said Omar Acuna from Nácori Chico, a small town in the Mexican state of Sonora. 'The whole project is about trying to incentivise the new generation to take back what is about to be lost.' By which he meant the myriad things than can be produced from the agave plant and other local resources. Todd Hanley, owner of Maynards, said the fair is about 'trying to promote cross-border business fertilisation with Sonora.'

In a Q&A session, Nabhan and Piñera extolled the potential of mezcal production in fusing tradition and innovation. 'It's like a jazz ensemble,' Nabhan said. 'They're playing off each other.'

Afterwards, I set off, California bound, invigorated by listening to people who were infused with optimism, not threatened by difference and the 'other', and who talked not about barriers but about sharing landscape, culture and business opportunities.

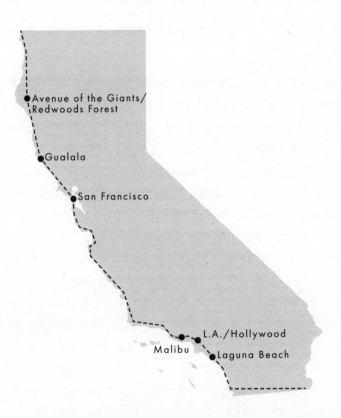

Avenue of the Giants/
Redwoods Forest

Gualala

San Francisco

L.A./Hollywood
Malibu
Laguna Beach

UNITED STATES

CALIFORNIA

AFTER TUCSON I RODE STRAIGHT WEST TOWARDS SAN DIEGO,
California, spending one night camping in Yuma, on the border with
Arizona. That evening, something happened that I believe is a regular
occurrence there: a mighty sandstorm blew up from further west. Visibility
was down to about 100m, which made the busy freight trains of the Pacific
Union line linking Los Angeles and Texas seem all the more ghostly.
During the night, they wailed their sirens at every level crossing, but you
could see nothing of them. You could only hear that mournful sound.

Next day, I saw the source of the storm: about 80km of pure sand desert that
got whipped up in late-afternoon winds caused, I assume, by the intense
heat earlier in the day.

San Diego appeared suddenly after I crossed the Cleveland National Forest, which was more upland scrub than anything else. Rather than enter the city, as time was cracking on and I needed to find somewhere to bed down, I skirted round it, finding myself soon on Highway 101, El Camino Real and the Pacific Coastal Highway.

A bit like the Wild Atlantic Way on Ireland's west coast, El Camino Real links places of Spanish heritage along the southern California coast that have existed for a long time. The road has been there for ages too – it's just been given a name. Highway 101 is also the coastal road and is sometimes El Camino Real at the same time. Every now and then, the road becomes the Pacific Coastal Highway, which is also known as Route 1. Confusing? A bit, but who cares! The way north is clear enough, and it skirts through attractive settlements and beautiful coastline. So far, I had gone only from Oceanside through San Clemente, Dana Point and Laguna Beach. The overwhelming characteristic there is upmarket style in shops, cars, homes – and money – lots of money – and lots of retirees.

In San Clemente, something I had noticed first in Texas crystallised for me: when I crossed the border from Mexico, and for the following few days, all the cafes and small restaurants I frequented were staffed almost entirely by older people – people from their early to mid-sixties and onwards, well into their seventies. In San Clemente I stopped at a roadside eatery that had a bit of character to it. It was the Sugarshack Cafe on the Camino Real, and it promised a good breakfast. There were about eight people working inside – waiting and checkout staff, plus those in the kitchen – and I think all were elderly. I looked at them, as I had others previously, and thought that they should be retired and enjoying their latter years, pursuing hobbies and the like, playing with grandchildren or whatever. But here they were, slaving away, mostly for tips. And then it struck me: most of them had to work because they lacked sufficient income, from either their social security pension or their occupational pension, if they had one. Of course, some may have worked simply because they liked the routine and didn't have other interests; but many, I suspect, didn't have that choice.

I sat in the Sugarshack Cafe eating breakfast and reading the *Orange County Register* when a story about Gene James caught my eye. It was a typical local news report. Gene, who was sixty-nine and had served on San Clemente City Council since 2019, and who was mayor in 2022, was retiring to Wyoming. Being on the council had been an 'honor of a lifetime and an incredible privilege', he told the reporter. He went on to express the sort of criticisms many aging people have when the world moves on: everything had changed in San Clemente. There was so much crime and congestion and a 'tolerance of vagrants'. He yearned for his and his wife's second home in Wyoming and its views of the Rockies and for their own water rights and the 'ability to live off the land'. So many – me included – could identify with that. But the kicker reason was the one that appeared really to galvanise Gene to leave California. He wanted 'most importantly, to own and possess firearms without fear of a state with intentions to seize them.' I sat there bewildered – again – at the gun madness in the States.

At Laguna Beach, a bit further on, a big sign caught my eye. Dissent, it said, and with it was a large poster in red, black and cream of a female face that reminded me of the Czech art nouveau painter and illustrator Alphonse Mucha. The sign was on the side of the Laguna Art Museum, and I thought I'd have a look.

Inside was a wonderful exhibition of posters by Shepard Fairey, the American artist who achieved much wider fame with his 'Hope' poster of Barack Obama, which came to define (visually) Obama's 2008 campaign. The exhibition at Laguna Beach was entitled 'Facing the Giant – Three Decades of Dissent: Shepard Fairey.' I counted thirty posters, and they were striking – mostly in the same style and using only red, black and cream. Several highlighted women's issues, others the cause of equality for black Americans. Others still promoted general equality. They have something of the flavour of socialist realism about them, or, as the gallery puts it, 'His bold, iconic images always convey a clear message, often depicting the struggle of oppression as a human experience and celebrating those who fight for change.'

They were well worth stopping for. There were many other beautiful, more traditional paintings in the gallery too – landscapes and coastal scenes in oil.

5 MAY 2023, HOLLYWOOD

Like so many roads through US cities, Santa Monica Boulevard goes on and on and on and for the most part is terribly unremarkable, but it grows eventually into Beverley Hills and, quite without warning, one side is suddenly all residential. On each side of Rodeo Drive (I assume it's *the* Rodeo Drive) there's a network of streets at right angles in which the front lawns and footpaths are manicured to within an inch of their lives. Strangely though, given the famous address, the homes are not the squillion-dollar over-the-top mansions I had expected: they were modest enough two-storey suburban houses, although in a hard-to-beat location and with roads lined with those extraordinarily tall palm trees you see in the movies. They're all beautifully kept, with flash cars purring in the driveways. But, really, I've seen flashier pads in parts of Blackrock, Foxrock and Greystones.

The boulevard careers on through West Hollywood, and at last comes to the junction with Highland Avenue – my target. I turned left and trundled up past the Sunset Boulevard junction to Hollywood Boulevard and the Walk of Fame, where the footpath slabs are memorials to stars, some great and enduring, some long forgotten and some notorious. Each pink-coloured slab has a name in brass embedded in it and a symbol relating to the honoured person's career – a TV, record, microphone or film camera. Where I stopped – by the Hard Rock Cafe, the TCL Chinese Theatre and the Dolby Theatre – there are slabs for Matthew Broderick, Sandra Bullock, Simon Cowell, Peter Frampton, Jerry Lewis, Barbara Walters, Britney Spears, Antonio Banderas and Mario Lanza, as well as (who could forget) Bill Stern, Susan Lucci, Billy Daniels and (unfortunately we can't yet forget) Donald Trump.

'Why Trump?' I asked a man making a living from taking pictures of tourists. 'Aw, man,' he said. 'I just don't know. Hard to figure.' And then we saw the little brass TV symbol under his name and supposed it's because of his TV series *The Apprentice.*

A busker was strumming a guitar and playing Eric Clapton, droning on about cocaine, which I guess was situation-appropriate. Another bloke in a Freddy Krueger mask and outfit was wandering about looking a bit disconsolate. Maybe it was because Spiderman was getting all the attention from the kids (and hence the few dollars from their parents for having his picture taken with them). Like, who wants to be seen with Freddy Krueger? Batman, accompanied by Wonder Woman, hove into view, and I took a pic. He was over to me in a flash, fist-bumping and 'Awesome biking!' me. Wonder Woman said nothing. I asked if I could take a photo of them close up. 'Sure,' they said, and struck a pose – and then looked for the dollars, which was fair enough. I opened my wallet and, to my horror, saw that it was all $20 and $50 bills. Wonder Woman gave a little squeak of joy. But then I found a five and heaved a sigh of relief. They seemed happy.

Just then a swarm of cyclists came down the boulevard – on both sides, taking over the whole road. Tourist buses and everyone else just had to stop and let it happen. There were guys doing wheelies all over the place and whooping and hollering. 'What's all this?' I asked one of them. 'We're just cycling, man. That's it, just cycling.' Fair enough …

I wanted to get up to the sign – the sign – but it took a while as I got lost in Studio City, where Universal, Warner Bros. and NBC all make their presence felt. But eventually I found Ledgewood Drive which, with Mulholland, winds this way and that up the hillside to the oversized letters. Ledgewood Drive is lined with nice homes but is hardly millionaire's row. Up close, or as close as one can get, which is about 100m below them, the letters of the HOLLYWOOD sign didn't look as large as they did from a distance, which was a bit odd. The hillside was scrubby and arid. The letters were impaled into the hill on stilts, and above them was a cluster of masts and reflective dishes, I assumed for phones and the like.

A little way down Mulholland, there was a patch of bare ground and some parking spaces and lots of people taking pictures. I took one of a young woman having hers taken by a child. She asked me to take one of them both on her phone. I did and then rode off back to the coast ...

Another one off the bucket list.

9–16 MAY 2023, SAN FRANCISCO

San Francisco is ridiculously beautiful. At every turn, up every hill, across every vista by the bay, the city is just stunning. And it's not a forced beauty. It's not beating you over the head like, say, Hollywood – 'Look at me, look at me!' – and yet you can't take your eyes off it. There's little that's vulgar about San Francisco, and there's much that's cool and classy – and an awful lot that makes one stop and linger to admire. It's laid back and not precious: the city just jogs along doing its thing. And if you don't like this bit, there'll be another bit round the corner that you'll love. I had only a few days in the place but was spinning. It's not as though I saw everything one must see as a visitor. In fact, I barely scratched the surface, but I still had the strong feeling that, if I were in my twenties, this is a city that would pull me towards it like a high-powered magnet.

On my first morning I went walkabout up Lombard Street and found myself at Sterling Park, an unkempt square abutting Hyde Street. A plaque at the entrance explained that it was dedicated to the poet George Sterling (1869–1926), of whom I had not heard. He was pally with a writer I like, Jack London. Sterling became the unofficial poet laureate of the city through his romantic verse, and a sample of it on a bronze plate at the park stayed with me as I explored over the following days.

> *Tho the dark be cold and blind,*
> *Yet her sea-fog's touch is kind,*
> *And her mightier caress*
> *Is joy and the pain thereof;*
> *And great is thy tenderness,*
> *O cool, grey city of love!*

'Cool, grey city' – as I read the line, a cable car trundled along Hyde, sounding its bell, passengers standing on the running board, hanging on as the little wooden wonder slipped down towards Fisherman's Wharf. I tried (and failed) to get a decent shot with Alcatraz Island in the background. But the scene – the cable car, the instantly familiar street and, of course, the vista out onto the bay – suddenly had me thinking, 'Wow! I'm in San. Fran. Sisco!' I jumped on a car heading in the opposite direction and soon found myself in Union Square, which is the end of the Powell–Mason and Powell–Hyde lines (there's one other, the California Street line). At Union Square there's a turntable, and they spin the cars round and send them on their way back to the wharf.

I didn't return immediately, though, because there was a fantastic busker singing for the cable car queue. Even though it was sunny, he looked cold and wore a beanie, a zipped-up black anorak and floppy, pyjama-like trousers, but he also wore new-looking white trainers. He wore raggedy knitted fingerless gloves, and there was something fragile about him, not helped by some missing teeth and a general demeanour that suggested that he was a vagrant or shelter-dweller – though he may have been neither. Despite this, he had some trappings of modernity: a mobile phone mounted on a tripod that was linked to Spotify, or some other playlist, and a speaker that allowed him in effect to perform karaoke. He had a terrific voice and rattled off a string of foot-tapping Motown numbers almost as good as the originals. Between him and the queue, there was an open bag on the footpath, and I can tell you it was bulging with dollar bills. I never got his name, but he got some of my money, and deservedly so.

I took the tram back to the wharf side. The cars run singly, but there's one along every few minutes or so. The guys who operate them should be on a bonus from the city's tourism promoters. They have that quintessentially American way of talking: firm but friendly. To someone maybe blocking the hop-on, hop-off entrance, they'll say, 'Sir! Step back into the carriage.' Or to someone standing on the running board and leaning out a bit too far to get a good shot of an oncoming car, there'll be 'On the left side! Mind the oncoming car! Don't want to lose no passengers here, ma'am.' They're not really scolding you, but at the same time you know they mean business.

Each car has two people running it, the grip operator – known as the gripman or simply the grip – and a conductor. The conductor inspects tickets or collects fares and jumps off and back on again at stops, making sure passengers alight or join the car safely. One is never entirely sure what the grip does, except that it involves a subtle blend of operating a lever that grips a cable running beneath the street, thereby pulling the car along, and applying a brake to prevent it running away. But it works, and he and the conductor manage to mix serious attention to the detail of their work with playful banter. An alighting passenger laden down with shopping may well be greeted by the conductor with 'Yo, ma'am! You didn't bring one for me?'

One evening, while walking to meet a new pal in a bar, I spied a grip or conductor lounging in a stationary cable car at the Taylor Street terminus. He had a fat cigar, and I asked him how many he smoked a day. 'Oh, this'll do me for at least two days,' he said, explaining that he smoked it only a bit at a time. I asked if I could take his photo. 'Sure,' he said, 'you go right ahead.' He looked the essence of cool!

I went on a bike ride round the city, including Chinatown and over the Bay Bridge to Berkeley, returning via the Golden Gate. I didn't stay long in Berkeley, just long enough to have some iced tea and a small mountain of delicious brisket in one of those food halls with multiple outlets. The way back round was over the Richmond Bridge, which gave me the willies. It's extremely long (8.9km) and high (56m), and on a bike you feel exposed. Unnervingly, in places where the road surface is a metal grill, you can also see right down to the water.

The Golden Gate Bridge was shrouded in San Francisco's famous sea fog when I eventually approached it – first by descending to Fort Baker (the former army camp on the northern shore at the foot of the bridge, which is now mainly a Coast Guard base, a few homes and a hotel) and then, still not having crossed over, from above, up in the Marin Headlands, where one gets a panoramic view of the bridge and the city beyond. The fog sneaked in like a cat, blanketing the sea and the bridge in a moving, frothy misty-grey. It changes shape every few seconds, and when it's there, so huge is the bridge itself that it affects the behaviour of the fog, forcing it up as it pours into the bay, before falling again. And as it envelops the area, fog horns on the bridge – three mounted on the middle pier and two on the south tower pier – blow their ghostly warning to shipping. I love the sound of it, and the look of it, and I got some half-decent photos, I think.

'You know the fog has a name,' said Rebecca, a Jewish cyclist (she told me she was Jewish within seconds of us getting chatting at one of the Marin viewing points).

'Eh, I didn't actually,' I replied. 'What is it?'

'Karl with a K,' she said.

'Why Karl?' I asked.

'Because that's his name,' she said, a totally brilliant answer to which there is no adequate response.

Crossing the bridge was uneventful – largely because Karl had stolen the view. But, up close, the orange towers from which the cables holding up the suspended roadway flow still appeared like giants in the mist. I rode across and took a right into the Presidio area, finding myself eventually in a small district named Sea Cliff. It's a warren of narrow roads and cul-de-sacs lined with some lovely homes, some of them backing onto cliffs above Baker Beach and China Beach and with views over the Pacific. I got off the bike at the end of one of the cul-de-sacs where there were steps down onto the beach. Standing there beside his car – a long thing like an old Jag that might have been a Buick – was Dave. He was wearing shades and a bush hat with the sides pinned up, which reminded me of Dennis Hopper in *Easy Rider*. He used to be a marine (Dave, that is) but was now in construction. Some of these houses – and they weren't mansions, just well-maintained two-storey semi-detached houses in a great location – must be worth three or four million, I ventured. 'More like twenty,' said Dave. He went on to tell me that Robin Williams's mother lived up the road (pointing towards Sea Cliff Avenue). And Sharon Stone 'had a place right there,' he said, pointing.

'We've had Spielberg too – had 'em all.'

After having a look at the beach, I rode off again, up the avenue, stopping soon after to take pictures of some of the houses. That was when I met Amanda from Islington in London, via her dog. We chatted – Amanda and me, that is – and before long she said, 'I've got to call Joe [her partner]. He's going to want to meet you.' And that's how I got to know Joe, another former marine and now head of global workplace security at Pinterest. He's a Honda and Triumph Bonneville rider, a frequent visitor to Ireland (where Pinterest has its European head office) and all-round nice guy. Next day, we met again in Sweetie's, a small neighbourhood bar in North Beach, famous for its art exhibitions and jazz nights. Joe and I talked bikes, careers in the marines, US politics, wives, pals and the Wild Atlantic Way.

I spent much of the next couple of days writing, exploring and realising that it's not just areas like Pacific Heights, Russian Hill, Cow Hollow, Marina and other parts of the city close to downtown and Fisherman's Wharf that have achingly beautiful buildings that are lived-in homes. The delightful clapboard houses, each a little different from their neighbour, most of them treasured and well maintained, are almost everywhere – certainly as far from the centre as Haight-Ashbury (of 1968 Summer of Love fame). They make walking along every residential street a joy, every building a delight to behold.

Before I left San Francisco, I spent a couple of days downtown in the Tenderloin district, observing homeless people and drug addicts (many of them living in tents on the sidewalk), and the people who are trying to help them. It was a fantastically depressing scene – people whose lives had been wrecked by addiction to fentanyl, a drug which is wreaking havoc across America. I spent a week in the hostel, exploring and writing, and on my last morning in the city, I went for breakfast in Mel's ...

17 MAY 2023, SAN FRANCISCO

If you're ever staying on Lombard Street as I did, the best place to have breakfast is Mel's Drive-In at Cow Hollow. It's at the Marina end of the street, which itself leads on to the Golden Gate Bridge about two miles away. I just knew that Mel's was going to be good, so I left it till my last morning in this impossibly beautiful city.

It did not disappoint.

I swung open the entrance door and walked inside. Carlos was there, behind the till. 'Hi, and welcome to Mel's,' he said. I was enveloped immediately in a wonderworld of Americana: stainless steel, chrome and more chrome and, facing me, right inside the door, a Wurlitzer jukebox, all lit up and banging out period-appropriate music. In front of the bar counter there was a row of one-legged bar stools, with the backsides of occupants rippling over the seat edges. All along the counter are little mini-Wurlitzers on which patrons can choose their favourite background music – Hank Williams, Roy Orbison, Buddy Holly, Frank Sinatra, Johnny Cash and, of course, Elvis (he lives nearby, I believe).

The bar counter runs front to back down the centre of the restaurant, which faces onto Lombard Street. Out the side is a car park. Years ago, waiting staff on roller skates used to serve patrons sitting in their cars. Not any more, sadly. The other wall, inside the restaurant, is covered in blow-up black-and-white photos from the 1940s and '50s. The men are all heavy overcoats and fedoras; the women have long baggy trousers and wear sunglasses. The scenes mostly show people arriving at or leaving places – nightclubs or political gatherings, maybe – or standing by a car, all bulbous fenders and oozing cool.

At the back is the kitchen. The hob hood has sunburst polished-steel panels. The chefs busy themselves cranking out plates of pancakes, eggs – 'Over easy, sir? Comin' up!' – bacon and toast.

I asked Carlos about the origins of the diner. 'The first Mel's opened on December twenty-third, 1947, at 140 South Van Ness,' he said. The diner featured in George Lucas's film *American Graffiti* (1973), whose Burger City was actually Mel's Drive-In. Mel's is even on the promotional poster. Competition in the 1970s drove Mel's out of business, but Steven Weiss, a son of one of the founders, revived it, and there are now eight outlets, in San Francisco, Hollywood and Los Angeles.

Carlos – Carlos Alexander Martínez – runs this Mel's and does a smooth job orchestrating the seating and serving. The place was buzzing with locals and tourists, though on that Wednesday morning at 9:15 it was mostly locals, I think.

Just then, Jessica sat down beside me at the bar. That's Jessica Quinlan (forty-three). 'I'm from Missouri,' she said just after ordering the first of what was to become two large glasses of champagne. 'I'm out here for a bunch of concerts,' she said, and we fell – plunged, might be a better description – into conversation. I was so sucked in to the riot that is Jessica's rock-and-roll life that my eggs and hash browns got cold, and I never even got round to trying the toast.

'Last Thursday we [Jessica and her boyfriend, Ben – 'he grows weed'] left Columbus, Missouri, and went to see Billy Idol in Kansas City and then went to the Rose Bowl in Pasadena for the Just Like Heaven festival. Tomorrow, we're going to see Gary Numan. I don't know if you know him. He sang the song "Cars". [I told her I knew it.] That's in Petaluma, California. Saturday, we're at the Cruel World Festival [back at the Rose Bowl]. Wednesday we have the Cure – I can't wait for that!'

Jessica used to be a dental assistant and at some stage also had a restaurant and an art gallery. 'But now I'm on disability [$1,400 a month, she said]. My ex-boyfriend tried to kill me. I had, like, kidney and liver failure, and I have vocal cord damage,' she said, explaining her husky voice.

'Are you going to have breakfast?' I asked.

'Nah, just champagne,' she answered. 'I'm going to take a shower and head to LA.' She was staying at the nearby Chelsea Inn Hotel, a choice on her part that was preordained by the script.

'You like champagne in the morning?' I asked.

'I do,' she said emphatically. 'I like beer too.'

We then had a political conversation. Jessica loathes Trump and all that comes with him – all that he represents about America right now and the way he and his supporters are affecting everything. 'They want women pregnant and in the kitchen,' she said. 'They don't want the gay people. I live in a country where so many people say, "We live in the greatest country." I'm sorry, you can pull a duck's neck as long as you want, but you're still not going to have a swan.'

For that phrase alone, I will love Jessica for ever. She downed what was left of her second glass and went off to her Chelsea hotel.

Within a day or two, I was heading back over the Golden Gate Bridge, this time going north, up 101, but then back onto the coast-hugging famed Highway 1 towards the redwoods. San Francisco will live long and fondly in my memory.

20 MAY 2023, GUALALA

The coast of central California as one progresses north takes one's breath away. It's ragged with cliffs and inlets where the Pacific – blue and sparkling on that sunny early-summer day – has carved out bay after little bay, and the land rushes down from the ridge of mountains parallel to the sea. a bottle of wine and a tin of something or other for dinner, knowing that wherever I found to camp probably wouldn't have a shop. As I got off the bike, a fellow approached me and started chatting – about biking, about the area and about what was I doing. And within a sentence or two, he was inviting me back to his house and suggesting that I could drink my wine there. I needn't worry about finding a campsite because I could sleep the night at his place as well.

He seemed normal, pleasant – and sane. But I still accepted his invitation by joking that, if I came back to his house, we'd both find out which one of us was the axe murderer. We laughed. But David (seventy-six) – and his fiancée, Shao-ying – turned out to be the sort of gracious, kind and interesting hosts who make casual and random twenty-four-hour encounters among the many things that make independent travel worthwhile.

I followed David's red Toyota pickup truck a couple of miles north up the coast to Anchor Bay and to his and Shao-ying's home on Fish Rock Road, a narrow road that was at a right angle to the coast and that went slightly up into the hills. A wooden name sign over the front door porch read Enchanted. And it was indeed enchanting – a beautifully designed and maintained timber home that backs onto a redwood forest, where the ground plunges into a small steep-sided ravine so that the entire house seems suspended amid the trees.

What is suspended among the trees is what David calls his 'Ewok outpost', named after the small furry creature in Star Wars that inhabits Endor, the fictional woods on the Moon. David's outpost is what my wife would call a 'gin platform'. It's a timber deck with seating bolted into the trunks of three large redwoods six metres up and from which the ground falls away almost vertically. Sitting there drinking Pepsi (as we did at least initially) was like sitting mid-air in the middle of the forest. Constructing it was 'probably the best money I've spent in the last thirty years', David said. He was a retired environmental compliance officer at Berkeley College and later at the San Francisco Medical Center, and he came here every day just to relax and watch the forest.

He bought four acres of it in 1977. The redwoods are everything you would expect: tall beyond belief, great, sturdy trunks reaching perhaps 30m, maybe 45m, ramrod-straight into the sky. At the bottom of the ravine there's a stream. The forest floor is covered in ferns and small flowering plants. In 2014 the home adjoining David's forest came up for sale, and he was able to buy it and decamp there for ever. As he said, when you're inside the house 'you feel you're in the forest rather than living next to it.'

The house is essentially a shingle-clad rectangle built on the shoulder of the valley and parallel to it. Picture windows at the rear bring the forest right into the house. It's three storeys, but because it takes full advantage of the steep-sided valley, it appears from the road to sit low, almost like a bungalow. It was built by the Californian architect, designer, muralist and painter Millard Sheets (1907–89). He earned his reputation designing large statement buildings for the Savings and Loan Bank in California, and during the Second World War he designed aviation school buildings in California, Arizona and Texas. He also designed huge mosaics for buildings and promotional posters for Trans World Airlines (TWA) and other companies in the travel business, such as American President Lines. And he did well financially from property dealings along the California coast near Anchor Bay.

The second owner after Sheets was another David. 'He was a psychic,' said the current David. 'He said he lived in the seventh dimension and was trying to progress to the twelfth. He was a little out there.' Well, it is California ...

The main living room, onto which the entrance door opens, is all windows to the forest and made of timber but not so dense that it's suffocating. The ceiling is as high as the roof, and so the room, with an open-plan dining area and kitchen, feels huge. I sat there as Shao-ying and David rustled up a delicious meal of ribs and an Asian chicken soup, which I suspect owed much to Shao-ying's Taiwanese background. We drank wine and, joined by neighbours David and Cindy, swapped stories of travel, life and politics.

Next morning, Shao-ying, an acupuncturist, showed me how to sit and stretch my spine, exercising each individual vertebra. David then whisked me off further up the coast to show me Bowling Ball Beach, so named because of the large spherical sandstone rocks that emerge out of cliffs that are being eroded. Movements in the Earth's crust upended the originally horizontal sandstone into vertical cliffs. This left parallel lines that look like they could be bowling lanes, hence, with the spherical stones, the name of the beach. David said there are only three such beaches: this one, another in Montana and a third in New Zealand.

The sea erosion is so severe that the days are numbered for several clifftop homes – all million-dollar places, in a stable seaside location – that will be rendered worthless. A little further along the road, we stopped at Alder Creek, an apparently humdrum small valley with a bridge over a stream that runs into the sea and a few ramshackle timber farm buildings. The land of the northern side of the bridge is part of the North American Tectonic Plate, while the land on the southern side is the Pacific Plate. And so I crossed directly over the infamous San Andreas Fault, that great rupture in the Earth's crust whose two sides are moving in opposite directions. Earth scientists predict that California will eventually sever its attachment to the rest of the US and sail off into the Pacific.

'Are there ever earthquakes?' I asked David.

'Oh, for sure. There was one a couple of weeks back.'

'Did you feel it?'

'For sure! Seemed like everything jumped a foot.'

Further along the coast still, we stopped for a goodbye sandwich at Elk, where the local garage and the small grocery store and cafe were straight out of central casting Americana. The garage has been going since 1901 and is still run by the Matson family. They have had several dealerships, including for Studebaker cars, a vintage poster which has pride of place inside the hardware and general store attached to the functioning garage and towing service. I bought a pamphlet of local poetry, and we got two paninis from the grocery (a pastrami and a smoked ham and pepperoncini), retiring to eat them sitting on a wooden bench overlooking the foaming turquoise Pacific.

I rode on to Eureka. How can one repay such spontaneous friendship and generosity as that shown by David and Shao-ying? I guess simply by saying thanks and offering the same in return.

25 MAY 2023, HUMBOLDT REDWOODS STATE PARK

Bikers and other travellers are wont to pronounce about Great Roads of the World. Well, California's coast road – sometimes identified as Route 1, sometimes as Route 101, which runs right up into Oregon and Washington state – is surely one of them. In northern California, where R1 leaves the coast and merges with the R101, part of it passes through the Humboldt Redwoods State Park, where, parallel to it, is what is called the Avenue of the Giants. It's only a little over 48km in length but this truly is one of the great roads of the world – not so much for the road itself but for what is all around it.

California's famed redwood forests are like cathedrals of nature. They show the sheer scale of things that can grow out of the soil if the conditions are right and they're left to their own devices. The redwoods love the coastal climate. The winters are cold, and in the summer, balmy sunshine is mixed with Pacific mists that drift inland and regularly drench the forests. Some of the redwoods are thousands of years old; some have trunks that, at their base, are several metres in diameter. They look like spears, a multitude of sentinels standing as tall as the eye can see. Their needles are tiny, much smaller than the average Scots pine needles familiar to us in Ireland, and the trees typically don't have many lower branches, so there's room for growth on the forest floor for ferns and other smaller plants. These really are coastal rainforests, full of lush growth and strength.

The Avenue of the Giants is narrow – one lane only in either direction for most of it – and full of bends. The redwoods extend right up to the edge of the road, so you ride carefully. Any contact with the trees would probably be fatal because the trunks are hard as concrete. The avenue hugs the banks of the Eel River, which appeared in flashes between the trunks as I rode. The water looked alternately turquoise and silver, or sometimes a frothy white where there were rocks. Sunlight streamed through the upper reaches of the trees, and the whole thing was like looking at nature through a zoetrope, the Victorian spinning drum with side slits showing objects that appear to move with the spin.

There's a sign at a place named Leggett that says Drive-Thru Tree, so I pulled in to the nearby petrol station and shop for a coffee break. There were two other bikers there, Kyle Koshman (forty-seven) and John Renquist (seventy-one), both living elsewhere in California. Kyle was riding an Africa Twin CRF 1100, while John was riding a KTM Adventure 1190. Kyle emerged from the shop with the advice, gleaned apparently from someone inside, that when we went down to the drive-through tree, we should say, 'Shelby sent us,' and we'd probably get in free. It's on private land and the owners have been making a good living from tourists for years. The usual fee is $15. None of us had any idea who, or what, Shelby is or was. But what the hell? We rode off together, down to the entrance and, lo and behold, 'Shelby sent us' worked and we were just waved through!

The tree is vast, probably fully three times the width of a car. A large square hole, or tunnel, was carved out of the centre of the trunk in 1937 by woodsmen working for the owners, Charlie and Hazel Underwood, whose family owns the tree still. The tree is alive and apparently thriving, despite being molested in this way and having goodness knows how many thousands of vehicles driven through it. When we arrived there was a car stuck half way, the driver trying to negotiate his way through delicately with two bicycles mounted on the rear, one of whose wheels was stuck and stopping the car moving forward. Eventually, the driver's wife removed the bikes and unblocked the tree, as it were. We followed through and did what must be done: take photos.

Kyle and John were two good biking companions for the afternoon, and so we rode off, at their invitation, and headed for lunch in Ferndale, a town just north off the 101 south of Eureka. It always interests me to know what other people do for a living, and it often surprises me too. Kyle's job is to certify as fit and competent people who ascend mobile phone and other masts. John is mad about flying and works for Skytypers Inc., a sort of daredevil outfit whose pilots use their planes to write promotional messages in the sky. Think Red Arrows meets Madison Avenue ... He has his own Cessna 180 and lives by an airstrip.

They were heading due south, and I was going in the opposite direction. So we parted after lunch, and I went north, camping overnight in the Elk Country RV Park and Campground, which was memorable for its large herd of elk that roamed the site freely. It was also the first place on my journey in which I became aware of ravens. These birds, which seemed to be everywhere I would go thereafter, right up to Alaska, are extraordinary. Friendly and clever, they chatter away as though talking to you, and many were indeed friendly with campsite managers.

But the ravens are also sneaky. In Elk I had bought for dinner a wrapped tray of chicken on skewers that were marinaded in satay, and I was looking forward to cooking them. I lay them on the wooden table beside my tent and went for a quick pee in the nearby toilet. But by the time I returned, the ravens had unpacked the raw chicken and eaten it all.

Next day, I was off up R101 again, soon stopping at a place called Klamath (population 632) in the hope of a coffee and maybe some eggs over easy and bacon. I didn't find any and instead saw the depressing sight of a hotel and casino that told me this was yet another Native American 'reservation' – what a horrible word – this one for the Yurok people. But there was a combined coffee shop and second-hand bookshop in which a young woman directed me to the visitor centre down the road. There, among much information, was revealed an ancient relationship with nature that the rest of the world has only recently begun to emulate, at least to some degree.

Northern California has the greatest diversity of Native American tribes in the state, and some ninety languages are extant. The largest tribe is the Yurok, of whom there are between 5,000 and 6,000. The visitor centre sells souvenirs and houses an exhibition about the Yurok. The first thing that struck me was how important the forest and the river, the Klamath River, was, and is, to the Yurok. 'The river is everything to me,' says a displayed quotation from Barry Wayne McCovey, a member of the tribe. 'It is my home, church, garden, highway, counsellor, friend, brother and provider.'

For thousands of years before the arrival of Europeans, the Yurok lived between the mountains and the sea, along the banks of the river, in the forest and by the Pacific coast, which is only maybe a mile to the west. The redwood tree was imbued by them with a divine characteristic: it was a sacred being, 'a woge, or spirit person, who created the earth', as the exhibition explains. The Yurok were river people, living off salmon – ne po y'or in the Yurok language ('that which is eaten') – and also eels.

Fishing was mostly done by men, I was told by Antonette ('but everybody calls me Teddy'), who runs the centre. She is enrolled as a member of the Pit River tribe in north-eastern California because her father is from there. 'Women are not supposed to go eel fishing,' she told me. 'I haven't understood why, but they say if a woman touches a man's eel hook, they have to burn it. So don't touch it. It's just something you learn at school.'

There wasn't much effect on the Yurok when the Europeans came – until the gold rush in the mid-nineteenth century, which, as the exhibition puts it, was the 'most troubling time in the Tribe's history.' The Yurok stood in the way of what the prospectors wanted, and wanted fast, and efforts were made in effect to wipe out the Yurok by killing their language. Families were broken up, and children were sent away to English-speaking schools as a way of killing the Yurok language. This system was the brainchild of Lt Richard Henry Pratt of the US Army, who founded the Carlisle Indian Industrial School in Pennsylvania. Pratt is credited with first using the term 'racism', in 1902, to criticise racial segregation – a view that appears to have gone hand in hand with support for aggressive assimilation. The aim of his school, of which there were 150 in the US by 1900, was to 'kill the Indian in him and save the man', as he said in 1892. The policy resulted in the deaths of many indigenous people the exhibition discloses that an astonishing 50 per cent of Yurok children sent to the schools in order to kill their native language themselves died. I couldn't see any explanation given in the exhibition for such a horrific rate of death.

In the 1970s, Yurok elders resolved to reverse the by then well-established trend and revive the language. It's now taught in public middle and secondary schools. 'Do you speak it?' I asked Teddy's three-year-old girl, Annelane, who was playing on the floor. 'She learns a little from flash cards at [play] school,' Teddy said.

A little further along Route 101, I stopped at a cafe opposite the Trees of Mystery, a tourist trap involving a bloke with a microphone and loudspeakers. Wherever he is, he's able to address people in the car park. 'Hey, bud, you heading off?' he broadcasts to one departing driver as another arrives. 'Well, have a great day ... Yo, lady! Welcome to the Trees of Mystery!' All around are the magnificent redwoods – pristine nature and reminders of a tragic history – but the sound of this utter fool bellowing through the air had me riding on as fast as I could.

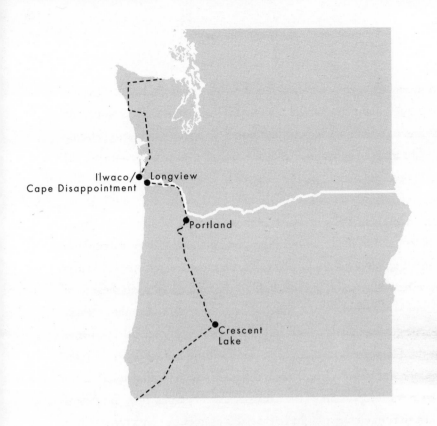

Ilwaco/ Longview
Cape Disappointment

Portland

Crescent
Lake

UNITED STATES

OREGON AND WASHINGTON

28–9 MAY 2023, SUNSET COVE CAMPGROUND, OREGON

Oregon is the America of youthful memory. It was fashioned in my mind in the waiting rooms of dentists and doctors, where, lying about, as distractions, were copies of National Geographic. And in those pages were the photographs – of the Rocky Mountains, of snowy peaks covered in pine trees, of blue lakes and rushing whitewater rivers from where bears plucked out salmon – many of the pictures taken in national or state parks, one of the greatest creations of the federal government. Coming here on this journey, it was a source of great joy to discover that this America really does exist. I hadn't seen bears yet, but I had eaten Pacific and freshwater salmon. As I came in to a cafe at the edge of a state park, two young deer were ambling along the street and footpath and through a gravel-topped cark park, as though they owned the place.

I thought before I went there that this America might exist in Oregon. And it does, many times over. After California's redwoods, I crossed the state line into Oregon, moving first north along the coast and spending the night in a campground at Indian Creek. I slept by a stream with the tent flap open so I could see the dying embers of my fire. Throughout the night, a family of wild turkeys in the field on the other side of the stream created a lovely racket, with bursts of their gobble-gobbling at each other.

Next day, I headed east into the mountains, along Route 138 through the Umpqua River valley and, gradually, ever more into forested wilderness – majestic wilderness that takes hold of the landscape. Soon there were fewer and fewer settlements. The road hugs the river, and at almost every turn a fresh vista of wild woods and rushing waters opened up. I was deep into the Umpqua National Forest and heading notionally for Crater Lake, one of Oregon's major natural attractions. As I progressed, there was evidence everywhere of the damage caused by forest fires. Swathes of hillside were inhabited now by burnt stalks of trees, but undergrowth had begun to return.

Dry Creek Stores appeared on a bend – the first shop, and petrol station, in many miles. 'Lovely valley,' I said to the woman behind the counter. She was Nancy Merchant, joint owner of the shop, with her husband.

'Yes, it is,' she said. 'Now, if we can only have a boater who doesn't set the forest on fire ...'

'Is that what happened?'

She went on to explain that in 2021 a boater – a lake fisherman with a boat on a trailer, of which there are many – was towing on the road, but his wheel bearings were shot. 'And he just kept going, sparks flyin' everywhere, and that's what started it. Had another in 2017, too. Don't need another.'

Later, when I came back to her about the fires, she explained that the boater actually pulled off the road to check his bearings problem, and the heat from the wheel caused the grass to catch fire, which eventually set the forest ablaze. 'That was the end of our summer business,' said Nancy. 'Shut the road down for three months.'

I can't confirm the details of Nancy's account, but Oregon's wildfires in 2021, including in her area of the state, saw the destruction of some 518,000 acres of forest. The cause of most of them is either unknown or lightning. Nancy's fire is known as the Jack Creek Fire, and online photos show a terrifying inferno that engulfed 4,600 acres. 'You could see it from our driveway,' said Nancy. 'It was pretty scary. We had probably one hundred firefighters here protecting our store, so we felt it was okay to stay.' The little shop is a felt-roofed log cabin and would have gone up in seconds if the blaze had got close enough. It's a miracle it survived.

As I headed towards Crater Lake, the air got noticeably colder, and soon there was snow on the mountains. Diamond Lake, a sister to Crater Lake, is sandwiched between two volcanic peaks, Mount Bailey (2,552m) and Mount Thielsen (2,799m). I was west of the Rocky Mountains proper but, snow-covered and rising above a pine forest, under a blue sky and with blue lake water below, Mount Bailey appeared to me as picture postcard Rockies. Unfortunately, but as I had been warned by Nancy, the road to Crater Lake was snow-covered and closed.

Route 138 brought me to Route 97, and I swung north on it and then west again on Route 58, where there were suggestions of camping sites round several lakes. Eventually, after several disappointments, I got lucky at Sunset Cove Campground, where all the sites were taken, but one had no booking ticket on display. A passing RV resident told me, 'That's a first come, first served – and the other guy just left, so it's all yours.' I was there only a few minutes before I saw a stream of disappointed hopefuls file past. The lake on which the cove sits is called Odell and was everything I could have hoped for: glassy calm and silvery, with forests right down to the water's edge and fishermen out on the water.

There were squirrels and chipmunks running about the place and lots of birds – crows and ravens, turkey vultures and Steller's jay. The ravens and crows are thieves, but the jay is a lovely, cheeky visitor – a little nervy but beautiful. Next door to me was the camp host, Vince from Cleveland, who was working and travelling with his four-legged best friend, Rickey.

The place was so nice, and Vince and Rickey such good company, that I spent two nights at Sunset Cove thinking how lucky I was to be there – but wishing my wife, Moira, was sharing it with me.

*

One of the things I noticed as I moved north up the west coast was that people became more and more pleasant – more liberal, more relaxed, more moderate, less angry, more comfortable in their own skin and more at ease with the rest of the world. But there's a terrifying amount of anger in the US right now. Some people are angry at just about everything and anything – about liberals or conservatives, about educated people or ignorant people ... They're angry and they'll tell you they're angry but usually in an inchoate way. They're just angry about 'them', them being something, or someone, other than themselves. Social media fuels it, as do demagogic, authoritarian politicians like Donald Trump, who stoke hatred and feed off it – the extremist and unhinged elements that currently control the Republican Party – and other right-wing libertarian interests who despise government.

It's hard to believe that the Republican Party of today is the party of Abraham Lincoln and Franklin D. Roosevelt. It has always amazed me that so many Americans see government as the enemy even though, because they live in a democracy, they elect the government and can change it at will. Yet, to them, elected government is the enemy, and those who entertain notions of a collective – of a society in which pain and gain are shared equitably – are to be pitied. If modern Europe has been fashioned in large measure by the idea, from the French Revolution, of liberté, égalité and fraternité, the US has been inspired by the Declaration of Independence's life, liberty and the pursuit of happiness. Today, there's a heart-and-soul battle in the US in which one side sees unbridled individualism as the answer to all problems. It isn't.

2 JUNE 2023, ILWACO, WASHINGTON

I scooted up Interstate 5 and went straight through, or rather past, the Oregon capital, Portland. My loss, I expect, but I just couldn't see any reason to delve into another city, so I kept on going – hopping over the Oregon–Washington bridge that uses Hayden Island in the middle of the Columbia River like a hopscotch square to get to the other side – which is Washington state.

I had been advised by Sue and Marci, receptionists at a huge lumber operation at Longview, that the Lewis and Clark Bridge (formerly the Longview Bridge) over the Columbia River, right by the mill, is, as they put it, pretty awesome, as is the one at Astoria. And, indeed, they both are. When the Longview Bridge was built in the 1930s, it was the longest cantilever span in the US. It's 800m in length and stands 64m above the river. The Astoria–Megler Bridge straddles the mouth of the estuary and is 6.7km long and stands 61m above the water. Opened in 1966, it's the longest continuous truss bridge in the US and completes Route 101, which runs essentially unbroken from Los Angeles to Seattle.

Earlier in the day, I checked out another bridge, also beautiful but rather different. From Odell Lake in the Oregon mountains back towards the coast, the road takes in the small town of Lowell, where, once again, I was reminded of just how young this country is in places. The bridge into Lowell crosses a reservoir, and it has a covered bridge made of timber. A picturesque bridge, it was completed in 1907, when Lowell itself was only about fifty years old as a settlement. In the mid-nineteenth century, about a thousand settlers – wagons of men, women and children from Idaho – got lost in the Willamette Valley while trying to trek to Oregon. They were eventually found by rescuers and, rather than go on, they decided to put down roots where their trail crossed the Willamette River, at what is now Lowell. They were subsistence farmers and loggers. One of them, Amos Hyland, also ran a ferry over the river and did well, as more and more people headed west and had to use his service. But so many complained about his fee that the timber-covered bridge was eventually built. It was designed to be strong enough to carry heavy logging traffic. It was rebuilt in 1953, when it was raised so that it wouldn't be drowned by a new reservoir then under construction.

Today, parents and their children fish from the side of the covered bridge, long since bypassed by a new structure. The old bridge is now used to tell its own story and that of the caravan of settlers. People who come to fish park their shiny pickup trucks in the car park just down from Lowell, now a tourist destination with cute shops and preserved buildings.

The story of opening up the west presented itself once again as I rode down off the great bridge over the Columbia at Astoria. A sign pointing to the right recommended visiting Dismal Nitch, which sounds hilarious but was not very inviting. I wheeled left, where the next sign was for Cape Disappointment, which didn't seem a lot better.

I was now on the Lewis and Clark Trail, which commemorates what happened after the United States bought Louisiana from France in 1803 for $15 million. The Louisiana of that time was some 828,000 square miles extending from New Orleans north and north-west, encompassing some fourteen of today's states, in whole or part, right up to Montana – in other words, basically the entirety of the central United States. Capt. Meriwether Lewis and Capt. William Clark were dispatched after the purchase by President Thomas Jefferson to lead an expedition of discovery across America to the north-west, and today's trail is a tourism offering that essentially piggybacks on their journey.

Cape Disappointment was so named by an earlier English explorer, Capt. John Meares. In 1788 he rounded the headland from the Pacific in search of the mouth of the Columbia and thought he had entered just another bay, rather than the estuary. Hence his disappointment. Approaching from the land side, however, Lewis and Clark were far from disappointed and carved the date of their find – 18 November 1805 – on a tree trunk. It was Lewis, apparently, who coined the memorable description of the small bay on the estuary where today one crosses its mouth. Trapped there by a storm for six days, he apparently dismissed it later as 'that dismal little nitch'.

Cape Disappointment did not in fact disappoint me – far from it. After crossing the bridge into Washington, I soon found myself in the small fishing town of Ilwaco. A row of timber- and shingle-clad buildings facing a harbour full of mid-sized commercial trawlers and sports fishing boats offered chowder and suchlike, but they were closed because it was Tuesday. (That really was a disappointment.) However, the Olde Towne Trading Post and Cafe was open, and the woman who runs it, Luanne Hanes, chatted to me, telling me that I really must visit the Cape Disappointment State Park.

It turned out to be the most beautifully laid out and maintained state park I had come across – so much so that I camped there for three nights and spent most of two days in Luanne's cafe, sitting to one side, writing. The cafe is a cosy and welcoming place and served great coffee and homemade soup. Crucially, it had Wi-Fi. Luanne and her customers were gentle people, the welcoming kind in whose company a stranger feels instantly at ease.

Straddling the mouth of the Columbia River Estuary, Oregon and Washington have created state parks that make the most of the sea, the landscape and the history of discovery. My stay at Cape Disappointment State Park really was fantastic – 231 sites for RVs, tents and also some yurts, all spread out over a vast area of sandy hillocks, clusters of pine trees and grassy areas for play, plus loos and showers with hot water. You can walk the length of great sandy beaches, or the park itself, or light a fire as the sun dies and sit there with a glass of something and take in the loveliness of it all. There's a soothing joy in listening to the sounds of nature – the low rumble of waves dying on the beach, a breeze rustling the trees and birdsong.

On my second morning, as I awoke, I watched a racoon waddle off into the undergrowth. The site but one to me was occupied by two gentle Canadians, Will and Cindy from Calgary, and their adventurous travelling cats, Jasper and Trixey. We had many easy chats over a few days, as the cats hunted mice. Jasper's and Trixey's calm manner and relaxed conversation whetted my appetite for Canada, which was just down the road.

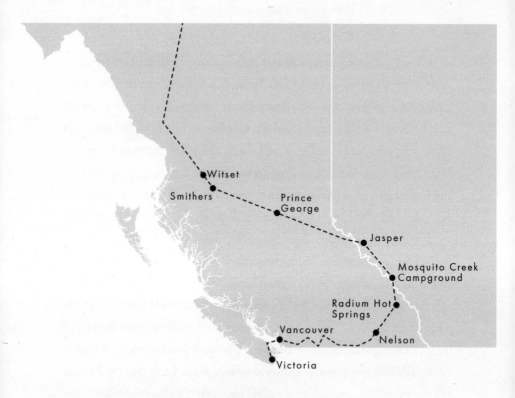

CANADA

BRITISH COLUMBIA AND ALBERTA

4 JUNE 2023, VANCOUVER, BRITISH COLUMBIA

It was early days, but Canada was already turning out to be everything I thought – I hoped – it would be: a place of extraordinarily beautiful countryside full of snow-topped mountains, their slopes blanketed by Douglas fir and spruce trees; rivers that are sometimes fat and meandering, sometimes blue-grey and rushing through forests and over boulders with an urgency suggesting that the snow that created them melted only the other day. And there's living nature – bird and mammal – everywhere. The place is full of people who are nice and calm and easy-going and, for the most part, of a fairly sensible and liberal outlook. They look south and see madness – not everywhere, but a lot of madness nonetheless, and so do I.

I arrived in Canada by taking the ferry from Washington state to Victoria on Vancouver Island. From there I went up Highway 1 (the Trans-Canada Highway) to Tunnel RV Park, where they do not normally allow tent camping; but a kindly manager took pity on me as night was closing in and allowed me to camp at an unoccupied RV site. 'Now,' she said after I had paid and she had explained where the toilets and showers (almost brand new) were, 'we do have a bear that comes occasionally at night, so don't leave out any rubbish, and if you do see him, stay out of his way, and he'll most likely just move on.'

'Okay ...' I thought.

I slept fine – no bear came, and so there was not, on my part, an 'Exit, pursued by a bear' moment. Next morning, from the RV next to me, there emerged a fellow full of chat and questions about what I was up to and advice about what I should do next. He was in his late sixties and had a gammy right ankle and foot. He used to be an all-purpose self-employed handyman. 'Doctor told me to retire,' he said, lighting a cigarette. 'I mean, I don't know that word, but he said I'd had too many heart attacks.'

The matter of the bear arose. 'Comes around regular, he does,' said my new friend, with whom I, with great bad manners on my part, neglected to exchange names. He wore a leather hat that I expect slept with him. As in, on him. 'You'll meet plenty in Alaska,' he said encouragingly about the bear issue. 'What you do, see, is take off your jacket, or whatever, and raise it above your head with both arms. Make yourself as big as you can and make a lot of noise.'

'Okay,' I said, visualising myself trying to reason with a bear by waving my T-shirt at him.

'Only other way is bring a friend with you who's slower than you,' he advised. 'That way you don't have to worry about anything.'

I showered, packed up and rode further on up Highway 1 to Jack Point and a ferry back across the strait that separates the city of Vancouver from its namesake island. The city has a beautiful setting, with multiple vistas of sea and mountain in almost every direction, lots of fine homes by the water's edge and both heritage and modern buildings downtown.

After a couple of nights in the city, I got onto Highway 1 once more and headed east, spending a single night at the Edgewater Bar Campground not far out. My tent pitch was on the bank of the Fraser River, which flows through Vancouver, where it's perhaps 100m wide. On the other side there are several railway tracks along which rumble great freight train caravans – up to a hundred cargo carriages at a time – of the Canadian Pacific Railroad company. The river is wide and slow-moving and has a silky sheen as the sun sets. Several families of Canada geese, adults and goslings, paddled up and down close to the shore, looking at the campers but not interested in us enough to come ashore. The sunset was simply glorious.

I was woken at 5:30 by a racket created by, I think, a robin. It was having a right old time with the glistening chrome hubcap on the wheel of the Centurion mobile home beside me. Seeming to look at its reflection, it had got excited and hopped up and down like it was dancing, before scampering up the left side of the tyre, all the while pecking away at the hubcap. Then it would come to ground again, peck at its reflection and dance once more, before scampering under the RV as though to go behind the wheel, playing hard to get. After a second or two, it would come out again, look at its reflection once more and start the excited pecking, dancing and tyre-climbing routine all over again. It stopped after about twenty minutes. I could think only of the Greek myth of Narcissus.

Thanks to the self-loving – or at least hubcap-horny – robin, I hit the road early, heading for Nelson, deep into eastern British Columbia, in an area Canadians call the Kootenays. On the way, Highways 1 and 3 pass through some fabulous countryside – huge mountains and rivers, lakes and forests aplenty, all epically beautiful.

At Eastgate petrol station, where I was trundling down the Crowsnest Highway, a biker named Funkymeter (that's what they said his name was, or 'Meter' for short) was on his knees trying to reattach the drive sprocket of his Suzuki DRZ 400. The nut came off, and with it the sprocket and chain, as he was cornering, but he managed to stay upright, which I'd say took a lot of skill. Any biker mechanics I've met have all been great improvisors, and Meter was no exception. He had removed one of the nuts attaching his front wheel to the forks and used it to reattach the sprocket. Then he put the damaged sprocket nut onto the front wheel, and it seemed to be holding ...

Meter was with six pals: Viv, Bish ('His name's Bishop, see?'), Rob, Justin, Brad and Jeremie. They were all from California or the Seattle area. They were on an eight- or nine-day on-road and off-road 900-mile jolly that began on Mount Rainier in Washington and would end in Whistler, British Columbia.

Rob, who was on a BMW G310R, was to travel the following year with his wife and two children. 'We're moving to Vermont, but first I want to travel to Spain and New Zealand. And Japan. Maybe Thailand too.' And why not?

Meter's sprocket fixing was helped by Bill Little and his son Darrin. Bill ('I did Europe in the '70s, and it was awesome!') had arrived to help, cavalry-like, in a long, gleaming vintage Pontiac. It looked brand new and had a dashboard with individual circular dials and an enormous gearstick like the driving levers from the cable cars in San Francisco.

'How old is it?' I asked him.

'1952,' said Bill.

'Ha!' I replied. 'Older than me.'

'And a year more than me too,' said Bill.

As a septuagenarian, I reckoned gloomily that the old Pontiac looked a lot better than old Murtagh. But then it was a long time since anyone was polishing my fender.

Jane, the unruffled woman who ran the unimaginatively named Food Store attached to the station, seemed delighted that a posse of bikers and a cool vintage car had taken over her forecourt. She told me she had a good friend who came from Ireland – or whose people came from there. Somewhere near Cork, she said, '"Bally" something, I think.' I told her there were five hundred million Ballysomethings in Ireland because 'bally' came from *baile*, the Irish word for town. This perplexed her.

But she was even more bewildered when she tracked down her friend on Facebook and, on her 'About' page, discovered that she came from Cóbh. 'Ah,' I said, 'yes, a very well-known place near Cork. It's pronounced "Cove".' The perplexometer needle pinged up again. But the friend did have a Bally connection: it was Ballyheigue in Co. Kerry.

I gave her a present of one of my shamrock stickers, and we hugged, laughing. She, and everyone else, posed for a photo. And with that, the lads sped off one way and I in the other, hoping to find a campsite. I imagine that once we had all gone, a sleepy calm returned immediately at Eastgate petrol station.

13 JUNE 2023, NELSON, BRITISH COLUMBIA

It was the middle of mosquito season, and sometimes, especially close to a river in the early evening, the little bastards have a field day. That was the case when I pulled in to the Kettle River RV Park and campsite, a beautifully lawned and well-maintained stopover in south central BC, almost on the border with the US. It had excellent showers and a laundry room with a table and chairs and wall sockets for recharging phones and laptops. More importantly, the laundry room was an escape from the early-evening mosquito hell. And, good god, when they're around, you really know about it. It's like you're being eaten alive, especially on your arms, neck, face and lower legs if they're uncovered. Luckily, I had a face mesh that worked well, but my arms remained exposed. Having got myself into the campsite, I put the tent up and retreated to the laundry room to write. Later, when the time came to sleep, I made a dash for the tent, making sure to open and shut the door flap as quickly as possible to keep the bastards out.

Next morning, I set off fairly early, but still, even at 8:30, the attack squadrons were at the ready. Once on the road, however, I was fine ... until Grand Forks, when a different problem emerged – one of my own making.

The first I knew of anything being wrong was when I saw the blue and red flashing lights in my mirrors. I had just gone through a crossroads junction that had a filter lane for turning left that was empty. I had nipped into it and, when the lights changed, nipped back into my lane to go straight ahead. A minor offence, judge, and no previous. The flashing lights were from an unmarked car of the Royal Canadian Mounted Police, the RCMP. I pulled over and a policeman, a youngish fellow who was initially quite stern, told me that I was wrong to use the left filter lane to pass cars queueing at the lights and also that, when I went off from them, I was about 10km/h over the speed limit, which I almost certainly was, but only because it was so low – 20 or 30km/h, I think – and I may well have been doing 30 or 40. Again, not a hanging offence, but, yes, an offence.

The policeman asked to see my licence, and so I reached into my pocket and withdrew my wallet. But at that moment I remembered that my Irish driving licence was out of date by about two months. I turned seventy on 9 April, and the licence expired on that date. While I had already renewed it online, the fresh licence remained sitting at home in Greystones, Co. Wicklow. I suddenly envisaged having to explain all this to the RCMP while they were already ticked off at my driving. So, thinking quickly, I placed my wallet on my top box (the luggage box immediately behind my back), something he didn't notice or at least never said anything about, and opened instead one of the side panniers to extract my international licence, which was still valid.

He examined it and continued to scold me for my behaviour. Then he started asking about the bike and what I was doing, and he told me he rode a bike as well. It was sort of an, 'I know that bikers sometimes do things they shouldn't' moment as well as a, 'Hey, I'm biker too! Tell me more!' moment. We chatted about what I was doing and about his job, and I mentioned that as a child I watched a TV series, RCMP, in which the 'Mountie always gets his man.' Did they still have those bright-red uniforms? Yes, he said, he had his, but it was only worn on special or ceremonial occasions. The more we chatted, the more confident I was that I was through that gap in the hedge. Sure enough, after a few minutes more, he handed me back the international licence while warning me to be more careful. 'Especially on major roads,' he said. 'We have special highway patrol officers, and they are not as nice as me.'

A let off, I thought, as I resumed the ride and as he turned off the road, back into the centre of Grand Forks and, I presume, his station. For me, the next town was Castlegar, the last one before my destination, the city of Nelson. I wanted to get some serious mosquito repellent before camping another night and so pulled in beside a Castlegar pharmacy for advice. Canadian pharmacies are great at this – helpful and with a common-sense approach. I took the pharmacist's anti-mosquito advice, selected a spray and went to pay for it.

I reached for my wallet and, to my horror, it wasn't there! Gone, missing! Oh, Christ. I knew immediately that this was a mega-disaster. Suddenly, I felt cold. All my cards, debit and credit, my press card and other ID and about $200 US and Canadian in cash, all gone and not easily replaced in a remote part of British Columbia. But where had I lost the wallet? 'Did you use your card already today?' asked the sympathetic cashier. 'Yes,' I said. 'I had breakfast not far from the mosquito campsite and must have left it there.' Apologising profusely, I left the pharmacy and ran back to the bike while racking my brain. My blood ran cold as I remembered taking it out for the RCMP patrol ... and then putting it on the top box and not replacing it in my jacket pocket.

The distance from Grand Forks to Castlegar is, I now know, 97.2km. It's a good road, skirting Christina Lake and passing over mountains, with some curvy sweeps and no rough surfaces. But still, 97.2km, and most of it done at I suppose 80–100 km/h I thought there was a good chance the wallet would have fallen off within a few feet of my restarting the ride after my encounter with the RCMP. I hoped that someone would have picked it up there and handed it in to ... the police. My calling in to the station would be an interesting moment, I thought. In the worst case it fell off maybe after five or six hundred metres further along the road and the contents burst all over the place. Either way, I had to retrace my steps to Grand Forks PDQ and hope to get lucky.

I ran up to the bike to depart, and as I was about to put on my helmet, I saw it. There was the wallet sitting on the top box where I had placed it, furtively, about an hour and 97.2km earlier. Nothing had slipped out, nothing was missing. It appeared not to have moved a centimetre.

Crisis over.

And so, somewhat against the odds, I came to Nelson, a lovely medium-sized city in the middle of the Kootenays, a stunningly beautiful part of south-eastern British Columbia characterised by mountains, rivers and lakes. Though it calls itself a city, for me it's town-sized, with a population of some 11,000 people. It sits on the Kootenay River, before it flows into the Columbia River, the largest in the Pacific Northwest and the one I had been criss-crossing since first meeting it at Astoria in Washington state, where it enters the ocean.

The best-known street in Nelson is Baker Street, which is lined with carefully restored buildings from the late nineteenth to mid-twentieth centuries. Most owe their existence to wealth generated by the surge, from the 1850s onwards, in logging and mining for gold, silver and copper. Europeans arrived there first in the early nineteenth century as fur traders linked to the Hudson's Bay Company and a rival, the North West Company. But the area was home to the Sinixt, Indigenous people who suffered in much the same way as all other American Indigenous peoples did when European origin settlers came their way.

The Sinixt have a prayer, the Prayer to the Four Directions, that reflects their relationship with the natural world. It is recited traditionally by the chief, who first faces east to acknowledge the creator, the Sun, who brings warmth, fruit, birds and animals, growth and happiness. Next, the chief faces north. The north changes the world, says the prayer, bringing snow, which melts and washes away into the rivers all the deteriorated stuff from the land.

'That's why we pray to the water, every morning and every night,' explained Snpaktsín (whose name means 'Breaking of Dawn'), according to a panel in Nelson's museum. 'You talk to everything. Everything is alive. If it wasn't for Father Water, nothing would live.'

Next, the chief turns west. 'That's where everybody is supposed to rest. You become a new man, a new woman in the morning.' Finally, the chief turns to the south. 'That's where all the good comes from. The animals, the birds that leave for the south return, the fruit will come, the roots will grow, and the salmon will return.' The prayer is yet another example of Indigenous Americans having a great closeness to nature and an appreciation of the value, to their own lives and to the Earth itself, of respecting it.

Gold was discovered in Kootenay in 1854. The first European settler was a man named Richard Fry, who came in the 1860s and married a Sinixt woman, Justine Susteel Fry, though Justine was not her original name. They had children, and their descendants remain in the area, according to Nelson's museum.

Mining came and went, but logging remains a huge part of the local economy. The Kootenay River has been tamed with dams and hydroelectric stations, and by the 1920s, tourism, based mainly on mountaineering and winter sports, began to take hold. In more recent decades, Nelson has become a place of note for other reasons: it has been a haven for retirees and for artists, and in the late 1960s and '70s about 10,000 US draft dodgers crossed the border into Canada to escape the Vietnam War. I'm told that about half of them remained and made their lives in Nelson. 'They brought with them their alternative, back-to-nature lifestyle,' said the museum guide Jean-Philippe Stienne, 'and that had a big impact on Nelson.'

Part of that legacy is that, today, Nelson is also the capital of cannabis production in British Columbia. On the way over to Victoria Island from Washington, I had fallen into conversation with a more than usually interesting man, a fellow biker named Cameron Derksen, who turned out to be one of the main fashioners of cannabis policy within the BC government. The drug was legalised entirely in 2018, and throughout BC there's now a burgeoning cannabis growing, processing and retailing industry – much of it centred on Nelson. Enthusiasts, of whom there are many, liken its potential to that of craft beer or wine and see a future in which tourists visit cannabis farms and sample different varieties of the drug, smoked, eaten like sweets or used in soothing oils or for medical purposes.

I visited Sweetgrass Cannabis, a farm on the edge of Nelson, and it was weird to see state-of-the-art indoor growing methods and equipment being used to produce and harvest a drug that, back home in Ireland, would get you locked up. But from what I saw in BC (as I wrote in the *Irish Times*), though cannabis is widely available – there's hardly a town or village without a licensed retail outlet selling it – society still functions, and the social order hasn't collapsed.

The jury is still out on BC's other great drugs experiment. In February 2023 the government also decriminalised (though did not legalise) hard drugs, addiction to which is now treated purely as a health, and not a criminal justice, issue. Possession and use of hard drugs no longer results in arrest and conviction. The initial result of the new policy is that parts of Vancouver are strewn with heroin and fentanyl addicts – comatose people lying across pavements or on benches in parts of the city. Fentanyl, a synthetic opioid, is 50 to 100 times stronger than heroin and morphine. In and around Vancouver's Granville Street, where I stayed, dozens of addicted people were living in hostels for the homeless or sleeping rough. Social services and medical outreach try their best to manage the situation and help addicts as much as they can. It's too early to know what success for this radical policy initiative would look like, and the data for such a judgement will probably not be available for years.

It's easier to make the call on cannabis legalisation. 'Is this good for society?' Cameron Derksen repeated my question. 'Time will tell. But the time and energy and money spent on arresting and putting into jail people for something less harmful than getting drunk on a Friday night hasn't been much good either.'

16 JUNE 2023, THE ROCKIES

I stayed in Nelson for about a week, much of it observing the cannabis situation, chilling in the town's small but central campsite and writing. After that I had a choice. I could go directly north-west and rejoin my original, if somewhat notional, route north from Vancouver – which was pretty much direct to Whitehorse in the Yukon, on to Dawson City and then left, as it were, into Alaska. Or I could go east from Nelson and experience the Canadian Rockies and then head north-west to Whitehorse and on as originally planned. Little contest, really. I mean, how could I come this close and not do the Rockies?

The road from Nelson first goes south past my friends at the Sweetgrass Cannabis farm before turning east and hugging the border with the United States until it goes up and over the Kootenay Pass. Along the way, the air was filled with white flecks of what looked like dandelion seeds, so much so that it appeared to be snow falling. I asked someone about this later, and they told me it came from cottonwood trees and was indeed a seed dispersal.

The journey from Nelson and up the pass was the start of several days of epic vistas that once again stopped me in my tracks. One after another, they came, and then another and another again. The views were breathtaking, and every time I said to myself, 'You can't keep stopping to take a photograph every time there's another great view.' I scolded myself and vowed to crack on and stop stopping. But within a few hundred metres, I was at it again. I just couldn't help myself. The result is that my phone now has over 13,000 pictures in it – all but a handful from this trip!

I took the Crowsnest Highway, also known as Highway 3, which has the bird as its symbol. As I rode up the pass, the fir and spruce trees began to thin out, and sheets of rockface took over the landscape. Coming down towards me were quite a few logging vehicles – always a lorry laden and pulling a fully loaded trailer and moving slowly downhill in low gear. At the top of the pass (and it's only 1,774m above sea level) there's quite a large flat and wide area, maybe the size of a dozen football pitches. There was a log cabin by the side of a small lake surrounded by pine trees. Truckers stop there and check their brakes before the descent.

The road comes down into a town named Creston, just east of which is a time-zone boundary line. I had a late breakfast in a diner, Ricky's All Day Grill. 'Oh, yes,' the waitress, Jennifer, said. 'Down that road there it's already one o'clock.' It was coming up to noon, and I was about to lose an hour. Still, I thought, I'll get it back when I turn west again and cross back over the line. Or does it not work that way? Jennifer was from New York but had been living in Canada since she was eight. She pointed out places of interest on the map when I told her where I was going. She said, 'I want to go to Alaska with a dog and see no one.' I asked her why. 'It's just the last of the wild land,' she said. 'Untouched. Rivers. Bears. I want to go there.'

The next stop for me was a petrol station, where three fellows from Saskatchewan – Nick, Adrian and Curtis – were giving themselves and their Harleys (two Road Kings and a Dyna Wide Glide) a rest. We chatted a bit and then they headed off. Another fellow was in the meantime inspecting my bike. He looked unusual, wearing a plaid shirt, dark workman's trousers held up by wide braces, and a pair of boots that rode up over the ankles and half way up his calves but that were only half laced so that the tops of the boots flapped open. He was about twenty and would not look out of place in the background of that renowned painting of 1930s mid-west farming, American Gothic.

'Nice bike,' he said, drawing the word 'nice' out as though savouring it.

'Thanks,' I said. 'Do you ride?'

'Just a 300. Just around the farm. Nothing like this. But I'd like to one day.'

His name was William, and we talked a bit about what I was doing. I then asked him about the farm.

'Twelve thousand acres, north of Edmonton,' he said.

I think he said they had cattle and sheep and also grew crops, but I was so stunned at the size of the farm that I didn't record that part of the conversation. He had come over to me from a transit van at one of the petrol pumps. I gave him one of my cards and a Tip2Top sticker, and as some women emerged from the station shop and began walking over to the van, he ambled off, thanking me. The women wore headscarves and long floral dresses. I followed them to the van and, after they got in the side door and were seated, asked if I could take their picture. 'Sure,' they said, smiling.

I asked if they minded my asking about them. They didn't, and I said they looked like they might be Amish. 'We're Hutterites,' said the woman sitting just in front of William. Her name was Carol. She had a big smile and bright eyes and was very unselfconsciously pretty. Her handshake grip was firm, and she looked me straight in the eye when we spoke. They had come all this way from the north of Edmonton for a wedding and were now heading home. I asked her what defined their faith, how it differed from, say, Catholicism or Protestantism. 'We're Anabaptists,' she said, 'which means you only get baptised when you decide you are ready, even if you are in your twenties or thirties.'

I had little experience of such people, but I did once know some Dippers in Co. Wicklow. The name, which is maybe what other people called them, rather than their own name, is derived, I think, from their practice of total-immersion baptism, usually in a river. I knew some when I was in my early teens in Avoca, and my memory of the women is that they were very shy. There were not necessarily oppressed (though they may have been), just withdrawn when out and about with their husbands, who tended to mix more with other men than with women of their own group. But Carol and the others were vivacious and outgoing. I would have loved to speak to them longer, but standing at a petrol station pump isn't ideal for interviews.

My resumed journey took me along Highway 93, more or less straight north towards where I would turn in to the Rockies at a place named Radium Hot Springs, which sounded like somewhere best avoided. But the weather was closing, the skies were darkening and rain was clearly on the way. I stopped at Fairmont, where there was a good campground, and got the tent up within minutes of the downpour. There was no point in even trying to cook dinner, so I satisfied myself with beer and peanuts while sitting in the tent before going to sleep.

I awoke next morning to find at least two inches of water sloshing against the sides of tent groundsheet, but hardly a drop of water got inside. It took a bit longer than usual to get going that morning, trying to dismantle and pack everything in a flooded site with intermittent rain, but I did and eventually came to the famed Radium. It's an unexpectedly Germanic place, with hotels named Tyrol and The Old Saltzburg. I kept going.

Highway 93 cuts deep into the Rockies via a narrow high-sided gorge at Sinclair Creek, immediately outside Radium, and later follows the course of the Kootenay River, threading a way between the steep mountains of Rockwell on one side and Hawk Ridge on the other – more vistas, more epic scenery. Just before entering Banff National Park, the road passes Marble Canyon, truly a wonder of the natural world. What today are the Rocky Mountains used to be a warm, shallow tropical sea in which the bodies of small creatures fell to the bottom, millions and millions of them, one on top of the other, until pressure and heat transformed the mass into limestone – just as limestone was formed in Ireland. That was 500 million and more years ago. About eighty million years ago the Earth's tectonic plates began moving in ways that pushed, buckled, bent and twisted that flat limestone into huge angular mountains. Finally, several periods of glaciation occurred from about two million to 15,000 years ago, and ice sculpted much of what we see today.

Vermillion Valley is a glaciated U-shaped valley. Running into it at right angles is Prospector's Valley, which was also glaciated but much less vigorously than Vermillion Valley. Prospector Valley was thus left hanging above Vermillion Valley and, as its glacier retreated, melt waters tumbling off it started drilling through the limestone at Tokumm Creek, attacking the rock at its weakest point, a joint. The result is the most extraordinarily deep but very narrow gorge, in which a roaring torrent of water is constantly deepening the fissure and scalloping great bowl shapes out of the side walls. It's extremely dramatic and beautiful. It's also terrifying where the river waters make their first plunge with a roar as the water bursts onto the rocks below.

A little further on, the road crosses the Continental Divide – a line running roughly north–south – in the Canadian Rockies. All water falling on one side of the line, the eastern side, will eventually reach the Atlantic Ocean, while all water falling on the western side will reach the Pacific. You can stand there, as I did, my right foot on the Atlantic side, my left on the Pacific side.

Just after Marble Canyon, I came to Castle Mountain Chalets, which has a petrol station and shop. Hot chocolate! The young woman behind the counter was chatty. 'Where are you from?' she asked me.

I told her and asked where she was from.

'Calgary. My dad's from Honduras, and my mom's Indigenous.' She asked my name and I asked hers. 'Tara,' she said.

'That's very Irish, you know.'

'Yes, and my other name is Patrick,' she said, and we both laughed.

The road comes down into the Bow River Valley, a major valley that traverses, south-east to north-west, Banff National Park, from Banff right up to Jasper, south of which Highway 93 becomes the Icefields Parkway, so named because of the number of glaciers that can be seen from it. But as I entered, the cloud was so low that I could see nothing but the road ahead, and only about 200m of it at that. The heavens opened again and, to make matters worse, it started to get really cold. Two days before, in Nelson, the temperature was in the mid-thirties. I'd say here it was below 10 degrees but over 5. Below 5, biking becomes painful for me.

I passed the less than encouragingly named Mosquito Creek Campsite and rode on for maybe five kilometres before giving up, turning back and camping there, getting the tent up and me inside just before a massive downpour. I slept fully clothed, anxious about how cold it could get as the night wore on. Still, I was thinking that it would be good training for Alaska.

In the morning the rain had gone and so too had the clouds. As I emerged from the tent – boom! Suddenly in front of me was the extraordinary sight of vast mountains that had been hidden the day before but were now visible. They towered over the valley floor, the Icefield Parkway and the Bow River, whose course it followed. In the rain and mist of the day before they had been invisible and, because I hadn't looked at a map, I had no idea they were there. They have a truly massive quality to them – vast pieces of bare rock, with glaciers visible and snow picking out every tiny horizontal ledge of the limestone, highlighting layer upon layer, like the layers of a cake. Their visual impact was only slightly diminished by a blue-grey haze caused, I think, by smoke from wildfires elsewhere in Alberta. When I look upon enormous creations of nature such as this – or on down-sweeping valleys covered in trees, with rushing rivers or with lakes, still and reflecting everything round them – I feel a profound sense of calm. I'm fulfilled by just looking at what is before me.

I got up quickly and rode on, eager to experience the fullness of this long valley before getting to Jasper ... and before rain or low cloud, or both, spoiled the day. At Bow Lake and Waterfowl Lake, both a few kilometres on, the water was that milky blue colour I hadn't seen since Torres del Paine and the Perito Moreno glacier in Patagonia. And the mountains behind the lakes were as dramatic and satisfying as anything I had seen in the Andes.

At Saskatchewan River Crossing, about 150km south of Jasper and where a turn to the right leads eventually to Calgary and Edmonton, there's a petrol station and restaurant, and I was desperate for a warm breakfast. I was put at a table by a window with a fabulous view of the mountains and beside an elderly couple in the corner. He was a little less robust than her, and she was doting on him. 'Would you like more syrup with that, dear?' she asked him.

'No, thank you. I'm doin' fine,' he replied.

They talked in that slightly too loud way that elderly people sometimes do. It's not that they want anyone else to hear what they're saying. Maybe it's just that they themselves are a little hard of hearing.

'Who's going to drive today, dear?' she asked.

'Well,' he said, 'I can do the first half, and you can do the second. Or you can do the first half, and I can do the second.'

'I'm happy with either,' she said.

And so they continued between mouthfuls of breakfast and largely inconsequential but pleasant chat. Every now and then, a rogue swallow caught the man's throat unawares, and he coughed and blew his nose. 'I don't know why it's like this this morning,' he said.

'Well, dear,' she said, 'you were fine during the night, but you were lying down then.' I'm not sure what led up to it, but at one point she pronounced, 'I suppose I can be Polish, and I could be German, but I'm so proud to be Canadian. I love this country.' And there was also something about having been married for seventy years.

After a while, when my breakfast arrived, I heard him ask me, 'What are you riding?' I turned round and told him.

'Ohh,' he said. 'I used to ride, but that was a long time ago.'

A little while later he got out of his chair, with her help, and, holding his walking stick tightly, made his way to the toilet, slowly and with measured paces. When he'd gone, the woman swung round to me, and I could see her properly for the first time. She had a beautiful face and a sparking smile. She was full of life.

'I envy you on a motorbike,' she said. 'It's lovely. He's had two strokes, but he's still moving.'

Benita was eighty-eight and was born in Kraków in Poland. 'Things were not good after the war,' she said, 'and so by myself, aged seventeen, I came to Canada on a slow boat and then across Canada on a wooden seat on a train from St John [in New Brunswick] to Alberta, where I was supposed to work on a farm.'

Instead, she worked in a hospital and, to save the 10 cent taxi fare to and from work, she walked. Vernon – he who had gone to the loo – and his brother ran a taxi business, and she always refused his offer of a lift, but eventually she accepted, and they went out and got married. 'Seventy years ago, last September 10th', she said. 'What are you writing all this down for?' she then said to me, and I told her why. 'Oh,' she said dismissively, but she carried on. In Kraków her father had driven a freight train, but he died young, aged fifty-five. She could remember her grandmother from back then but not much more about that life long ago. She remembered her grandmother feeding a goose and massaging its throat to help it swallow.

Vernon then returned and pulled up a chair to join the conversation.

'This getting old is better than the alternative,' he pronounced with slight weariness. His brother used to have a Harley-Davidson 45 – 'no shiny parts, from the Army', he said. 'Any kid that wanted one could have one' after the war. His brother was more into bikes than he was; the brother also had an Indian with a sidecar. 'Likely sold it for fifty dollars,' said Vernon. 'Don't know what it would cost now.' (I checked: there was one on eBay for $17,500.) Vernon's big thing was cars. 'I had a '39 Ford coupe,' he said.

In the early 1950s, when Alberta's oil boom was starting, he worked in that before setting up the taxi business with his brother, 'until I met Benita and we decided to get married.' Then he worked for a hospital and then for a gas utilities company as an installer and all-purpose fix-it man. When he retired they bought a small sailing boat and moved to Vancouver Island. 'We sailed it around and around,' said Benita, 'and we loved it. Boy, we loved it!'

They have five children, five grandchildren and three great grandchildren. 'They're much more careful nowadays than we were,' Benita explained, apparently a reference to the low number. Benita asked me whether I was going to do the Dempster Highway, the road that runs from Dawson City in the Yukon north to the Arctic Ocean and the Northwest Territories. I said I might do some of it, but I was committed to riding the Dalton Highway from Fairbanks to Deadhorse, in Alaska, which is further north than the other.

'The Dempster Highway is lovely,' she said. She had only to 'close my eyes to think of it. Lovely.'

And then they got up to leave, ninety-year-old Vernon and Benita, a sprightly eighty-eight. Vernon picked up his walking stick in his right hand while Benita linked arms with his left arm, and together they walked slowly across the dining room.

'Now,' one of them said, 'are you driving, or am I?'

As they were shuffling away from me, the restaurant sound system was playing 'Harvest Moon' by Neil Young. Still in love ...

And as they walked away, I turned round to look out the window at the mountains again. But I couldn't see them. Must have been something in my eye ...

19 JUNE 2023, JASPER AND SMITHERS

I spent two nights in Jasper, at Whistlers Campground, which has an astonishing 781 camper van and tent sites ... and a lot of elk wandering round. Jasper is an all-year resort town and a favourite among people in their twenties and thirties. It's set in the middle of a valley floor, the confluence of three wide valleys deep in the Rockies, close to Mount Robson, which, at 3,954m, is the highest mountain in the Canadian Rockies. Three roads lead in and out of the town: south back down the Icefields Parkway is Banff and Calgary; east is Edmonton; and the road west goes back into British Columbia and on to Prince George, slicing across the province to the north-west and on ultimately into the Yukon.

West was the way I went, and on the morning I left Jasper, along Highway 16, the day didn't seem to know what to do with itself: one minute the sun was beating down on the mountains, picking out all the interesting visual details; the next, gloomy clouds were creeping in and, with them, the rain. By the time I got to Mount Robson, the day had settled on being fine, but the mountaintops still had clouds sitting on them.

At Mount Robson there's a pit-stop information shop for tourists. All the coaches pull in, and if you want to go trekking, there are several ways to get round the back of the mountain, where its glacier sweeps down into a lake. Behind the shop there's a large grassy area in front of a forest of aspens and pines that blankets the flat earth running for a couple of kilometres to the foot of the great mountain. And it really is magnificent, even if its peak was shrouded in low cloud, much to the dismay of the serious-minded photographer, with their camera mounted on a tripod and just waiting for that charitable puff of wind that would clear the peak.

The mountain looked like a series of triangular peaks, each one stacked against the other and each rising a little higher until the summit itself emerged. And the horizontal stratification of the limestone was picked out in near-perfect detail by a dusting of snow that remained even though we were by then halfway through June. To the Indigenous people, who knew the mountain long before anyone else, those horizontal lines were like a spiral, and so they called it the mountain of the spiral road.

Having spent several days and most of a week in Nelson, I really wanted to get back on track. So after paying due respect to Mount Robson, I hit the road north-west for Prince George and stopped again really only twice. The first was to say hello to a moose grazing in a field. An adolescent, I think, it seemed put out at my attention but wasn't sure whether to run away. Instead, it did a little circular trot of anxiety before deciding, sensibly, that I was just another biker. It carried on grazing. The second stop was to examine an abandoned 'little house on the prairie' near the settlement of McBride, a tumbledown wooden house that would make a great retirement restoration project ...

Prince George, when I finally got there, didn't present its best face. The highway skirts round the edge of the town, by the railway tracks and associated post-industrial gunge, and so I just carried on, hoping to stumble across a campsite. After about 20km a sign said Northland RV park, and so I pulled in. Noreen, the woman who ran it, said they really didn't do camping, just trailer homes on one side of the site and RVs on the other. It was getting late and I must have looked disappointed because, after asking me where I had come from and my telling her my travel story, she said, 'See that green patch over there?' pointing to a lawn on the RV side. 'You can camp anywhere over there, and I won't charge you.' And then she asked me how old I was!

Noreen and her husband, Ernie, bought the place a few years back, 'and then some Chinese with a lot of money offered us a lot of money for it, and so now I just manage the place for them and live here.'

'Here' was a very nice and cosy trailer home that had all of Noreen's and Ernie's bits and pieces, a small office for the RV business and a nice patio and awning for when the weather was good.

Further up the RV site lived her friends Mike and Wendy, in their RV, which had a little fenced-in garden for their two small dogs, and a man shed in which Mike, a trucker, had a sofa on which he sometimes fell asleep and a TV with a pull-down sheet on which he could project films.

Next day I awoke to hear the intermittent patter of raindrops on the tent. I got up fast so that I could dismantle everything and pack it all away before it got soaked. Hitting the road, I set as my target destination for the day a place named Smithers, 370km from Prince George, plus the 20km back there from Noreen's place, so close to 400km. It was a lot of biking, but I really needed to crack on and break the back of the 1,200km between me and the Yukon.

The only stop I made en route was in a place called Vanderhoof, where, in an outdoor shop for game hunters and fishing, I bought bear spray – a belt-mounted holster and aerosol can filled with Mace, or pepper spray, a last resort deterrent against unwelcome attention.

'You going all the way up 37?' a man named Mike asked me about the road that branches north off Highway 16 and heads pretty much straight north, all the way to the Yukon. I said I was. 'Used to truck up there regular. You'll see lots and lots of bears. Be careful.'

I got to Smithers at about 18:00, exhausted but okay. The municipal campsite was nicely laid out and well kept and was by the river in a lovely setting. That evening I saw my first bear – far off upstream on the riverbank. It was a medium-sized bear, as far as I could make out, minding its own business and well out of bear-spray range, even if I wanted to zap it.

Next day I had a memorable encounter just north of Smithers, at a place called Witset (formerly Moricetown). Near there a roadside sign told me that Highway 16 – the 720km link route all the way west between Prince George and the port city of Prince Rupert – is also the Highway of Tears, so named because, since 1970, between eighteen and forty women hitchhikers along it vanished or were murdered. Many of them, some of whose bodies were recovered after their murder, were young Indigenous women. The number of victims is disputed. The RCMP accepts that up to eighteen women were victims of separate individual attackers, while Indigenous organisations assert that more than forty women have been attacked, some murdered and others missing, their fate unknown. Girls, warns the sign, don't hitchhike on the Highway of Tears. Beneath the words are pictures of three missing women:

Delphine, who vanished in June 1990; Tamara, last seen hitchhiking on 16 in September 2005; and Celicia, a cousin of Delphine's, missing since October 1989 and last seen near the road.

The long road across BC's interior plateau passes through many different Indigenous areas, most of them plagued by poverty. As it hugs the Bulkley River at Witset, the river below tumbles into falls. A few people had stopped and were looking at what I assumed was a pretty sight, so I pulled over.

Down below, at the Moricetown Falls, there were two fellows, one holding a long pole with a net. He was fishing. There was a side road that went right down to where he was, and I parked the bike there and got a closer look. The river there is wide and bends into a graceful curve as it approaches a gorge, heralded by large rocks opposite each other, forcing the river into a narrow trough, which it passes with great force and speed, frothing and roaring all at once. The two men were down on the rocks, where I joined them. They were Myron, who had the pole and net, and Warner, who was just watching. Both were Wet'suwet'en people, whose members, about 2,000, Myron said, live in the Witset Canyon. There's a channel beside the main fall into the canyon, and the water there slips into a large pool and moves on through it, much slower than the main body of water. In that channel, too, a ladder has been built through which fish can swim upstream with greater ease than battling through the main river as it tumbles down the canyon.

Myron was dipping his pole and net deep into the pool, stirring it and then pulling it out. Nothing. 'No salmon yet,' he said to me. 'Next month. Then they'll come. First week of July.'

'Will there be many?' I asked.

'Lots,' he said, but not as many as years ago, apparently.

The annual salmon run is a great occasion for the whole community. When the salmon come, people come to the gorge, to the rocks where we now were, on either side, and use nets on long poles to catch the fish.

'Do the bears come too?' I asked.

'Sure, they come! You can see 'em on both banks up there,' he said, pointing a little upstream where the river was wide and the water a bit shallower. 'We got bangers [explosives], bear bangers, and they run back up the banks when they go off, but then they get used to them and pay no notice when they go off. It's the way.'

He said I should come back and see it all, maybe on my way back down from Alaska. I told him I'd like to, and I really would! I thanked him for chatting and took a couple of pictures, and we parted company. 'You betcha,' said Myron by way of goodbye. 'See you soon.'

Back up on the highway, and looking down at the gorge, another man was sitting watching the river. His name was Willie. 'Been fishing there forty-five years,' he told me. 'We're part of a dying breed down here. Each year we have maybe ten poles on either side [of the gorge], and there's just less salmon.'

He looked across at the far bank of the river and up and down this side too. 'This used to be all village houses along here,' he said. 'But they modernised it. Built new houses up there [he indicated behind, on the far side of the highway], and this is a historical site now.' I wasn't sure whether he was pleased about that or lamenting something lost. He said that Myron got a sockeye salmon the previous Thursday.

There was no real centre to the village, as far as I could see, but there was a petrol station about 200m on that overlooked the village and the gorge. Arnold, an Indigenous man, and Scotty, who was European Canadian in origin (lots of Irish and Scots in his background, he told me), joined me on a bench by the road.

Arnold looked over at a patch of ground where a digger had removed the shrubs and grass and scoured up the soil but then ceased work.

'See, they stopped,' Arnold said.

'I told 'em,' said Scotty, 'told 'em there was people buried there. But they didn't listen, just went right on ahead and did it. And dug up bones. Just like I said they would. And now they've stopped. People buried all over here,' he said, with a sweep of his arm, making an arc across the whole area.

The plan was, apparently, to create a trek walkway around the village. Scotty was adopted by an Indigenous person some thirty years before. I didn't know whether he meant formally adopted or just taken under their wing, in the friendly way these things sometimes happen. We talked about the salmon.

'They're in,' Scotty said with certainty. 'Can smell 'em now. You smell 'em?' he asked me, as if seeking confirmation. 'They're there, that's for sure.' I couldn't smell anything except my coffee, but I told him Myron got nothing that morning when he went looking, though apparently he had got lucky the Thursday before.

'Well, they're there,' said Scotty, 'maybe resting in the pool down there [pointing to part of the river below the gorge]. They're here. I can smell 'em.'

He said there's fewer salmon because of bad fish husbandry. 'One of the elders said to me years ago, "If you take from the river, you have to put back in the river." They ain't putting nothing back. Nothing about over-fishing. It's all about the spawning beds ... Used to be colder here, too, in winter. Minus fifty maybe. Now it's only ever minus thirty. Snow only up to here.' He indicated his waist with an open palm, as if to suggest it used to be much higher.

*

I rode and turned up Highway 37, on through Hazelton and into Gitanyow, a village off the highway that's famous for its totem poles. There are maybe twenty of the giants on a green in the centre, all carved with strange squat figures, fat little men, or that's how they looked to me, and animals – birds, birdmen and dogs – on ageing and weathered poles perhaps 18m tall.

Highway 37 carried on northwards, and me with it. Through valleys and forests, past rivers and lakes of great beauty ... and evidence of fewer and fewer people. I admitted to myself that I was a little nervous. Next stop: the Yukon.

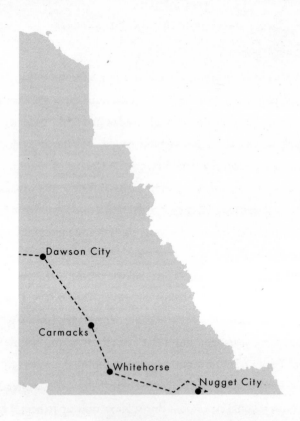

CANADA

YUKON

21 JUNE 2023, WHITEHORSE

There are times riding Highway 37 deep into British Columbia and nearing the crossing into the Yukon when everything you see all round you, and I mean for kilometres and kilometres, appears to be utterly devoid of people and of any sign of their existence. It's unsettling, which I didn't expect. Rattling along the highway with the noise of my engine purring contentedly under me, but not seeing another soul, car, lorry or biker, for maybe 80km, I felt very alone inside my helmet. I knew there would be times, the further north I got, when the sense of isolation would be great, but I had not expected to be bothered by it. And then I rode a long stretch and noticed, in the verge, sticks with orange signs. Eventually, I stopped to see what they were – 'Caution', they read, 'fibre optic cable' – and realised that human activities are never really that far away.

As I moved through north central BC, in the far distance, Tuktsayda Mountain (2,276m) was snow-covered and looked impressive, but it was the landscape closer to hand that held my attention. It was undulating between rivers and lakes and was dominated by fir trees, as well as by aspens, with their distinctive trembling, or quivering, leaves. The firs are Rocky Mountain firs, Engelmann firs or Balsam firs; but they were ugly things: tall but not huge, with little bulk or volume and, if anything, somewhat scrawny. They look black – if not bleak. The lower branches don't grow outwards much, and neither do the upper ones, leaving the impression of a uniform width, as opposed to the triangular shape, wide at the bottom and narrow at the top, of other trees in the pine family. The firs grow in great forests stretching all over the landscape or are scattered individually, peering above lower growers, giving it a sort of giraffe neck quality.

I spent the night at the Kinaskan Lake campground, which is confusingly sited on the shore of Lake Natadesleen, just beside the other one. It was stunning – tent sites right down on the water's edge, beautifully calm, with that glassy surface as the sun sets.

Next morning I watched a spruce grouse padding about my neighbour's RV pitch, pecking away at the ground, hoping for breakfast, before I hit the road without having had any myself. I stopped at a petrol station and eatery near Iskut and, walking inside, was greeted by a 'Wo-ho! Look at this, man!' from one of three bikers already seated at a table, followed quickly by questions about who I was and where I was from. The speaker was a large fellow with an ebullient personality – one of a team of three from Los Angeles: Dimples (because she has them), Smiley (her partner, and he does) and X Man (also known as Xavier), the group's entertainment officer and the one who started asking the questions – even before I could! We quickly settled into conversation and shared breakfast (X Man insisting, generously, on paying for my two pancakes and coffee).

'I'm a bum, Peter,' said X Man when I asked him what he does. But he went on to say, 'I used to be in the USMC, the United States Marine Corps, and then I drove the subway tram.' He went on to tell me he was a Marine machine gunner. 'That's an MOS 0331. That's what they called it. I was in Desert Shield. That's what they called that before it became Desert Storm. The [Marine Corps] brought me around the world.'

Outside, we did some pictures and decided to ride a while together. I told them I wanted to stop at Boya Lake, which is a few hours up the road and had been recommended as one of BC's 'must see' places.

When we did just that, it was a knockout for beauty – a turquoise gem twinkling in the sunshine and surrounded by pine forests. X Man et al. were suitably impressed.

Next stop was the Yukon border sign, where stickers were applied, photos were taken and Smiley rode his GS up the muddy bank to the foot of the sign, as if he'd done it ten times before. He hadn't and was inordinately pleased with himself.

We rode on to Watson Lake, to the sign forest there. Begun in 1942 by a homesick GI, it's now home to thousands of place name signs from all over the world, assembled on poles and in circles, a bit like a maze. Another good photo op.

The guys were into biking huge distances. They thought little of covering 700km a day – far more than I was willing to do. Having done four hours' biking and 340km to get to Watson Lake, they were going to press on to Whitehorse – another five hours and 440km. I just didn't trust myself to do that sort of distance and kept thinking of the friend of Luis, the BMW guy in northern Chile who looked after me there. There was a wrecked GS in Luis's workshop, and I asked him about it. 'A friend,' he said, 'was in the Atacama. Drove too far and fell asleep. Lost his leg in the crash ...'

I'd prefer to avoid that fate, and so, after a few kilometres more, I bade farewell to X Man, Smiley and Dimples, who rode on and, some days later, made Prudhoe Bay and got home safely. I bedded down for the night at the Nugget City RV and Campground, just inside the Yukon. I couldn't quite believe that I was actually in the Yukon. For me, the very name 'Yukon' is associated with a particular landscape and weather of great

extremes – a place where people and nature struggle, where survival is far
from guaranteed, a place made famous by the poetry of Robert Service
('the Bard of the Yukon') and the prose of Jack London, chronicler of the
'great white silence' and the epic struggle of the man trying to light a fire.
For me, London's very name has magic and romance all over it. However,
on that evening, the most memorable thing was finding a squirrel sitting
on my motorbike seat, like it was ready to hit the road, rummaging for
chocolate it could smell in my fleece pocket lying there. And not a bother
on it when I came into its view ...

Next day I made straight for Whitehorse along the Alaska Highway
and a campsite just before the city that specialises in catering to bikers. It
looked unpromising at first – or maybe worse even – but it was shaping
up to be a fantastic place and maybe the best biker pit stop in the Yukon.
It's the project of sixty-seven-year-old Bruce Martin from Vancouver but
who was a longtime Whitehorse resident. In May 1986 he was 'working
at a young offenders facility in Alberta and came here as a volunteer in a
correctional facility.' He never really left, he told me. He'd always been into
bikes – Hondas and Ducatis, and he once owned a 900 Mike Hailwood
replica. Down in Vancouver one day, he noticed the huge number of bikers
heading north – 'Counted seventy-five of them,' he said – and thought there
was a business opportunity in there somewhere. From late spring to early
autumn, hundreds of bikers set out north through British Columbia and
into the Yukon, where they'd do Whitehorse to Dawson and maybe the
Dempster Highway to the Arctic Circle and Tuktoyaktuk in the far north
of the Northern Territories, or they'd head into Alaska and do much the
same, maybe even tackling Dalton Highway to Prudhoe Bay.

'I want this to be a full-service facility for the long-distance rider,' he
said. 'I want to have everything here that a guy like you needs, and I want
you to leave here saying you'll come back and also recommend it to other
riders.'

The place was basically a building site, but you could see where it
was going. Set inside four acres of scattered pine trees were twenty-five

almost-finished walled tents – a room like a square yurt – each of which would have two beds, electricity and USB chargers and a front-porch boardwalk patio. The walled tents were roughly in a semicircle round a large central brick patio with a fire pit, a fully kitted out communal kitchen, loos and showers. There would also be twenty tent camping places. And there would be a workshop in which bikers could strip down their machines and fix whatever needed to be fixed. A big draw, I think, will be the already functioning restaurant, the Wolf's Den, and the full-service bar.

Workers were all over the place when I camped – sawing, drilling, nailing, screwing, assembling and testing just about everything in sight. Another month or so and they'll be all but done. Bruce (and a partner, Chris Saunders) had already sunk Can $1.2 million into the project, but I think it'll work. Being inherently biker-friendly (cars are not allowed to enter!) is a big draw. But so too are the charges: $110 a night for a two-bed wall tent and $35 per person for a tent site is good value.

Bruce is pitching for the older market – bikers from their forties upwards – and is not interested in 'squids'. 'Squids?' I said, baffled. 'Yeah, too much money, shorts, no helmet, and they're pulling wheelies downtown.'

I asked him, as a biker experienced in the region, about the Dalton. 'I've heard of bikes that got stuck in the mud and left there, right in the middle of the road. They waited till it dried up, and they could basically chisel it out and continue riding ... It happens. Or you hit a bear or a moose or some other dumbass.'

Hmm ...

22 JUNE 2023, CARMACKS

After Whitehorse I took Highway 2 – the Klondike Highway – straight north towards Dawson City. The Yukon is 480,000km2. To give that some context, France is 551,000km2, so the Yukon is big. Really big. But the population is only a little over 44,000 people, almost all of whom live in or around Whitehorse, the capital city, which is close to the border with British Columbia. Dawson City, 533km to the north of Whitehorse, has a population of under 2,000. Not a lot of people live between the two, and those who do usually have a particular reason. Other than the Indigenous people, they may be doing some sort of government work or highway maintenance, or they may be a wildlife and park ranger. Or maybe they just don't want to be near many other people, and being remote is their personal balm. Up here, you can be trundling along the highway for hours and see no one. Between you and the horizon, whichever way you turn, there's nothing but forest and mountain. And you quickly realise that, in the great scheme of all that is around you, and all that is not, you are quite insignificant.

As you set out on the Klondike Highway (the very name excited me!), notices advise you to start the journey with a full tank, and they also tell you where the next petrol station is – usually a very long way off. My bike, the R1200 GS Adventure, has a massive fuel tank – thirty-three litres, which is enough to last me close to 500km, depending on speed and weight – so I usually don't have a problem. I started early but then lost time as, after maybe 80km, I remembered that I had left my laptop behind at Bruce's place in Whitehorse. Once I remembered, I knew where I'd left it – tucked under a seat on the veranda patio where I was the night before – and I was confident that it would still be there. I went back and got it, but the best of the day's biking was gone.

I spent the night at the Coal Mine Campground in Carmacks. I couldn't see any evidence of coal mining, but the camp was on a bend of the Yukon River – a mighty thing to see! It was moving with great speed, like a big green-grey snake of swirling eddies, with forest debris being swept along. During the night, there was a fork lightning rainstorm, with jagged shards of light flashing across the sky and sometimes striking the ground. Rain bounced off the tent, but I still felt secure and dry. When it stopped, a rainbow appeared across the river …

Next morning was bright, dry and clear, and I set off early. Just after Pelly Crossing, a bridge over the Yukon River, the road rose to an upland forested plateau, much of which had been burnt to almost nothing a year before. Large swathes of the surrounding countryside were huge patches of black where the fires, almost invariably started by lightning of the sort I watched the night before, had been allowed simply to burn themselves out. But suddenly, in this desolate place, there appeared cars parked on the side of the roads, or in small areas off it – flat places where sand and gravel had been gouged out, maybe for road building. I stopped when I saw two youngish people rummaging in the back of their car and asked what they were doing. 'Mushroom picking,' they said. I expressed surprise – and ignorance – noting the devastation of the fire and asking when it occurred. 'Last year,' said the man. 'Yes, it was bad – but good for the mushrooms!'

A little further on, at one of the larger sandpit clearings, I spotted a sign. Mushroom Buyer, it said, with little white-on-black drawings of mushrooms, as one might see in a children's story book. I pulled in.

There were a couple of large RV caravans and the detritus of shambolic living – broken stuff and useful stuff all lying round in a mess, with children's toys also strewn about and a tarpaulin hanging off the side of one caravan, just flopping there and seeming to cover nothing in particular. In the distance, further into the pit, were a couple of cars parked beside tents, but no one was visible. And by the entrance itself, opposite the big RV, there was a robust square beige tent, like something you'd see in a military camp.

Through a flap, a child emerged, smiling at me and curious, and then a man. He was the mushroom buyer, and he explained what was going on. 'The forest burn,' he said with a French Canadian accent, 'and the year after, you go into the forest and pick mushrooms!' I asked what type, thinking they were probably for smoking, and he said they were morel mushrooms, the best of which were the blonds and the greys, he said. 'Last year was a really good season in BC because of the fires there.'

His name was Phil Lemieux. 'French Canadian?' he said, throwing my question back at me. 'But of course!' he said, in that very French way. He was originally from Montréal but had been living in BC for fifteen years. This was his life now. He bought from the pickers, paying them in cash, and sold on to a BC company, West Coast Wildfood. He said about

40 per cent of the pickers were travellers, people from all over the world who moved about all the time, going from harvest to harvest, picking for a living. The rest were opportunists, just picking because the mushrooms were there. After the morels were all harvested, he would go to where the next seasonal wild food could be had. 'Now it is morels and afterwards huckleberry and then chanterelles or pine mushrooms ... Sometimes I'm done by my birthday [19 November], and then for the winter I work in the vineyards [in BC], pruning the vines, until the mushrooms come again.' He paid the pickers $6 a pound for morels.

Some days later, I met a French Canadian woman known as Melissa of the Bush who is a morel picker. She said the mushrooms sold at market for between $25 and $30 a pound. She picked and tried to sell directly to the consumer, cutting out the buyer–suppliers to take a greater slice of the money. 'I love doing it,' she said, 'to be out in the wild, in the bush, with my dog ...'

25 JUNE 2023, DAWSON CITY

Dawson City is a ramshackle place – half falling down, half done up – but, for all that, fantastically attractive. Bits of it are like every Western movie you've ever seen. The roads are unpaved, just compacted gravel, mud and grey dust. There are no footpaths, as we know them. The sidewalks, where they exist, are boardwalks, sometimes buckled this way and that because the ground beneath them has given way. In the summer the place can be baked by the sun and, next minute, drowned in torrential rains. In the winter, in the snowy, icy silence, the temperature falls to −50°C, and everyone waits for that moment in the late spring when the ice on the Yukon River, there since the previous November, cracks, unjams itself and floats away again. With the extremes of the weather, it's a wonder the city's buildings of timber and corrugated iron have survived a few decades, let alone for over a century now.

Dawson City today is great fun and full of history, of which it's making the best it can, having been created in a world that no longer exists but that is enduringly fascinating. It was built on a river bend a little down from where the small Klondike River flows into the mighty Yukon River and on the only piece of flat land around – a frozen swamp, not far below the Arctic Circle. It grew from nothing almost overnight into a teeming mass of 30,000 people at the height of the Klondike gold rush in the 1890s. 'Mania' is the only word that describes what it must have been like. It was, instantly, an American city sprung up in Canada; but despite the frenzied pursuit of money, in the gold rush years there were no murders and few thefts. Guns were banned and the RCMP were a visible, restraining presence. And then, within a few years, it was all over, and Dawson City shrank rapidly, dwindling to as few as 300 people in the mid-twentieth century.

In what a film narrator at the local museum described as 'one demented summer' during the gold rush, you could buy anything in Dawson City – shovels, axes, tents, top hats, silk dresses, oysters and champagne. And in Paradise Ally, and several other establishments, helped by the likes of Bombay Peggy, Madame Zoom and Ruby Scott, you could indulge your every fantasy. One woman was desired so much that she was bought for her own weight in gold. In Bombay Peggy's it's alleged today that one madam who went topless had breasts so large that she slung them over her shoulders.

The Klondike gold rush exploded in 1896 like a giant Roman candle, fizzled with a bright burning madness for two or three years and then went out. In the process of exploding with people – mostly men hungry for riches – the lands of the Indigenous people, the Tr'ochëk Hwëch'in, were overrun, prompting Chief Isaac to move them downriver to a place named Moosehide. It's only in recent decades that they have moved into Dawson in any number, and the Canadian government has agreed a final legal text, recognising them and their longstanding, though hitherto largely ignored, rights over lands in the region.

Dawson today is still recognisably the place it then was, though without the naughty bits. It's locked in by winter for most of the year, but it has bounced back in population and is nudging towards 2,000 inhabitants today. All but one of the streets remains unpaved, so that when it rains they're like a gloopy, slippery ice rink. Where there are no boardwalks, you just walk along the roadside. Many of the original buildings – hotels and bars – remain and function more or less as before, and the shops, many of them originals and with original signs, all face front onto the street and have authentic tall square gable fronts. Some of the timber buildings are falling down, mainly because the permafrost, the permanently frozen ground 6–24m deep that starts a little below the surface, has melted. This happens either because of global warming or something specific, such as the building sitting directly above the ground and warming the ground beneath it. For that reason, new or rebuilt and restored buildings are placed on wooden stilt foundations, which themselves sit on a raised gravel plinth to distance the building from the permafrost.

St Andrew's Church, a substantial timber structure built in 1901, is keeling over and has been abandoned to its fate, a slow-motion death that one day will see it topple, if it's not knocked down first. Not far away, two neighbouring buildings have slumped over into each other and now prop themselves up. They're known as the 'kissing houses'. Another building near my campsite on the edge of town, a two-storey warehouse-style commercial structure sporting the name Mueller Electric, remains standing only because it's leaning against a cottonwood tree.

A strong belief that gold in great quantity was to be found in the gravel of the area's many creek rivers, which combine eventually to create the Klondike, brought approximately 1,000 miners into the area from the late 1880s to the mid-1890s, many of them from San Francisco. But there was no big find, no eureka moment, until 17 August 1896, when three men – George Carmack, an American; his Indigenous brother-in-law Skookum Jim Mason; and Mason's nephew Dawson Charlie – were out hunting in Rabbit Creek and stumbled on a huge amount of coarse gold grit – a layer 'as thick as cheese in a sandwich', it was said. They staked their claim, renamed the valley Bonanza Creek and got digging.

The outside world knew nothing until the following winter had passed and a ship, the Portland, arrived in Seattle in July 1897 laden with gold. In that first year of mining, two tons of it, worth some $1 billion, was extracted from Bonanza Creek and from others nearby – by panning, by digging down, using fires to melt the permafrost and then digging horizontal tunnels. Light a fire, melt the ground, dig and bucket the result up to the surface for washing in water to reveal – you hope – gold dust. 'Paydirt' they called it. When the Portland docked and revealed its cargo, the whole west coast of America, and places further afield, went berserk.

'Gold!' screamed the newspaper headlines, and some 100,000 people, many from California, set out for the Klondike in a mad scramble, half of them failing to get there, turned back by the extreme weather. Those who made it first went by boat, up the west coast to Skagway in southern Alaska, from where they set off on foot north-east and into the frozen Chilkoot Pass. The successful, hardy and really determined ones continued across lakes and down rivers to Dawson, where some 7,000 homemade boats arrived within days of each other.

'Overnight, Dawson was the largest city north of Seattle and west of Edmonton,' explained Lucy Welsh, a knowledgeable, funny and engaging Parks Canada guide, one of several who lead visitors on walking tours round the town. As you travel from the south-east, from Whitehorse, travelling along the Klondike Highway, the first indication of something unusual appears a few kilometres before Dawson itself: huge mounds of river rubble at Bear Creek. For maybe 10km on each side of the road, there are mounds of rounded stones, gravel and sand, piled high up to perhaps six metres. These are the tailings from river dredging, long since ceased, and long since drained of any precious metal. The great mechanical river dredges came after the initial gold rush, of course. In the first flush of the rush, it was panning. Within weeks, much of the area's natural beauty was ruptured as the landscape was violated. Thankfully, as far as I could see, it has mostly recovered.

Lucy took us to the bank that sprang up, the Bank of British North America, first occupying a tent and then a building on a corner, just as banks everywhere love, looking sturdy, safe and trustworthy. In fact, it burnt to the ground several times (any gold inside was saved by the safe), fire being the bane of the city, until the bank was clad in corrugated metal sheeting, thereby creating, in effect, a firebreak between neighbouring buildings. The bank has been restored perfectly, with the counter and teller positions behind wire mesh and lighting just as they were a century and a quarter ago. The tellers took the little sacks of grit and gold dust the miners brought in and, out back, the contents were melted, burning out the impurities, and decanted into ingot moulds. Once it was weighed, the miners were paid in cash, which the clever few squirrelled away or invested in the town (some bought hotels or set up other businesses). Or they took it south to San Francisco and bought mansions. Others blew it all in the city's bars and brothels.

Not far from the bank is the fully restored Red Feather Saloon, complete with a long bar counter, foot rail and spittoons. Behind the counter a triptych of mirrors doubtless reflected a packed bar most nights, a portrait of Edward, then Prince of Wales, looking on, perhaps wishing he were there, given his reputation. Miners who brought their gold dust in with them, to show off or use as payment, sometimes allowed bar staff to dip their finger inside as a tip or just to let them feel it. In the process, specks of dust escaped and fell to the ground, accumulating to such an extent that when the Red Feather Saloon, and other bars in the city, were knocked down or restored, traces of gold, reflecting the shape of the bar counter, were found in the ground beneath the floorboards, according to Lucy.

One of the few women to join the gold rush was Belinda Mulrooney. She was born in Co. Sligo but grew up in Pennsylvania, where her father was a miner. Belinda came to Dawson City via a sandwich business she started in Chicago, an ice-cream parlour in San Francisco and a stint as a steward on a steamship plying between California and south-east Alaska. She earned extra cash selling goods to passengers, and when the gold rush happened she stocked up and headed through the Chilkoot Pass, arriving in Dawson with hot-water bottles and bolts of cloth, which she sold with a 600 per cent markup.

Aged just twenty-six, Belinda made enough money overnight to open a cafe and start a cabin construction company. Profits from these enabled her to build a hotel, The Grand Forks. Knowing that almost all her customers were miners, she ensured that the hotel's floorboards were swept daily and that what was gathered was run through a sluice. The gold dust thus retrieved earned her $100 a day – every day! Perhaps not surprisingly, she became a millionaire in the process, the first Dawson woman to do so. She made and lost several fortunes, making a success of two failed banks – one in Dawson, the other in Fairbanks – and married and divorced a fake French count. She lived out her years in Seattle, where she died in 1967, aged ninety-five.

Everyone in Dawson wanted to know what was going on in the outside world, and so a newspaper emerged, the Dawson Daily News, which managed to keep going until 1957.

A contemporary tradition has its roots in the harshness of the gold rush days. A miner named Louis Liken, who was also a fur trapper and rum runner, got frostbite and, to prevent gangrene, axed off his frozen toe. He pickled it in a jar, leaving it under the floorboards of his cabin, for reasons he knew best. It lay there long after his demise, until the 1970s, when it was found by Capt. Dick Stephenson, who one evening at a bar – possibly a long evening, by the sound of it – dreamt up the wheeze of a cocktail involving the severed appendage: the 'sourtoe cocktail'. 'You can drink it fast. You can drink it slow. But the lips have got to touch that toe!' Thus was born a Dawson City tradition, a 'must do' ritual for visitors. Sour toe is a clever play on the word 'sourdough', which locally means a person who has been living in the Klondike for a time, at least one winter, as opposed to a blow-in, as we would term it. The ghastly drinking process involving the cocktail is alive and thriving today at the Sourdough Saloon in the city's Downtown Hotel.

Every evening from seven, seventy-five-year-old Terry Lee, with a salt-and-pepper beard and looking like an old sea dog, plays the role of Capt. Dick, initiating new members into the Sourtoe Cocktail Club. Initiates must down a shot of liquor of their choice, into which the severed limb has been dropped. Their lips must touch what does indeed look very much like a small, pickled and very old toe. My turn arrived as my name was hollered across the bar, and I sat down in front of Capt. Terry, successor to Capt. Stephenson, who died in 2019. '*Conas atá tú?*' Capt. Terry asked in Irish in a flash. '*Tá me go maith*,' I replied with, in my view, commendable speed and lack of surprise. It turned out that Terry used to work in Glenealy, Co. Wicklow, for a man named Don O'Sullivan, trying out various tree types from Canada, pines mostly. Before that, he worked on ships but was soon burnt out, as he says himself. He then got into forestry, which pitched him into a state forest-exchange programme in Ireland. He's been in Dawson on and off for forty-four years. 'Some people come here to escape,' Terry told me. 'Some people come here to see and experience and return home. I am in the latter group.' And so, when the snows come, Terry heads off – to the Philippines ...

With a theatrical flourish, Capt. Terry used a pair of tongs to pick a slimy black thing from a plastic box and drop it into my glass of Yukon whiskey, uttering the traditional edict: 'Drink it fast or drink it slow, but your lips must touch the toe.' I did, and they did: a slug-like but rigid thing bounced off my upper lip as a shot of Yukon Jack slipped down nicely, easing my discomfort. And as a result, I now have a certificate verifying that I'm member number 105,966 of the Sourtoe Cocktail Club ... and with that, I was out of there!

*

Jack London was twenty-one and rather aimless in San Francisco, working on boats and thinking about writing, when he caught the Klondike bug. He headed to Dawson with the others and spent a winter in a log cabin in Henderson Creek. Today the cabin has been reassembled in Dawson, beside the Jack London Museum and a little way down from another cabin on 8th Avenue, one rented by the poet Robert Service, who also fell under the spell of the Yukon. For him the Yukon had 'beauty that thrills me with wonder | It's the stillness that fills me with peace'.

London's museum is a small wooden building of one room filled with photographs of the man and dedicated to his memory. The tiny cabin beside it is fascinating: a single-room hovel with two raised wooden lath beds covered in caribou pelts and with a small wood-burning stove. Joann Vriend, a potter, gives talks about the man and his time in the museum and early on reminded us of the opening lines of *White Fang* (1906), one of his great animal stories, in which he refers to the 'savage northland silence'. London spent a winter in the creek, panning for gold but failing to find the riches he craved. Instead, he turned to his natural talent, writing, and became the first American author to be a millionaire. 'But he never had any money,' said Joann. 'He liked to live large,' as she put it rather well. He cranked out at least fifty short stories and magazine or newspaper pieces from 1900 until his death, from kidney failure and alcoholism, aged just forty, in 1916.

I feel certain that his story 'To Build a Fire' had an influence on Hemingway's *The Old Man and the Sea* – the themes are just too similar for that not to be the case. London certainly fired my lust for travel, and for this part of the world, when I read him as a teenager. And when I looked now at the Yukon landscape, or at Alaska's, even in the summer I knew exactly what he meant when he set *White Fang* in 'vast silence' that 'lay over the land'.

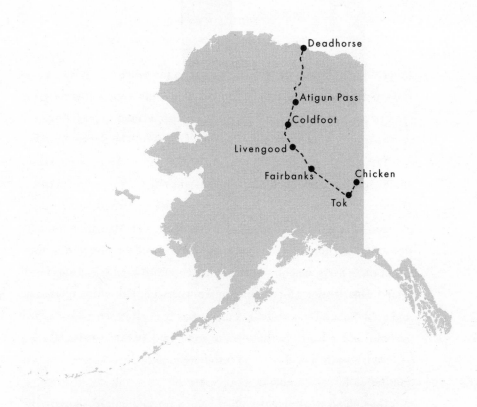

UNITED STATES, AGAIN: ALASKA

26 JUNE 2023, CHICKEN

The fastest and easiest way to get to Alaska from Dawson City is to go to the north end of Front Street and, from there, hop on the free ferry that will take you across the Yukon River, and you're on your way.

The ferry isn't a huge thing, just one of those flat-bottomed crafts that look the same, front and back. There's no quay or slipway: the ferry simply approaches the Yukon's shingle bank, and then a roll-on, roll-off platform is lowered. The ferry maintains power so as to hold its position against the flow of the river, and once the vehicles are off, a new batch drives on and is taken back in the opposite direction. On the other side, the other end of the ferry lowers its platform, and they drive off again. Simple and effective.

I got on with a huge RV, a giant the size of a tourist bus. The RV also had a rig on the back on which sat an enormous Harley. The RV was so large (and heavy) that it took most of the deck, and mine was the only other vehicle allowed on with it. We got to the other side in minutes – though the pilot of the ferry had to sail at an acute angle across the great river to counter the strength of its flow, which wanted to push him well downstream. I headed off, onto the Top of the World Highway.

This is the road essentially west out of Dawson, and it rises quickly up the mountainside and proceeds right along the ridge of the mountain range, giving great views to each side of the road but especially to the north, where a huge and lengthy chain of snow-covered, angular Alaskan mountains dominates the horizon. The road is mostly unpaved, or 'untarred' as they say in these parts, meaning that it's densely compacted gravel and mud. Grand when it's dry, a bit of a nightmare otherwise. Thankfully, it was dry, and even though I was a bit nervous, especially in places where stones had accumulated at bends in the road, or sometimes in linear strips because vehicle wheels had pushed them into long mounds, I soon found myself tootling along contentedly at about 80km/h.

The upland areas were devoid of habitation, and indeed, in parts, the road was above the treeline and the mountaintops were almost bare. After maybe three quarters of an hour I realised that I had foolishly forgotten to fill my tank before exiting Dawson. I had already decanted my spare cannister into the tank and was now showing a range of ninety-five miles in the tank – about 140km. The first petrol station was about 160km away. I flagged down a lorry coming towards me and asked the driver how far it was to the next petrol station. When he told me, we both realised that I might just about make it ... but I might not.

'I've got a can,' said the driver. 'I'll give you some.' His name was Jesse, and he was a firefighter paramedic from Juneau, the Alaskan capital to which he was driving via the Yukon after attending a course in Anchorage. 'Getting education up here isn't always easy,' he explained. He was training to be an ER nurse. 'Lots of us up here drive around with cans, and we usually end up filling other people's vehicles.' He topped up my tank with maybe five litres but generously refused my offer of $20 and continued on his way home. My fuel range was now 190km, easily enough to get me to the next station.

Next stop for me was one of the more than 120 Canada–US land border crossings. It's known as Poker Creek Port of Entry and proclaims its pride at being the most northerly land border port of entry into the US. It's a small enough place – one line for entering, one for exiting and no queue. I pulled up to the booth, as urged by a uniformed border policeman standing on the road. A colleague inside was doing the active checking. 'Passport,' he said, and I obliged. He flicked through it. 'You have an Esta?' he asked. 'Esta' stands for Electronic System for Travel Authorisation and can be used, instead of a visa, by travellers from certain countries, one of which is Ireland.

'No,' I said, 'I have a visa. It's there in the passport.'

He asked what I was doing and where I was going. I told him I was travelling to Prudhoe Bay and that I was a journalist – which is also written on the visa. He said I was not entering on an I visa, which is the sort that was issued to me, allowing me to work in the US, though not for any US company. I said that was what had been issued to me for the purpose stated at the time.

'Well,' he said sternly, 'you are not working as a freelance journalist riding a motorcycle to Prudhoe Bay.'

'That is exactly what I'm doing,' I replied with a certain defiance in my voice.

'No,' he said firmly. 'It is not!' And with that, he ordered me to park my bike and report to the office round the corner. He then slammed the booth window shut.

I parked where I was told, all the time thinking, 'This is going to be interesting,' because I knew I was 100 per cent in the clear. I had all the required permissions, and their records, if they bothered to look, would prove it.

Another policeman, named Brandenburg, who was, I suspect, the other man's senior, took over when I entered the office. He didn't say much, but on his computer he called up information, which I assume meant anything that was under my name and held by the Department of Homeland Security, which manages security and entry at US ports. That information should include details of my visa, and maybe even a copy of the supporting letter from the *Irish Times*, plus my track record of using the visa, which amounted to my entering the US via Texas from Mexico, last 14 April, on exactly the same basis that I was travelling now. I told Officer Brandenburg that my visa had been issued by his embassy in Dublin for the precise purpose that it was now being used: my travelling, from Tierra del Fuego, since November 2022, through the United States to Alaska while working freelance for the *Irish Times*. He asked whether I had any documentation, anything from the *Times*. I said I hadn't, but I had my press card and my personal travel card giving details about the journey. I gave him both and mentioned that I had been published weekly by the paper since starting my journey.

He stood there, scrolling the screen, saying nothing, until he asked me how long I'd be in Alaska. I said maybe two weeks but added that I really didn't know. I had to get to Prudhoe and then return to Fairbanks. At that point I would try to work out how to get back to Ireland, but I suspected that I might have to get back to Vancouver and that there were flights from there directly to Dublin. He really didn't engage with me but kept examining his screen. And then, without saying anything, such as announcing a decision, he just handed me my passport, press card and business card, still without saying anything, until eventually he pronounced, 'That's it.'

'That's it? I can go?' I asked.

'Yes.'

No 'Welcome to the United States' or 'Enjoy Alaska' or 'Well, that's some journey. Have a good time!' Just 'That's it.' I'll say this: unlike his colleague, he wasn't an arrogant prick, but it was a close-run thing. It was only a few hours, but I was already missing Canada – and the Canadians.

The first settlement I reached in Alaska was a place named Chicken, and it had a petrol station. 'Why Chicken?' I asked the young man at the pump. 'Well,' he said, in the manner of a man pulling up a bar stool and leaning forward into his listeners, 'the way I heard, at the time of the gold rush, all these miners were around, and this place was called Ptarmigan then, and the post mistress got fed up correcting the envelopes because the miners weren't good spellers, see, and so one day she said, "Right, that's it. We're calling it 'Chicken' from now on." That's the story, anyways.'

I'd love to believe that this is true. And, hey, this is America, so it might well be.

27–28 JUNE 2023, FAIRBANKS AND STARTING THE DALTON HIGHWAY

Well, this was it.

I had reached the city of Fairbanks in Alaska, and the last road was calling. Would Jack London have felt 'the call of the road', I wonder? Movement, the road, going west are all core themes of American literature and writing, and with them, that other great theme, dream and disillusionment. I had dreamt of this journey for quite a long time – if not this one exactly, certainly the idea of just taking off and going away for a long time, absorbing and coping with whatever was thrown at me. Or not. And in doing that, I have been blessed with an indulgent wife who has tolerated me and whom I missed more than I can say. Ditto my children. And the dogs. But nothing that happened in the past eight months or so had disillusioned me – the opposite, if anything. All along the way, people asked me, 'What have you learnt'? And my answer was always the same. 'That people everywhere, all people, are mostly good and decent and kind and just want what everyone else wants, or already has: a reasonable life and a chance to work and live in peace and have a bit of a laugh every now and then, and they'll go out of their way to help you.'

I had thought about this last leg of the journey, and not thought about it, if that makes sense. I had thought about it by way of wondering, daydreaming, if you will, what it would be like; and I had not thought about it in the sense that I hadn't researched it that much or planned it really at all. I just knew where I was going: from Fairbanks straight north along the Dalton Highway to Deadhorse, the oil settlement at Prudhoe Bay on the

FROM TIP TO TOP

edge of the Arctic Ocean. The Dalton Highway was an unpaved gravel road (hardpacked at best, mud at worst) that was more than 700km long and served the Alaskan oil industry and not much more ... apart from timber workers, bikers and other adventurous sorts who want to do it, well, just because it's there.

I kept meeting people who asked where I had booked to stay along the way. And the answer was that I hadn't but that I was confident that I'd get in somewhere. I hoped so, because you can't camp up there in Prudhoe ... there's the problem posed by grizzly bears that see us and our detritus as a source of food.

I would have liked to have spent a number of days there, trying to absorb the place and get a sense of it and the people who live and work there. I imagined them to be oil industry types, roustabouts, geologists, engineers, workforce managers and others – misfits who maybe work in the industry or just somehow hang round it in the way loose-end people often hang round the edges of everything. And there would be Indigenous, anti-oil or pro-environment campaigners and then the people who know there's a living to be made out of serving the rest of them – hostel or hotel people and bar owners, if bars are allowed up there. Who knows? But if you are allowed to stay only some miles back from the edge of the Arctic Ocean, some miles down the road from Prudhoe, and can only go there in a shepherded tour, I wasn't sure I'd get much of a sense of the place. We would see ...

I stayed my final night before starting on the Dalton in Fox, an area a little north of Fairbanks, at a campsite called the Northern-Moosed RV Park. It's a small place, a bit ramshackle but clean and run by a genial host, Ritch. It was $25 for a site and access to toilets and a shower ... and to his house-cum-office, which has a kitchen, washing machines, a TV and, crucially, plug sockets for charging phones and laptops.

After putting up the tent and settling in, I was sitting in the laundry room writing when a new camper walked in. 'Are you in charge?' he asked. 'No,' I said, 'but look for the small fellow with white hair and a big Santa

Claus beard.' Ritch must have heard me because, a few minutes later, he presented me with a postcard. It showed a Santa Claus figure who looked remarkably like Ritch, wearing seasonal garb, sitting in a chair and making a list. 'North Pole AK,' it said on the front – a reference to the town a few miles south that styles itself (rather ridiculously) as North Pole and is little more than a string of Christmas shops. It must provide Ritch with a seasonal winter nixer.

At about 22:00, I got into my sleeping bag and went to sleep ... and woke at 4:00. It was completely bright as, at that time of year this far north, the sun doesn't fully set. The Dalton begins about 130km north-west of Fairbanks. On the way, the countryside becomes more and more empty of people and dwellings. Just after Fox, there's a messy roadside property typical of its type and not at all unusual in the States. There was stuff strewn everywhere in front of the house, right beside the road – barbecue bits and pieces, a ladder, bicycles, tyres, planks, chopped wood and tarpaulins, several of them keeping out the elements. Still, I guessed it was someone's cosy pad inside.

Not far from there I got my second glimpse of the famed Trans-Alaska Pipeline. My first sighting was just before Fairbanks, where it crosses the Tanana River via a suspension bridge built especially to hold it. It's quite a sight. Now, on the way to the Dalton, I saw it several times, snaking overground on stilts through the countryside and the forests and along a pathway cleared especially for it. It looks neat and tidy ... and vulnerable to attack.

I passed a sign that said Arctic Circle Trading Post and turned in, with high expectations. But I found myself in front of the Wildwood General Store, a log cabin outpost that was closed. Beside it was, oddly, a wooden shed proclaiming Lemonade Stand. It too was closed. Just after Livengood Creek and a timber roadway bridge, the Dalton emerges from the wilderness and is strangely small, or should I say narrow, at the start. Not much wider than a single track, it has a jet-black gravel top but one that seems well packed down and – famous last words – easy enough to ride. I took a selfie before setting off down it.

Coming out of Fairbanks, at a place named Hilltop, there's a big official noticeboard warning would-be users of the Dalton. It is 414 miles long (666km), says the sign. 'Though considered to be the trip of a lifetime,' it continues, 'it involves real risks and challenges.' Big trucks have a right of way (so stay out of their way, the message implies), never stop on bridges or hills or curves. There are no grocery stores, banks or medical facilities. There's no mobile phone service outside of Coldfoot, which is a staging post about halfway to Deadhorse and is also the last settlement just before Prudhoe.

WiFi is extremely patchy between here and the Arctic Ocean. Heading off, I told friends, 'You may not hear from me for a while …'

29 JUNE – 1 JULY 2023, DEADHORSE

The Dalton Highway is perhaps the greatest adventure-biking road accessible to mortals like myself. It's named in honour of James P. Dalton, an Alaskan mining engineer and oil prospector in the tundra area between the Brooks Range of mountains and Prudhoe Bay, which is known as the North Slope. He worked with the US Navy's Alaska oil-exploration project and during the Cold War helped create the Distant Early Warning Line, or DEW Line, a necklace of radars running from Greenland across North America to western Alaska. The highway was built not by him but by the Alaskan oil industry after confirmation that there was oil in Prudhoe.

The Dalton was initially a haul road for building the 1,300km pipeline. Finding the oil was like a second Alaskan gold rush: the road was built in an incredible 154 days, with 32 million cubic yards of gravel essentially dumped onto the ground and compacted in a line from Livengood to Prudhoe. The pipeline that followed took just three years to build, from March 1975 to May 1977. Crude oil began flowing, at 37.7°C, in 1977, and it takes two weeks to reach Valdez. Construction workers, some of whom were Irish, could earn $1,000–1,500 a week. Today, the average pay in the oilfield is $150,000 a year.

The pipeline is visible everywhere between Fairbanks and Prudhoe because it runs almost entirely above ground, on steel stilts about 3m tall, sometimes in a straight line, sometimes zigzagging to help it survive earthquakes. The oil-carrying pipe is 1.2m in diameter, but it's sheathed in protective and insulating material, making it look fatter. Lots of signs warn the curious to stay away from it and not to climb onto it. The pipeline is a scar on the landscape, but I can't say that it has destroyed it – it's there, yes, but then so is everything else: the scenery, the forests, the plants and the wildlife, and when the oil runs out, the pipeline is supposed to be removed.

Once I got onto the Dalton, just beyond Livengood, some 134km north of Fairbanks, I settled into the final ride of this adventure and soon found my anxiety easing. The gravel was hardpacked and, crucially, there weren't greats drifts of it into which a front wheel might sink, causing the bike to slew and maybe topple over, me with it. In no time at all I was tootling along at 50km/h, even when the gravel gave way to stretches of hardpacked mud.

Fairly early on there were major roadworks, perhaps about 20km long, where there were lots of diggers, earth-movers, dozers, traffic cones, red flags and traffic restrictions. Sometimes one side of the road was closed to traffic and a stop/go system operated for the other side, with cars and lorries being led, when they were allowed to proceed, by a pilot car with a large Follow Me sign on the back. There wasn't much traffic – sometimes a lone car, sometimes two or three in convoy; sometimes big Ford or Ram pickup trucks; occasional articulated lorries with long lengths of steel or piping; a few petrol tankers – but it wasn't Friday evening rush hour, not anything like it.

It started to rain and my heart sank. The mud surface turned slippery, and tyre track gullies formed from the lorries. But, as I'd learnt by this stage, the best tactic is to keep going at a steady, if reduced, speed, 20 or 30km/h, for instance, sometimes standing on the pegs for balance and control. I had good tyres on – Heidenau K60 Scouts – and they held up really well.

The roadworks ended, the pilot car pulled over and I was through – elated not to have fallen over. I felt that now I really could do this: I was up to the challenge. I felt great and this feeling was reinforced when I reached Yukon Crossing, an early staging post 224km out from Fairbanks, where the

Dalton crosses the mighty river. And it really is mighty here – enormously wide, a couple of hundred metres, I'd say, and starting to enter its old man stage as it moves towards the Bering Sea.

Just after the timber-floored crossing – the only one over the Yukon in Alaska – there's a campsite called Five Mile Campground, which is, by strange coincidence, five miles after the crossing. Amid a blizzard of mosquitoes kept at bay by a face net, I got the tent up. A couple, Bret and Kacey, and their big friendly dog, Lila, were camped beside me, sleeping in a pop-up tent on the roof of their car. They love travel so much that they decided to sell their home and, well, travel. Bret is a supply-chain strategy consultant for retailers, and Kacey works in IT on something known as 'air tagging'. They can do their jobs anywhere ... and so decided to do just that! They sold everything and hit the road.

The midnight sun keeps it daytime all the time there at that time of year, and so I went to sleep in sunshine and woke up in it too. In between, it rained like hell, and so I was nervous about the road once again, but the first challenge was how to get up and dressed without being eaten alive by the bugs.

Leaving Five Mile Campground, I saw that there was an airstrip right beside the road, with two huge yellow X markers stapled into the runway. Soon after, the road rose gently to a plateau named Finger Mountain – so called because of the granite protrusions that in some instances resemble an upright finger sticking out of the bog-like ground. Views of the mountains to the north and east were obscured partly by long streaks of low early-morning clouds; but through them it was still possible to see snow-flecked mountaintops and winding rivers in the flat floor valleys between them.

Further on, the road passed the only home I noticed outside of a couple of settlements on the whole Dalton. It was a two-storey house, sitting across from what looked like an old log cabin, on which a sign read, Old Man Alaska. Although there was a car, the gate was chained, and a sign said No Trespassing. Someone wants to be alone, apparently.

At the crest of the next hill, which is named, ominously, Beaver Slide, just before I started to descend, a driver coming up lowered his window and shouted out a warning: 'Muddy! Really muddy ...' I started the descent fearing the worst but, again, everything was okay – his side of the road looked like a thick-gravy plasticine, but on mine the ground was firm and easily driven.

I reached the Arctic Circle – 318km north of Fairbanks – my second time to cross it (the first being north of Bodø in Norway about forty-four years before). Lukas, a young American, was there by the big Arctic Circle sign, latitude 66°33'. On a bicycle and heading for Ushuaia, in the extreme south of Argentina, he wanted to hike to the Refugio Charles on Isla Navarino. I told him of my experience. At the sign too was motorcyclist James from New Zealand. It was his second time riding in this part of the world. 'What did your wife say when you said you were doing it again?' I asked. '"Don't come back", he said, and, by the sound of it, I don't think he will. After Ushuaia he was planning to come back up and do the Northwest Territories of Canada.

At Coldfoot, 414km from Fairbanks (and 390km from Deadhorse), there's petrol and coffee, and food, if wanted. I asked the woman behind the counter how far it was to Deadhorse. 'Five to twelve hours,' she said, 'depending how fast you go.'

It was coming up to midday, and so I reckoned I could do it in seven or eight hours – lots of time, especially with twenty-four-hour daylight. And this part of the journey proved to be the most magical, the most jaw-dropping, part of the whole Dalton. There's a valley, much of it with a tarmac road, that passes massive mountains – bare rock with jagged edges and coloured rockfaces, towering over rivers and lakes, a raw landscape from which trees are slowly being banished as the road surges northwards. One of the mountains is Sukakpak (1,338m) – jagged and angular, it juts upwards like a broken plank sticking out of the Earth. Opposite it is another, a long-bare escarpment above the treeline, an enormous mountain of grey rock with rust-coloured minerals bleeding from it. The valley leads into the Atigun Pass, the final mountain hurdle through the Brooks Range, where the partly snow-covered mountains are black and look doom-laden and where landslides are a menace preventing any stopping on the road. I'd been warned by a guide at the Arctic Visitor Centre in Coldfoot that this could be the most difficult part of the road, with unstable gravel and lots of mud. But it wasn't a problem: the bike handled it without demur, even though heavy rain had appeared, making it almost impossible at times to see clearly ahead.

I was travelling down onto the rolling landscape that would soon drop onto tundra flat as a pancake, and Deadhorse was but 270km away. And as I neared the end, the struggle between land and ocean saw the landscape become more and more blotched, with rivers and lakes and bits of estuary – the wild, bare, windswept Arctic, inhabited only by low-growing tundra shrubbery and flowers, birds, caribou and other mammals ... plus transient oil workers and adventurous visitors.

Deadhorse is a bit like a twenty-first century version of a Wild West town, and it struck me as a place where anything could happen. Well, almost anything: there'll be no gunfight at the OK Corral saloon, because, well, there ain't no saloon in town. Deadhorse is dry, totally dry, because of the dangers that alcohol poses. Oil drilling operators and the heavy industrial contractors who serve them cannot afford a worker operating below par the day after a night on the tiles, not to mention a drunk worker. And so in Deadhorse, there's very little that constitutes a town, just one shop, selling hardware mainly, and souvenir stickers and T-shirts as an afterthought, and an there's unmanned petrol station. There's no main square, no church – in fact, there's no public square at all. There are places to work, heavy industrial places – land-based oil rigs and the contract operations that serve them – and a few places to sleep and eat. There are a couple of hotels – bunk houses, really – with canteens rather than restaurants, and that's about it.

The place didn't exist in any shape or form before oil, which was discovered in 1968, having long been suspected of being there. When oil was found, the place contained an estimated twenty-five billion barrels of it, the largest reserve in North America and more than twice the amount in Texas.

Production began in 1977, after the completion of the Trans Alaska Pipeline System, which delivers crude oil to Valdez on southern Alaska's Pacific coast.

'So why "Deadhorse"?' I asked a tour guide of the oilfield about the name. He said one version was that, if you got this far, your horse would surely be dead. But the other was that a haulage company involved in bringing gravel for the highway had as their motto, 'We'll move anything, even a dead horse' and thus was born the town that ain't a town.

Some weird things do happen in Deadhorse, I'll say that.

I was on the bike at about 8:00 heading for Deadhorse Camp, a sort of hostel, from where I'd join the tour of the Prudhoe Oilfield. Mine was the last of three vehicles approaching a bend in the road, when the first car came to a halt. The bus in front of me, which was behind the car, also stopped. And so did I. I didn't know why we'd all stopped, and then the car started to reverse, and I saw the reverse lights of the bus light up. I started to shuffle myself backwards, still not knowing what was going on. And then I looked ahead, where the road turns sharply left and where we were all about to go. There was a bear – a very large brown bear – ambling along with no obvious sense of mission, from what I could see, but ambling towards us nonetheless. It was a grizzly, which I could tell by the hump on his back about where its shoulder blades are – a defining characteristic. It really was large, about the size of a short-legged but overweight bull, and although it was ambling with a lumbering motion, it had that way about it that had me thinking, 'It looks like it could run very fast if it wanted.'

I pulled over to the left side of the road and started fumbling urgently for my phone to take pictures as Mr Grizzly moved along the right side, where the vehicles were and where another vehicle had just joined the queue behind me. I could see that people in the cars were agitated, and the bear apparently tried to open one of the doors, grabbling the handle in its mouth. My efforts to video Mr Grizzly failed miserably as, simultaneously, I realised that I too had better high tail it out of there, which I did, making a two-second video of the nearby petrol tank and the road surface. But not the bear.

'Oh, you're the guy who was on the bike!' exclaimed Sher from Oregon when she arrived at the camp, also for the tour, she having been in the car that pulled in to the bear queue just behind me. Her outburst had a sort of, 'We thought you were going to die!' ring to it. 'Oh, my God!' she said. And then we had the, 'Where are you from?' conversation, and Sher and the other twenty or so people about to embark on the tour, plus the guide, were all very congratulatory about my journey. 'Yes,' I said, 'it's been a long one, and this is the end ...'

I had pulled in to Deadhorse the night before, 797km north of Fairbanks. My odometer was showing 37,204 miles, not kilometres, because the bike was bought in the UK. Of those, 13,941 miles were done before I started this trip. So I reckoned that, so far, my adventure had clocked up 23,263 miles, give or take. That's 37,438km, and at that juncture, I didn't really know what my feelings were. I had a detached conversation with myself in which I said, 'Well, there you are now. You've done it,' to which I replied to myself, 'Well, yes, I suppose I have.' I fell silent, not knowing what to think or say to myself next.

Officially, no one lives in Deadhorse. The population is all temporary – some 5,000 oil workers and about the same number of contractors, according to a tour guide. The contractors have names like Haliburton (the Dick Cheney-linked company of notoriety in Iraq and Kuwait), Worley (chemicals), Schlumberger (general oilfield services) and M-I SWACO (drilling fluids). The oilfield has 1,400 wells, of which 800 are active. It's 241km across, that is, east–west, and 24–32km deep from the Arctic Ocean shore inland.

Huge installations are scattered across a flat, barren landscape, many behind wire fencing with acres of gravel yards round them in which there are stacks of pipes and bits of equipment, some redundant and ready for scrap, others their replacements. And despite all the heavy industry, nature is everywhere.

Interestingly, wildlife seemed unperturbed by all this human activity. 'On the right,' said Jack, our guide and bus driver for our oilfield tour, 'caribou.' And there, strolling between huge lumps of frontier industry, were half a dozen of the beautiful animals, most of them with impressive antlers. An arctic fox, with its dark summer coat on, appeared bounding across the tundra. 'He'll be looking for birds' eggs,' said Jack. 'On the left, a Brent goose – now, he's quite rare. Those over there are cackling geese. They look quite like Canada geese but have a shorter neck ...'

We saw great white-fronted geese, a snow goose, a tundra swan, long-tailed sea ducks and a red-necked phalarope. Jack said that polar bears are not really a problem in Deadhorse, contrary to what I had been told, but that grizzlies are. That much I knew from experience. Polar bears do hang out over at a seawater treatment plant, further away, said Jack.

He then took us down to the sea – Prudhoe Bay, the Arctic Ocean – gritty sand and seashells, a peaty shoreline and lots of driftwood timber lying about. It looked like a beach almost anywhere, and yet there I was, on the edge of the Arctic Ocean, in bright sunshine, at the end of an almost eight-month odyssey from Isla Navarino, at the extreme far south of Chile, which I had left on 22 November 2022.

I'm not a great sea swimmer, but I had to get in at Prudhoe Bay – I knew that for sure, as did three or four of the others. When I did, I plunged in and swam out a bit and then stood up, the shock of the cold banished by the moment itself. Those who didn't get in stood on the beach cheering me, and that's when it hit me – that's when I felt a bit emotional. This was truly the end. More than 200 days riding the bike, almost every day. And now it was over.

I spent the night in the 432-room Aurora Hotel, mainly serving contractors. It's a building with all the charm of a prison block, and I ate microwaved turkey and rice, not having a celebratory beer. I looked across the tundra at the Brooks Range, clear and sharp in the sun, despite the distance.

Once again, I rode through the Atigun Pass, through valleys, passing the majestic mountains, the rushing rivers and the turquoise lakes. The day was bone dry, and on that long, flat, compacted mud section of the Dalton near Yukon Crossing, I stood on the pegs, leant forward and hit 70mph.

On the pegs. Doing seventy, aged seventy.
Top of the world, Ma, top of the world.

EPILOGUE

Getting home wasn't quite as simple as just going down the way I came and hopping on the first plane back to Dublin. For a start, I nearly didn't get out of Deadhorse. At Prudhoe Bay's one filling station, my credit cards were rejected, and I got back along the Dalton only thanks to the kindness of fellow-bikers Olaf Roepke from Austin, Texas (via Germany) and his pal Spence Gerber, also from Texas, who paid for a tank of petrol and also stood me dinner in Coldfoot.

Back at the Northern-Moosed RV Park & Campground near Fairbanks and completely broke, Steph, who was married to Santa Claus Ritch, said I could stay for free by working in her garden. And so, like I was a character in someone else's novel – a hard travellin' hobo workin' for my vittles – I spent an afternoon clearing a patch and feeding a large mound of her garden cuttings into a shredding machine. Thankfully, my cards were sorted easily enough, and next day, I headed south again, more or less back the way I came – covering 3,200km in ten days.

At Duffy Lake, just before Vancouver, I had the weird experience of running into Myles and Brigid Mitchell, a couple from Louisburgh in Co, Mayo. Truly, the world is a small place. And that's one of the things that hits you after a journey like this – 45,000km through fifteen countries over eight months and crossing two continents, from the bottom of one to the top of the other. The world is indeed small and the people in it are mostly – overwhelmingly – good, kind, decent and helpful and just as interested in you, as you are in them. They're like us and not some sort of 'other' of whom we should be suspicious and fearful. I knew that already, but in depressingly fractious times it was comforting to have it reaffirmed. Over all those roads and through all those different countries, nothing untoward happened to me and I never really felt threatened or truly fearful for my own safety. Nothing happened to disillusion me about people – the opposite, if anything. Of course, some people can be suspicious of strangers, but by engaging, talking, listening and sharing inconsequential things like stickers, we can evaporate suspicion and prompt smiles. Being Irish was a huge plus: those who have heard of us like us; those who have not are curious and want to know more. Many have half a notion: 'It's where men wear skirts, no?' was a common misconception. 'That's Scotland,' I'd say.

The motorbike was a great icebreaker, and even when surrounded by the angry and protesting poor, as in Peru, who always asked me how much the bike was worth, I never felt threatened or in danger once we got talking. Latin America's poor, and the migrants passing through Central America, are exactly the same as migrants everywhere – like everyone else, they just want the chance to work to build a decent life.

The negative portrayal of them by some in the United States is shameful. Of all the countries I visited, the US is the one that frightens most. So many people there have a lust for guns, the need for which is utterly unsupported by empirical evidence, or the experience of other countries anywhere. And so many people who ought to know better are willingly flirting with a would-be tyrant, while showing simultaneously a depressing disdain for facts, truth and reason. It will not end well.

As I delivered my bike to an air freight company in Vancouver, I marvelled at its performance. Throughout the entire journey, there was not a single mechanical issue, despite everything I put it through. It had four services – one in Punta Arenas, one in Antofagasta, one in Bogotá and finally one in El Paso – and went through three sets of tyres. I set out from Dublin with a new pair of Metzeler Tourance Trail Enduros, which lasted from Ireland to London and on to Buenos Aires, Punta Arenas and Puerto Williams and from there, through Argentina and Chile, to Antofagasta. There I got a set of Continental TKC 70s, which took me across the Atacama and through Bolivia, Peru, Ecuador, Colombia and all of central America, to El Paso. In Texas I got the set of Heidenau K60 Scouts that got me to the Arctic Ocean, back down to Vancouver, to London and home.

The end came very suddenly. After handing over the bike, I sat down in the air freight office and asked could I use their WiFi. Sure, they said, and so I opened the Skyscanner app on my phone. It was 10:30. There was a WestJet flight to Calgary that afternoon at 15:30 and a connecting WestJet flight to Dublin at 19:55, landing at 10:55 next morning, 12 July. The cost was US$354 (€335).

At that price, I didn't hesitate and clicked the buy button. Seconds later, my ticket was confirmed.

'Holy fuck,' I thought, 'I'm going home.' It had been 214 days on the road, and in a matter of seconds it was all over. No regrets. Ever.

Next evening, July 12 2023, I walked in on Moira unannounced. We embraced and it was wonderful to be back.

But still, every now and then, my mind drifts, and I hanker for the road.

ACKNOWLEDGEMENTS

I could not have done this trip, and so much more, without the love, support and tolerance of my wife, Moira, and our children, Patrick and Natasha, and their respective partners, Beibhinn and Tristan. And as they all managed so well without me, I think I should do more …

I could not have done it also without the support, financial and otherwise, of my former editor at the *Irish Times*, Paul O'Neill, whose successor, Ruadhán Mac Cormaic, continued that support. Ditto to Mary Minihan, my commissioning editor at the paper whose unruffled professionalism, sorely tested at times by me, shone through and made my life easy, if not hers.

Many thanks also to Gill Books, who ran with the idea, backed up their support with a generous advance and whose editors, designers and publicity people, Sarah Liddy, Isabelle Hanrahan, Charlie Lawlor, Ruairí Ó Brógáin and Mia O'Reilly, have been great to work with. This book is a compilation of my pieces for the *Irish Times*, edited blogs from my trip website, Tip2Top.ie, and extracts from my notebooks. The website, fronted by Nick Bradshaw's photo of me riding in the Wicklow Gap, was created by Ben Duffy of Portview Digital, adapted subsequently and operated by Cathal Byrne of Arrow Design, whose patient help to me en route was heroic.

My near neighbour and fellow biker Noel McMullen of Maxol kindly contributed to my sponsorship but sadly, the wind kept ripping his Maxol stickers off my panniers! Matthew Lambert of Landy High Pressure Washers of Yorkshire, and Louisburgh, had better luck. When, in April 2020, I had to abandon the bike in Punta Arenas because of Covid, and return to Ireland, Greystones neighbours Owen and Paula Owens kindly lent me their Honda Shadow 600 to help keep me sane.

Before setting out through the Americas, and along the way, I got sound advice and encouragement from fellow bikers Geoff Hill, Ken McGreevy, John O'Kelly and Howard Bell. And also from Tom McDonnell of

Maddocks of Bray, Co Wicklow, who made sure my bike was mechanically up to the challenge at the outset. And what a bike it has been: not a single mechanical issue throughout the whole trip. I'd never have got going at all had not Stephen Hingston of Devon sold it to me in the first place and, true to his word, it was a great buy.

Thanks too to the fellow bikers – among them Michael Brinch of Roskilde in Denmark, Fernando de Rossas of Mendoza in Argentina, Jason Espinosa from San Antonio in Texas, Mario Werner from Heuston in Texas, Joe Ordona of San Francisco, Kyle Koshman and John Renquist, from California, Cameron Derksen of Vancouver, Canada, Dimples, Smiley and X man from LA, Bruce Martin of Whitehorse, and Olaf Roepke and his pal, Spence Gerber, both from Austin who saved my bacon in Deadhorse, Alaska – and others, too numerous to mention by name, I met along the way and who befriended me and showed me kindness. Much practical advice came from Irish diplomats, not least Ireland's then ambassador to Chile, Paul Gleeson, his staff and several other Irish diplomats, notably Fiona NicDhonnacha of Colombia. All were unfailingly helpful. My extended family and many good friends were in a WhatsApp tracker group, through which they kept an eye on me, offering support, advice and suggestions along the way.

I blew a small fortune, but what the hell? Hostel accommodation, which was what I used for most of South and Central America, averaged around €20 a night. State and National park camping in the US and Canada was usually around $25 a night. RV parks charged around $40 a night for a tent site, though one, in Malibu Beach, hit me for $90! Airfreighting the bike from Bogota to Panama City cost $1,200. In February 2020, motofreight.co.uk, and their super-efficient Kathy Wood, air freighted the bike from London to Buenos Aires for £1,640 (equal in October 2023 to about £2,000, or €2,290) and got it back to the UK from Canada for €2,945. From there, in July 2023, I rode it to Holyhead where Stena Line generously gave me a free ride home across the Irish Sea.

Thank you all.